AF760991

Global Issues Series

General Editor: Jim Whitman

This exciting new series encompasses three principal themes: the interaction of human and natural systems; cooperation and conflict; and the enactment of values. The series as a whole places an emphasis on the examination of complex systems and causal relations in political decision-making; problems of knowledge; authority, control and accountability in issues of scale; and the reconciliation of conflicting values and competing claims. Throughout the series the concentration is on an integration of existing disciplines towards the clarification of political possibility as well as impending crises.

Titles include:

Berhanykun Andemicael and John Mathiason
ELIMINATING WEAPONS OF MASS DESTRUCTION
Prospects for Effective International Verification

Mike Bourne
ARMING CONFLICT
The Proliferation of Small Arms

Roy Carr-Hill and John Lintott
CONSUMPTION, JOBS AND THE ENVIRONMENT
A Fourth Way?

John N. Clarke and Geoffrey R. Edwards (*editors*)
GLOBAL GOVERNANCE IN THE TWENTY-FIRST CENTURY

Malcolm Dando
PREVENTING BIOLOGICAL WARFARE
The Failure of American Leadership

Toni Erskine (*editor*)
CAN INSTITUTIONS HAVE RESPONSIBILITIES?
Collective Moral Agency and International Relations

Brendan Gleeson and Nicholas Low (*editors*)
GOVERNING FOR THE ENVIRONMENT
Global Problems, Ethics and Democracy

B. K. Greener
THE NEW INTERNATIONAL POLICING

Roger Jeffery and Bhaskar Vira (*editors*)
CONFLICT AND COOPERATION IN PARTICIPATORY NATURAL RESOURCE MANAGEMENT

Ho-Won Jeong (*editor*)
GLOBAL ENVIRONMENTAL POLICIES
Institutions and Procedures

APPROACHES TO PEACEBUILDING

Alexander Kelle, Kathryn Nixdorff and Malcolm Dando
CONTROLLING BIOCHEMICAL WEAPONS
Adapting Multilateral Arms Control for the 21st Century

W. Andy Knight
A CHANGING UNITED NATIONS
Multilateral Evolution and the Quest for Global Governance

W. Andy Knight (*editor*)
ADAPTING THE UNITED NATIONS TO A POSTMODERN ERA
Lessons Learned

Kelley Lee
HEALTH IMPACTS OF GLOBALIZATION (*editor*)
Towards Global Governance

GLOBALIZATION AND HEALTH
An Introduction

Nicholas Low and Brendan Gleeson (*editors*)
MAKING URBAN TRANSPORT SUSTAINABLE

Catherine Lu
JUST AND UNJUST INTERVENTIONS IN WORLD POLITICS
Public and Private

Robert L. Ostergard Jr. (*editor*)
HIV, AIDS AND THE THREAT TO NATIONAL AND INTERNATIONAL SECURITY

Graham S. Pearson
THE UNSCOM SAGA
Chemical and Biological Weapons Non-Proliferation

THE SEARCH FOR IRAQ'S WEAPONS OF MASS DESTRUCTION
Inspection, Verification and Non-Proliferation

Andrew T. Price-Smith (*editor*)
PLAGUES AND POLITICS
Infectious Disease and International Policy

Michael Pugh (*editor*)
REGENERATION OF WAR-TORN SOCIETIES

David Scott
'THE CHINESE CENTURY'?
The Challenge to Global Order

Marco Verweij and Michael Thompson (*editors*)
CLUMSY SOLUTIONS FOR A COMPLEX WORLD
Governance, Politics and Plural Perceptions

Bhaskar Vira and Roger Jeffery (*editors*)
ANALYTICAL ISSUES IN PARTICIPATORY NATURAL RESOURCE MANAGEMENT

Simon M. Whitby
BIOLOGICAL WARFARE AGAINST CROPS

Global Issues Series
Series Standing Order ISBN 978–0–333–79483–8
(*outside North America only*)

You can receive future titles in this series as they are published by placing a standing order. Please contact your bookseller or, in case of difficulty, write to us at the address below with your name and address, the title of the series and the ISBN quoted above.

Customer Services Department, Macmillan Distribution Ltd, Houndmills, Basingstoke, Hampshire RG21 6XS, England

---

The New International Policing

B. K. Greener
Massey University, New Zealand

palgrave
macmillan

© B. K. Greener 2009

All rights reserved. No reproduction, copy or transmission of this publication may be made without written permission.

No portion of this publication may be reproduced, copied or transmitted save with written permission or in accordance with the provisions of the Copyright, Designs and Patents Act 1988, or under the terms of any licence permitting limited copying issued by the Copyright Licensing Agency, Saffron House, 6-10 Kirby Street, London EC1N 8TS.

Any person who does any unauthorized act in relation to this publication may be liable to criminal prosecution and civil claims for damages.

The author has asserted her right to be identified as the author of this work in accordance with the Copyright, Designs and Patents Act 1988.

First published 2009 by
PALGRAVE MACMILLAN

Palgrave Macmillan in the UK is an imprint of Macmillan Publishers Limited, registered in England, company number 785998, of Houndmills, Basingstoke, Hampshire RG21 6XS.

Palgrave Macmillan in the US is a division of St Martin's Press LLC, 175 Fifth Avenue, New York, NY 10010.

Palgrave Macmillan is the global academic imprint of the above companies and has companies and representatives throughout the world.

Palgrave® and Macmillan® are registered trademarks in the United States, the United Kingdom, Europe and other countries.

ISBN-13: 978-0-230-57390-1 hardback
ISBN-10: 0-230-57390-8 hardback

This book is printed on paper suitable for recycling and made from fully managed and sustained forest sources. Logging, pulping and manufacturing processes are expected to conform to the environmental regulations of the country of origin.

A catalogue record for this book is available from the British Library.

Library of Congress Cataloging-in-Publication Data

Greener, Beth K., 1977–
The new international policing / Beth K. Greener.
p. cm. – (Global issues series)
Includes bibliographical references and index.
ISBN 978–0–230–57390–1
1. Police–International cooperation. 2. Criminal justice, Administration of–International cooperation. 3. Law enforcement–International cooperation. 4. Crime prevention–International cooperation. I. Title.

HV7921.G74 2009
363.2–dc22 2008050840

10 9 8 7 6 5 4 3 2 1
18 17 16 15 14 13 12 11 10 09

Printed and bound in Great Britain by
CPI Antony Rowe, Chippenham and Eastbourne

For Anateira and Tamaira

Contents

List of Figures

Acronyms

AAP	Australian Assisting Police (Papua New Guinea)
ADB	Asian Development Bank
ADF	Australian Defence Force
AFP	Australian Federal Police
AIA	Afghan Interim Administration
ANA	Afghan National Army
ANAP	Afghanistan National Auxiliary Police
ANCOP	Afghan National Civil Order Police
ANDS	Afghan National Development Strategy
ANP	Afghan National Police
APEC	Asia Pacific Economic Cooperation
ASEAN	Association of South East Asian Nations
ASEANAPOL	ASEAN Police Chiefs
ATA	Afghan Transitional Authority
BCPP	Bougainville Community Policing Project
BPS	Bougainville Police Service
B/RCTs	Brigade (Army) and Regimental (Marine) Combat Teams (Iraq)
CAP	Community Auxiliary Police
CENTCOM	Central Command
CEP	Community Empowerment and Local Governance Project (East Timor)
CEPOL	European Police College
CIVPOL	UN Civilian Police (pre-2005 name change to UNPOL)
CPA	Coalition Provisional Authority (Iraq)
CPATT	Civilian Police Advisory Training Team
CSFP	Common Security and Foreign Policy (EU)
CSTC-A	Combined Security Transition Command – Afghanistan
DCAF	Democratic Control of Armed Forces
DDR	Disarmament Demobilisation Reintegration
DEA	Drug Enforcement Agency
DMU	Detainee Management Unit (East Timor)
DoD	Department of Defense
DPKO	Department of Peacekeeping Operations (UN)
ECHO	European Commission Humanitarian Office

ECP	Enhanced Cooperation Program
ePRT	Embedded Provincial Reconstruction Team (Iraq)
ERRF	EU Rapid Reaction Force
ESDP	European Security and Defence Policy
ESIF	European Security and Intelligence Force
EU	European Union
EULEX	EU Rule of Law Mission (Kosovo)
EUPOL	European Union Police Mission to Afghanistan
FALINTIL	Armed Forces for the National Liberation of East Timor
FBI	Federal Bureau of Investigation
F-FDTL	FALINTIL-Forcas de Defesa de Timor Leste or Timor Leste Defence Force
FPU	Formed Police Units
FRY	Federal Republic of Yugoslavia
ICC	International Criminal Court
ICITAP	International Criminal Investigative Training Assistance Programme (US)
IDG	International Deployment Group (AFP)
IDP	Internally Displaced Persons
IFOR	Multinational Implementation Force (Kosovo)
INC	Iraqi National Congress
INP	Iraqi National Police
INTERFET	International Force East Timor
INTERPOL	International Criminal Police Organisation
IPAC	International Policing Advisory Council
IPM	International Police Monitor (Haiti)
IPMT	International Peace Monitoring Team
IPS	Iraqi Police Service
IPSF	Interim Public Security Force (Haiti)
IPTF	International Police Task Force (Bosnia)
IPU	Integrated Police Units
ISAF	International Security Assistance Force (Afghanistan)
ISF	International Security Forces (East Timor)
ISG	International Service Group (New Zealand Police)
JEMB	Joint Electoral Management Board (Afghanistan)
JSDF	Japanese Self-Defence Forces
KFOR	Kosovo Force
KLA	Kosovo Liberation Army
KPC	Kosovo Protection Corps
KPS	Kosovo Police Service
KVM	Kosovo Verification Mission

MACP	Military aid to the civil power
MINUGUA	UN Verification Mission in Guatemala
MINURSO	UN Mission in Western Sahara
MINUSTAH	UN Stabilisation Mission in Haiti
MIPONUH	UN Civilian Police Mission in Haiti
MNF	Multinational Force (Haiti)
MNSTC	Multi-National Security Transition Command
MOOTW	Military Operations Other Than War
MP	Military Police
MSU	Multinational Specialised Unit
NATO	North Atlantic Treaty Organisation
NZDF	New Zealand Defence Force
NZPOL	New Zealand Police
OAS	Organisation of American States
OECD	Organisation for Economic Cooperation and Development
OEF	Operation Enduring Freedom
ONUC	Operations des Nations Unies au Congo (United Nations Observer Mission in Congo)
ONUMOZ	Operations des Nations Unies au Mozambique (United Nations Operation in Mozambique)
ONUSAL	Operations des Nations Unies au El Salvador (United Nations Observer Mission in El Salvador)
OSCE	Organisation for Security Cooperation in Europe
PAP	People's Armed Police (China)
PCC	Police Contributing Country
PDD	Presidential Decision Directive (US)
PICP	Pacific Islands Chiefs of Police
PNC	Policia Nacional Civil (El Salvador)
PNG	Papua New Guinea
PNTL	Policia Nacional de Timor Leste (East Timor/Timor Leste)
POLRI	Indonesian Police Force
PPF	Participating Police Force (Solomon Islands)
PRPI	Pacific Regional Policing Initiative
PRT	Provincial Reconstruction Team (Afghanistan)
RAAF	Royal Australian Air Force
RAMSI	Regional Assistance Mission to Solomon Islands
RCMP	Royal Canadian Mounted Police
RNZAF	Royal New Zealand Air Force
RPNGC	Royal Papua New Guinea Constabulory

RRP	Rapid Reaction Police (Angola)
RRR	Reform, Restructuring, Rebuilding
RRU	Rapid Response Unit (INTERFET)
RSIP	Royal Solomon Islands Police
SAARC	South Asian Association for Regional Cooperation
SARPCCO	Southern African Regional Police Chiefs Cooperation Organisation
SCAP	Supreme Commander for Allied Powers
SCO	Shanghai Cooperation Organisation
SCU	Serious Crime Unit (East Timor)
SFOR	NATO-led Multinational Stabilisation Force (Bosnia)
SIPF	Solomon Islands Police Force
SMART	Support, Monitoring, Advising, Reporting, Training
SNP	Somalia National Police
SPU	Stability Police Units
SRSG	Special Representative of the Secretary General
SSR	Security Sector Reform
SWAPOL	South West African Police (Namibia)
TCN	Troop Contributing Nation (ISAF Afghanistan)
TIP	Transition Integration Programme
TNI	Tentara Nasional Indonesia (Indonesian Army)
TPIU	Trafficking and Prostitution Investigation Unity (UNMIK)
UN	United Nations
UNAMA	UN Assistance Mission to Afghanistan
UNAMET	UN Assistance Mission to East Timor
UNAMIR	UN Assistance Mission in Rwanda
UNAVEM	UN Verification Mission Angola
UNCJS	UN Criminal Justice Standards
UNCRO	UN Confidence Restoration Operation (Croatia)
UNDP	United Nations Development Programme
UNEF	UN Emergency Force (Gaza)
UNFICYP	UN Force in Cyprus
UNHCR	UN High Commissioner for Refugees
UNITAF	Unified Task Force (Somalia)
UNMIBH	UN Mission in Bosnia and Herzegovina
UNMIH	UN Mission in Haiti
UNMIK	UN Interim Administration Mission in Kosovo
UNMISET	UN Mission in Support of East Timor
UNMIT	UN Integrated Mission in Timor-Leste
UNOSOM	UN Operation in Somalia (I and II)

UNOTIL	UN Office in Timor Leste
UNPA	UN Protected Area
UNPOL	UN Police (post-2005)
UNPREPDEP	UN Preventive Deployment Force (Macedonia)
UNPROFOR	UN Protection Force (Croatia/Bosnia)
UNSC	United Nations Security Council
UNSCR	United Nations Security Council Resolution
UNTAC	UN Transitional Authority in Cambodia
UNTAES	UN Transitional Administration in Eastern Slavonia, Baranja and Western Sirmium
UNTAET	UN Transitional Administration in East Timor
UNTAG	UN Transition Assistance Group (Namibia)
UNTEA	UN Temporary Executive Authority (West New Guinea)
USCON	US Constabulary (West Germany)
USIP	US Institute for Peace

Acknowledgements

I would like to first of all thank Palgrave Macmillan for taking this research project on. I would also like to thank those who invited me to a number of very useful workshops in 2007 including: a workshop on future directions for Pacific Policing at the behest of the Pacific Islands Chiefs of Police (PICP) in March; the Third UN International Policing Advisory Council (IPAC) meeting in Canberra in August as hosted by the UN Police Division and the Australian Federal Police (AFP); a roundtable on Australian and Economic Union (EU) policies towards the Pacific region hosted by the National Europe Centre with help from the School of Diplomacy at the Australian National University (ANU) in Canberra and a workshop on Community Policing in Three Dimensions in December as co-hosted by Regulatory Institutions Network (REGNET) ANU and the Berkeley Centre for Criminal Justice. From October to November 2007 I had the opportunity to give talks to the Liu Institute at the University of British Columbia and to War Studies, King's College, London and would like to thank those who joined in some lively discussions there. During this trip to the northern hemisphere I also had a chance to talk to a number of officials and serving personnel from North Atlantic Treaty Organisation (NATO), the European Commission, the European Council and UN Police Division in New York and would like to thank all those who gave their time and opinions but who did not necessarily want to be named. Also thanks to the AFP for letting me observe Pre-Deployment Training (PDT) in mid-2008 and to the New Zealand Police (NZPOL) for many useful discussions, both of which greatly helped me better understand operational aspects of policing abroad. Chapter 6 is a revised version of an article published as B.K. Greener-Barcham, 'Crossing the Green or Blue Line? Exploring the Military-Police Divide', *Small Wars and Insurgencies*, 18/1, March 2007, pp90–112 that is reprinted by permission of the publisher (Taylor & Francis Ltd, http://www.tandf.co.uk/journals). Every effort has also been made to secure permission for use of the figures reproduced here.

More specifically (and my deepest apologies if I have forgotten anyone), I would like to offer a very big thank you to: Jon White, Jacqui Goodwin, Cam Ronald, Tony McLeod, Tony Annandale, Hamish McCardle, Roly Williams, Andrew Carpenter, Jared Rigg, Rolf Landgren, Gerard Beekman, Kevin Steeves, Ugo Solinas, Mark Kroeker, Andy Hughes, Tony

Murney, Juani O'Reilly, Abby McLeod, Robbie Langdon and the PDT team at AFP, John McFarlane, Adam Bycroft, Greg Fry, Peter Grabovsky, Bill Tow, Pauline Kerr, Paul Keal, Bu Wilson, Eirinn Mobekk, Alice Hills, Eboe Hutchful, David Bayley, Andrew Goldsmith, Otwin Marenin, Paul Kernaghan, Brian Job, Richard M. Price, Andrew Mack, Rachel Kerr, James Gow, Robert Perito, Jamie Shea, Andrew Budd, Predrag Avromovich, Benoit Dupont, Samuel Tanner, Philip Cunliffe, Arrigo Velicogna, Martin Smith and David Brown.

In more general terms I would also like to send out a thank you to Lionel Banfather for letting me sleep in his front living room in London, and to recognise the generosity of Debika Pal and Claire Trivedi for a similar favour in Washington DC. Thanks to Massey University for grants to help release me from teaching duties to complete the manuscript, and to my School for taking me on in a year when I had many trips to and fro. Thanks too to my immediate family, Mum, Dad and my sister Kate for support along the way. And last of all thanks to Will for, amongst numerous other things, asking the hard questions in a very gentle way.

Any mistakes are, however, of course mine and mine alone.

1
Introduction

> *I have no doubt that the world should eventually have an international police force which will be accepted as an integral and essential part of life in the same way as national police forces are accepted.*[1]
>
> U Thant, 1963

Demands for civilian policing tasks to be carried out in peace operations have increased dramatically in recent years.[2] This has resulted in a concomitant increase in the number of police professionals being deployed to peace operations to carry out those policing tasks, as well as an increase in the range of international, regional, national and private sector actors providing those police professionals. At the same time, there has been an ongoing deepening and broadening of just what those 'policing tasks' can potentially be, to the point where we now see executive in-line policing roles and deeper police reform efforts as normal or typical functions for international police. These combined developments of: an increased role for police in peace operations, rising police numbers and a growth in actors who look to contribute police to international operations, and a broadening and deepening of policing tasks in this setting constitute what I call the 'new international policing'.

Up until the start of the new century there was a 'curious' neglect of civilian police as promising but underutilised agents in international peace operations.[3] Into the new millennium, however, the importance of civilian policing as a vital and often neglected component of peace support (and other) operations has begun to be recognised by a number of international actors. In recent times, for example, the UN Department of Peacekeeping Operations has raised the status of policing in-house, the EU has expanded its policing capacity and activity in Europe, and a number of countries have created their own standing police capacity in order to be able to respond to international security situations that require a police presence.[4] In addition to such institutional expansion, the growing importance of international policing has been demonstrated in other ways with executive policing missions in Kosovo and East Timor, and with the establishment of the first major police-led international peace mission – the Regional Assistance Mission to Solomon Islands (RAMSI). The situations in Iraq and Afghanistan have further served to demonstrate the significance of police in international missions, with some asserting that in Iraq 'policekeeping' should have been the main focus for the intervening forces.[5] This consolidation of policing as a vital part of international peace operations represents a major shift away from previous eras where 'civilian police issues were typically more of an afterthought': police played more minor roles, were overshadowed by others, particularly the military, and were not often the subject of academic study.[6]

We are, therefore, witnessing an era of increasing international policing in terms of scale, institutional arrangements, and roles and expectations attributed to civilian police in peace support and other like deployments. However there is much more to the picture than these operationally focused aspects of international policing as such activity both represents deeper shifts in the contemporary international system and contributes towards them. The consequences of the new international policing stem from the fact that policing operations are qualitatively different operations that signal and symbolise changes in the international order. The use of police professionals from one state to police the citizens of another raises broader questions with regards to such things as sovereignty, authority, and norm transfer.

The purpose of this book is therefore threefold. First it seeks to bring the increasingly important role of police as international actors to the attention of those working in the international relations field. Second it seeks to highlight to police personnel and experts in the policing field the significance of broader changes in the international arena; changes with regards to vital issues such as sovereignty and intervention that have prompted (and are in turn shaped by) this increasing international police presence. Lastly this book seeks to ascertain the remits, the limitations, and the main issues at stake in contemporary international policing efforts today.

Outline of the book

David H. Bayley once asked whether the term 'international policing' would 'cover the study of police forces in several nations or activities of the Federal Bureau of Investigation (FBI) internationally, or the growth of collaboration among police forces in Europe, or even UN peacekeeping in Bosnia?'.[7] 'International policing' might conjure images of instances of imperial policing – the US in the Pacific, in the Philippines, and in Latin America, or British police in the British Empire.[8] Alternatively it could be thought to refer to developments such as the early creation of the International Criminal Police Organisation (Interpol) which acts as 'a global conduit for police communication'.[9] In the present context, however, international policing refers to the use of external police personnel in countries that are host to peace support operations, or with regards to other state-building exercises (such as invitations to undertake police reform efforts) that similarly involve external agents. In this book, post-conflict operations take centre stage predominantly because they are the mainstay of more recent international policing operations launched and because, as Otwin Marenin notes, 'post-conflict societies provide greater opportunities to rebuild security systems from the ground up'.[10] This is in contrast to those more specific foreign assistance programmes to police forces which have often focused on basic order and effectiveness questions, rather than on broader accountability measures, the improvement of police-community relations and more fundamental forms of change.[11] As increasingly comprehensive and complex policing efforts have been undertaken in recent post-conflict situations, focusing on these allows for more detailed analyses of the ramifications, problems and prospects of developments with respect to international policing operations. As noted at the outset the term 'new international policing' therefore refers to an increase in the scale, institutional support, and roles and expectations attributed to civilian police in international peace support and other like deployments.[12]

This book joins analyses of academic literatures, official documents and statistics together with interviews with decision makers and policy commentators. It is also informed by interactions carried out in other settings such as academic roundtables and informal discussions with personnel working in this area. In particular, this project looks to meld history, theory and practice. Just what is different about the new spate of international policing deployments cannot be determined without an understanding of what has gone before. We shall see, for example, that 'although the extent of involvement in executive policing in Kosovo and East Timor was unprecedented, there were tentative forerunners from the very early days of UN peacekeeping'.[13] Yet it is not enough to merely lay out a historical exposition or narrative pertaining to these and more recent deployments. There is a real need to try and grapple with the broader ramifications of international policing developments – particularly in terms of international security issues and other wider aspects of international relations. In exploring this new international policing phenomenon, the book is divided up into two main thematic parts. The first part provides an overview of the development of the new international policing in practice, whilst the latter part discusses what these practical issues pertaining to the new international policing mean in more conceptual and theoretical terms.

Chapter 2 begins by constructing a brief history of the emergence of the new international policing. Though not an exhaustive history it illustrates how international policing operations have changed over time and sketches possible reasons for these changes. It also identifies just who has been undertaking such policing projects, pointing to a number of recent institutional changes at national, regional and international levels, all of which underscore an increased capability of different policing agencies to operate abroad.

The following three case study chapters then assess this new international policing in much more detail. Chapter 3 analyses the watershed deployments to Kosovo and East Timor where executive policing was put into practice from the very inception of both missions, Chapter 4 then investigates a recent regional police-led deployment to Solomon Islands and Chapter 5 briefly addresses additional key deployments in Afghanistan and Iraq. In the first of these three chapters, the case studies of East Timor and Kosovo demonstrate the kinds of issues arising from UN mandated and UN driven executive policing projects in post-conflict situations where the local government is incapable of providing that policing role. The case study in Solomon Islands highlights issues arising when regional police forces are invited in at the behest or agreement of the government in charge to help shore up or restore law and order. And the case studies in Afghanistan and Iraq show what kinds of issues arise from situations whereby the policing part of the mission is operating without a prior invitation (though later in conjunction with new government authorities), and where policing is being carried out in what essentially is a conflict rather than post-conflict environment.

These chapters also begin to highlight the ways in which police deployments are different from military ones. Chapter 6 therefore begins to explore more conceptual issues by asking if the new international policing is qualitatively different from military involvement in peace operations. In focusing on the police-military divide this chapter first of all demonstrates that in traditional models the tasks, mandates, ethos, training and so on of police and military were quite distinct. The chapter then assesses more recent challenges to this police-military divide: in particular the claims that the police are becoming more militarised, the military are becoming more constabularised, and that developments since September 11 have eroded the internal/external distinction on which the police-military divide depends. However whilst these considerations do illustrate some significant ways in which the police-military divide is changing, this chapter argues that this is far from a complete convergence, and indeed that there remains an important distinction between police and military forces.

The final chapter then brings practical issues together with these conceptual phenomena. It first of all outlines the kinds of operational challenges that are faced in the new international policing era, before moving to discuss broader political ramifications of this phenomenon. As 'policing is inherently political' there is an even greater onus on contributing states to ensure that we are not more accepting of such international deployments just because they seem less overtly threatening to the international order.[14] There remains a need for reflection about just why and how such deployments should proceed, and thus we must keep at least one eye to the broader ramifications of such deployments – after all, policing deals with the very fundamental matters of governance, social justice and the ordering of collective existence. Just as Sandra Whitworth has suggested that in order to assess peacekeeping more comprehensively, we need to begin by questioning the assumption that peacekeeping is necessarily 'good', similar questions must be asked in relation to what is happening in international policing too.[15] This is perhaps doubly so given concerns to limit the 'military footprint', given assumptions that policing is necessarily a positive function, and given the apparent assumption that 'blue' will be better than 'green' in addressing a number of security issues prevalent in the world today. So whilst it is correct to say that 'the presence of uniformed, international civil police in a community can increase the sense of personal security of local citizens who would be intimidated by or opposed to the presence of armed, foreign troops in their community', we need to ask how, if at all, the rise in international policing represents any kind of qualitative shift with regards to broader concepts of intervention.[16] The book thus ends with a consideration of how the emergence of the new international policing has impacted upon international order, upon ideas as to how we may police the globe, why, for whom and just what this means for understanding our international system today.

Summary

The term 'new international policing' refers to an increase in the scale, institutional support, and roles and expectations attributed to civilian police in international peace support and other like deployments. Over the course of this book we will see that the new international policing phenomenon has arisen as states (whether acting bilaterally or through regional or international arrangements) have acquired:

1. An increasing ability (capacity and capability) to police others' jurisdictions narrowly defined in operational terms.

In doing so this has created:

2. A growing division of labour between police and military, and an increase in status and importance for policing and related institutions as international actors.

These claims will be discussed and defended in Chapters 2–5 and 6 respectively. And as we shall see in Chapter 7, at a higher political level the phenomenon also presents:

3. The potential for states to police world order more broadly defined.
4. A challenge to, and at the same time a reinforcing of, the concept of statehood – a challenge because a state may be required to relinquish aspects of sovereignty to allow others to police it, yet at the same time a reinforcement as it can lead to improving security of that state by contributing to the strength of the state (plus contributors increase the external security of their own state by improving the internal security of others).
5. The opportunity to make use of the police/society interface in others' countries to both disseminate one's state's own norms and to take a better understanding of the policed state's norms back to one's own. This contributes to a broader agenda of standardisation, together

> with the pursuit of common policing principles and norms at a global level. This also thereby feeds into a transmission belt for liberal agendas at a fundamental level. In liberal societies it is the police who uphold the rule of law and protect democratic values such as individual human rights. Though police are only part of the puzzle they are nonetheless a very important one, acting as both the guardians of public welfare and the public face of authority. The new international policing is not, therefore, a neutral phenomenon but rather part of a larger normative project that seeks to spread liberal values across the globe.

Over the course of this book, we shall therefore map the development of the new international policing through historical analyses and detailed case study investigations, before drawing out both the operational and theoretical consequences of this important international phenomenon.

2
A Brief History of International Policing

The claim that we are witnessing an era of new international policing is underpinned by the fact that operational demands for policing in peace operations have increased substantially through the Cold War and post-Cold War years, and this in turn has necessitated a concomitant increase in the number of police professionals being deployed to peace operations to carry out those policing tasks. In addition to this there has been an ongoing deepening and broadening of just what those 'policing tasks' for these police professionals actually are – in particular, there has been a significant move towards executive policing and deeper police reform efforts. The present chapter highlights the development of the core themes of the new international policing through a brief history of international policing from the Cold War through to the end of the 1990s.

This chapter begins by showing that, post-World War II efforts in Germany and Japan not withstanding, the norm during the Cold War years was for international policing tasks to be very restricted in scope and scale. And indeed institutional support for police efforts in peace operations was similarly limited for many years, with the name CIVPOL for civilian police only being coined in the late 1960s and with development of the position of police commissioner to coordinate policing efforts in UN missions being institutionalised in Namibia in 1989. For many years, then, international policing efforts involved a few police professionals who often had to work within a heavily military-dominated environment and who were restricted to limited support, monitoring, advising, reporting and training (SMART) tasks. Yet into the 1990s this norm began to be challenged as UN police were first of all charged with overseeing reform efforts in Mozambique; then actively undertook police reform efforts in El Salvador before being deployed to places such as Cambodia and Haiti where local governance mechanisms were effectively non-operational, leading to the development of executive policing missions in these missions. Similarly this extension of policing roles in such situations has been paralleled by an increase in the numbers of actors involved in providing police professionals for these kinds of missions. This chapter therefore also outlines how the more traditional usage of less intrusive bilateral training programmes and UN-only peace missions has begun to be challenged by the rise of regional and national actors.[1] This investigation into changes to policing and policing institutions up until recent times sets the scene for the following case study chapters which explore the challenges faced in international policing missions in much greater detail.

Post-war reconstruction to fledgling UN missions

Occupational forces set in place at the end of World War Two in Germany and Japan were charged with re-establishing effective and legitimate police, judiciaries and penal systems. Indigenous police were used for law enforcement under US control at a local level (town or city) with separate US units at a regional level (army units that received military government and police duties training).[2] The US Army established a US Constabulary (USCON) in charge of public security in Western sectors in Germany, and here power resided with the US commanding officers not the local German authorities.[3] In Japan the Japanese civil police remained in place, controlled by the Japanese Home Ministry, though the Supreme Commander for Allied Powers (SCAP) removed some senior police officers, separated police from military and reduced a previously very broad 'policing' mandate which had included tax collection and intelligence gathering amongst other things to law enforcement only.[4] Following the departure of the occupying parties both the Germans and Japanese went back to their traditional organisational patterns; with the Germans moving to make police accountable to states, and the Japanese deferring to the national government.[5] This post-war reconstruction of policing within Germany and Japan was therefore predominantly directed by the US military with significant indigenous input and was part and parcel of post-war efforts to support fledgling democratic practices. These were, however, highly unusual cases of the reconstruction of severely economically and institutionally damaged countries and these fundamental state-building exercises were not to be repeated for many decades.

In addition to these extraordinary US-directed post-war reconstruction efforts, the UN began to become involved in policing issues in its nascent peacekeeping operations. The United Nations Observer Mission in Congo (ONUC) was created in 1960 to assist local police to maintain civil order. ONUC originally utilised a small police unit from Ghana but this unit soon got caught up in local politics and had to be removed, being replaced by a 400 member Nigerian police contingent that was withdrawn at the end of 1965.[6] These police forces were deployed to provide aid to the civil power because the national police had staged a mutiny, but this UN effort in the Congo was not highly successful.[7] The second post-war instance of international policing was the 1962–63 UN deployment to West New Guinea. Here the UN Temporary Executive Authority (UNTEA) administered West New Guinea for eight months, and deployed a Security Force, installing a British officer in charge of the local police. Another instance of international policing during this decade involved the UN Emergency Force (UNEF) of 1956–67 which on occasion had to undertake crowd control operations during its deployment to Gaza where it was effectively maintaining law and order following Israeli troop withdrawal.[8] Similarly, the first UN force in Sinai was at times referred to as a 'police force'.[9] These early UN peacekeeping efforts therefore at times incorporated some policing tasks but these police professionals were an undifferentiated component of a wider UN peacekeeping effort, and such policing roles were fairly small in scale and mandate.

Increasing police involvement in UN missions

In contrast to these smaller and more specific deployments the UN involvement in Cyprus was much larger in scale and much longer in time frame. It was during the deployment to Cyprus that police began to become a much more important part of UN peace missions. At the end of 1963 intense conflict between Greek Cypriots and Turkish Cypriots followed political action that appeared to be facilitating union with Greece. British troops attempted to stem the violence but casualties continued and the United Nations Security Council (UNSC) voted to respond to the request by the Cyprus government for assistance. UN Force in Cyprus (UNFICYP) began operations in March 1964 with the original policing contributions consisting of police from Australia (40 officers), New Zealand (20), Austria (34), Denmark (41), and Sweden (39). The primary task of the peacekeeping force was to prevent a recurrence of the fighting to allow for a climate for compromise and a political solution, and policing tasks more particularly focused on liaison between communities, observations and cooperation with Cypriot police and the separate Turkish Cypriot police element.[10] These were tasks that required police rather than military expertise. Although the UN Secretary General's special representative (SRSG) had proposed sending a military police unit, the military commander had suggested adding a civilian police unit instead. It was, therefore, during this mission that the term 'CIVPOL' was coined to ensure civilian police were differentiated from military police.[11] These CIVPOL policing efforts in Cyprus helped to dampen violence and create a much greater sense of security but the commitment was clearly going to be long term and, indeed, the deployment to Cyprus continues today.

From this significant deployment in Cyprus the use of police abroad in UN and other missions began to pick up pace. The United Nations Transition Assistance Group (UNTAG) helped facilitate the electoral process and independence within Namibia; a process that represented the culmination of a long and difficult attempt to free Namibia from German and South African domination.[12] UNTAG was a significant policing deployment in terms of the sheer numbers of police involved, the unprecedented attention in organisational terms paid to the policing component of the mission and in terms of the overall impact of the policing part in aiding the success of the mission too.

UNTAG was authorised by UNSC Resolution 435 that enabled UNTAG to assist the SRSG:

> to carry out the mandate conferred upon him by paragraph 1 of Security Council resolution 431 (1978), namely, to ensure the early independence of Namibia through free and fair elections under the supervision and control of the United Nations.[13]

CIVPOL were involved in Namibia under this UNTAG mandate in a supervisory and human rights role, undertaking major public information and outreach programmes as well as ensuring that the South West African Police (SWAPOL) maintained law and order in a professional and non-biased manner.[14] The mission to Namibia was thus a watershed in a number of ways. The role of UNTAG police was:

> different in nature and more comprehensive in scope than any previous United Nations mission. The UNTAG police came under the direct control of the special representative rather than being administratively attached to the military component, as on other

> missions....The main functions of the UNTAG police on this mission included:
>
> - taking measures against intimidation or interference with the electoral process;
> - helping to create conditions where free and fair elections could take place.[15]

Perhaps most significant with regards to the UNTAG deployment was the notion that the CIVPOL presence in Namibia was 'more significant than the military presence in encouraging a sense of day-to-day security and impartiality in running the country'.[16] Given that this sense of day-to-day security and impartiality was one of the major goals of the mission it underlined the important role that police could potentially play in such UN missions. This was also the first time in a UN peacekeeping mission that CIVPOL personnel were coordinated by a Police Commissioner reporting to the SRSG – and this organisational shift underscored some increase in status for police within a UN peacekeeping setting.[17]

However, as in times past insufficient attention was paid to the significance of this policing role in the opening phases of UNTAG. UNTAG met a number of problems with regards to a lack of coordination and cooperation between civilian and military components, with one major issue at the start of the mission being that:

> The changing situation in Namibia over the decade before UNTAG was deployed had seen a decrease in the importance of the military and an increase in the importance of the police component. While there was a last minute reduction in the military component and a small increase in the number of police monitors, this realignment was insufficient to meet the needs of the operation. As a consequence, the number of police monitors needed to be increased threefold once the operation was underway.[18]

Moreover, despite the ambiguous allowance that would enable such personnel to 'take measures against intimidation or interference with the electoral process', the effectiveness of CIVPOL was mixed. As Roger Hearn notes, in the formative months of the deployment CIVPOL were limited in their ability to act against violence, with one local resident commenting that 'If UNTAG got beaten up he would wipe off the blood from his face, take notes and do nothing'.[19] This situation did improve but signalled the need to have sufficient personnel together with adequate logistical help, amongst other things, if a mission was to achieve its objectives.

UNTAG was, at that point in time, unprecedented in its focus on facilitating democratic processes. In part because of this more complicated mandate Namibia cemented the importance of police in these increasingly complex UN peace operations as such operations required a more nuanced response. Although there was no major recognition paid to the importance of police in terms of major UN reviews or external commentary at the time, the increase in police numbers underscored that police could well become increasingly important actors in such situations. Thus CIVPOL numbers numbered a mere 35 in early 1988, but over 1,500 CIVPOL from 25 countries served in Namibia.[20]

From here policing operations continued to snowball. A deployment to Panama in 1989 was part of the much larger US actions intended to remove Manual Noriega from power but these police actions faced significant deployment gap problems.[21] A longer term though fairly modest policing programme also began in 1989 in Papua New Guinea. The Royal Papua New Guinea Constabulary Development Project lasted for 16 years from 1989 to 2005 and involved Australian expertise in aiding capacity and institution-building, especially in management.[22] Similar bilateral efforts were also being established by the US in Latin American countries at this time though these also tended to focus more narrowly on technical or technological matters.[23]

By the end of the 1980s, then, police professionals were being deployed in bilateral programmes or through UN auspices to undertake a variety of tasks such as election monitoring, community liaison, and monitoring and advising of local police forces. Civilian police in UN peacekeeping operations were now identifiable as 'CIVPOL' and, as demonstrated through the appointment of a police commissioner in Namibia, had begun to be recognised as an important and qualitatively different part of peacekeeping operations. This role of police in international missions was, moreover, set to increase further into the 1990s.

Pushing the boundaries of the SMART model

At the start of the 1990s CIVPOL were deployed to the second UN Angola Verification Mission (UNAVEM II) to help monitor the neutrality of the Angolan National Police during the election period. The UN mission that had begun in 1991 was initially stymied when war broke out following the ambiguous election results. However UNAVEM's mission was finally extended to monitor the ceasefire in November 1994. This mission was significant because it again saw an increased role for police. A total of 260 CIVPOL members from 21 member states were mandated to verify and monitor the activities and armaments of the Angolan National Police, and to verify the demobilisation and induction of soldiers into the Police or into the Rapid Reaction Police (RRP, a paramilitary type of force).[24]

A quietly undertaken but vital CIVPOL role also unfolded in 1991 in protecting humanitarian relief supplies for Kurdish populations following the Gulf War, though much of the broader provision of security role was a military responsibility.[25] Also of interest but again little known was the 1992 deployment of police observers from Commonwealth countries to South Africa – ostensibly acting as a catalyst for change with regards to policing issues.[26] This latter deployment can therefore, with the benefit of hindsight, be said to be significant in that it was supportive of the development of democratic policing norms.

A UN Protection Force (UNPROFOR, a force which involved military, civilian and policing elements) then deployed to three UN Protected Areas (UNPAs) in Croatia in 1992. UNPROFOR was tasked with 'creating' the conditions of peace required for negotiating an overall peace agreement for the former Yugoslavia.[27] The role of CIVPOL monitors was significant in that they were tasked with overseeing the activities of local police forces and ensuring that basic human rights within the UNPAs were protected.[28] In September 1992 UNPROFOR's area of operations was extended into Bosnia where the emphasis was on delivering humanitarian relief and the provision of protection when directed by UN High Commissioner for Refugees (UNHCR), and it was later replaced by the UN Confidence Restoration Operation (UNCRO) which operated from 1995 to 1996, terminating with the establishment of the Croatian administration. The length of involvement of international policing forces in the Balkans, under both UN and EU banners, highlights that such missions may be very protracted affairs.

In the United Nations Operation in Mozambique (ONUMOZ) that followed in 1992 CIVPOL again had a very broad mandate. In instances similar to those outlined above CIVPOL were to: monitor police activities, verify details of police forces, monitor citizens' rights and civil liberties, and to monitor the election campaign.[29] However ONUMOZ was also a precursor to later training and police reform missions as the civilian policing component was to 'monitor and verify the process of reorganisation and retraining of the local Quick Reaction Police' – though ONUMOZ itself did not conduct the training.[30] ONUMOZ therefore had political, military, humanitarian and electoral responsibilities that required those deployed to pacify a conflict-ridden country and to help transform the government from a single-party state to a multiparty democracy.[31] ONUMOZ was also noteworthy in that no major power from the region, from the permanent five or from any other important country took a leadership role in the operation – either as troop contributor or political patron – and this may have helped ensure a higher level of acceptability of the mission.[32] Yet despite this CIVPOL personnel still found themselves facing a myriad of problems: the local police forces were very underpaid, and often corrupt; suspects were detained awaiting trial for an average of two years; a lack of resources bedevilled police, the courts and the Attorney General; deaths and instances of torture in custody were fairly common; detentions frequently occurred without legal reasons; and CIVPOL personnel were themselves often unsuited, with a number of personnel unable to drive or to speak any of the official languages, and some were of a nationality disliked by the host country.[33]

In El Salvador in the early 1990s CIVPOL police undertook another unprecedented step. Reform and training were now part of the CIVPOL agenda as a new El Salvadorean police force was to be brought into being, helped in particular by the United Nations Observer Mission in El Salvador (ONUSAL) Human Rights and Police Divisions, and by police advisers brought in by the United Nations Development Program (UNDP).[34] Previously the local police (National Police, National Guard, Treasury Police) had been part of the Ministry of Defence, were trained by military instructors and had a tarnished human rights record. Paramount in this exercise in police reform in El Salvador was thus the downsizing of military influence.[35] The new National Civilian Police was to be completely independent from the armed forces and under civilian control. The new police academy called the National Academy of Public Security opened in September 1992, and the Policia Nacional Civil (PNC) began to be deployed in March 1993, replacing the National Police within two years and bringing to a head the peace process that had begun with initial talks in April 1990.[36] One theme highlighted in this situation was the importance of a civilian policing approach to cement a civilian rather than military ethos. And much effort was made throughout the peace process to ensure that there was clear discussion as to what the new police force should be like, encouraging a strong commitment from both government and rebel leaders to bring this police force into being.[37] From this example of successful reform, then, police involvement in UN operations continued to deepen.

The emergence of executive policing

The UN Transitional Authority in Cambodia (UNTAC) mission in the early to mid-1990s presented civilian police with a unprecedented profile in a post-conflict peace operation. Following the signing of the Paris Peace Accord on October 23 1991, and the passing of United Nations Security Council Resolution – UNSCR 745, UNTAC began operating in 1992. UNTAC eventually came to be a very large mission in terms of police numbers with total CIVPOL numbers reaching 3,600 personnel contributed by 32 countries.[38] The significance of this mission lay in the fact that although CIVPOL were initially limited to monitoring local police to ensure the maintenance of public order, they later received limited executive authority.[39]

In terms of significant characteristics of this deployment, the military component in UNTAC was ostensibly there to provide a 'neutral political environment' and key tasks included: monitoring the ceasefire, disarmament, regroupment, and demobilisation of factional forces. The civilian police component, on the other hand, was tasked with 'stabilising the security situation', and, as noted, an important part of this particular role was the regulation of existing police forces in Cambodia.[40] Major issues arising from UNTAC included a lack of clarity about how these apparently separate roles could be demarcated from one another in terms of day-to-day operations, and the relevant jurisdictions of the two agencies. This highlighted the difficulties in establishing a clear division of labour between the two forces, particularly as military affairs tended to dominate to the extent that military aspects of the mission 'pervaded almost every aspect of UNTAC's mandate'.[41] Another problem was the lack of planning and preparation for the civilian police aspect of the peace operation in general.[42] Indeed a number of commentators have stressed the lack of overall emphasis on security sector reform.[43] And further questions remain over how successful the mission actually was – with continuing factional strife, a bloated military capacity, inefficient bureaucracy and a fragile economic status leading to concerns that further international involvement may be necessary in the new millennium.[44]

The situation in Cambodia was most significant, however, in that police were given the authority to make arrests mid-way through the operation – executive policing received its first mandate. However as Annika Hansen suggests, the implementation of the CIVPOL mandate (which involved the supervision and control of State of Cambodia (SOC) police) was sidetracked when conditions became more unstable and local police were unwilling to cooperate leaving the UN 'decidedly apprehensive' about the practicality of an executive policing role.[45] Part of the reason for that apprehension was the patchy performance of the CIVPOL contingent, with a number of officers being repatriated because of unacceptable behaviour.[46] This helped lead to the development of the United Nations Criminal Justice Standards for Peacekeeping Police Handbook. This was released in 1994 with the help of CIVPOL members who had served in UNPROFOR and UNTAC, in the hope that it would prove useful in future UN operations 'acting as a catalyst for change in law enforcement and police behaviour, as well as a guide for effective and fair criminal justice administration'.[47] The Handbook covers the role of police as it relates to fulfilling duties imposed by law, serving the community, protecting persons against illegal acts, and respecting and protecting human rights. It also outlines the procedures for lawful arrest, the use of force and firearms, trials, the handling of victims, refugees, detainees and prisoners, and the need for law enforcement officers to resist corruption, the use of torture, illegal executions and genocide. Some efforts to increase basic standardisation of policing under UN auspices were therefore underway, but the UN were not the only actors engaged in international policing efforts at this time.

Increasing involvement of other actors

The joint police-military mission in Haiti, like the mission in Cambodia, met with mixed success and – like Cambodia – saw the eventual introduction of executive policing. In addition to police efforts in Haiti 'the UN focused on training an effective police force, and the United States, Canada and France, among others, have provided assistance for building a judicial system', and it is significant that in this case these basic political institutions had never really functioned properly before.[48] This mission was also notable in that it was both a coalition and UN police force.

The initial US-led Multinational Force (MNF) was comprised of 920 International Police Monitors (IPM) from 26 countries who were authorised by the 1993 Governor's Island Accord to carry sidearms, to arrest and to use deadly force when necessary (this included US contributing personnel who were often commercially contracted private operators who wore US government uniforms and carried US government weapons).[49] In planning for the UN part of the mission, Dante Caputo, the UN Secretary General's special envoy for Haiti, had moved swiftly to call for a 500-strong international police presence by early 1993, and over 800 police officers joined some 6,000 troops in the UN deployment (UN Mission in Haiti – UNMIH), in January 1995, and took over from the MNF.[50] Forces deployed to Haiti were effectively there to help facilitate the restoration of democracy in a member state, and one of their biggest challenges related to police reform as local police had previously been dual-role personnel who simply donned police or military uniforms to suit the occasion.[51]

This was thus another important deployment as it was the first time that CIVPOL explicitly had 'police development' included in its mandate which began with the recruitment of an Interim Public Security Force (IPSF) made up of vetted Haitian police.[52] And, like the US part of the mission, UN police also had executive authority. Important elements of the mission that encouraged successes included: the unity of purpose demonstrated by those involved in the mission, the usefulness of pre-mission training, the use of the 'four men in a jeep' concept (whereby an MP (Military Police) driver, an IPM and an IPSF officer travelled together with an interpreter) and, not to be underestimated in thinking about coordination and jurisdiction issues, a comprehensive political-military plan for the US Government agencies involved.[53] Here too the involvement of US Army Special Forces and Military Police was thought to have helped to prevent a 'security gap'.[54] Yet although the reformed police force at first performed reasonably well, by 1999 it was under fire for heavy-handedness and was plagued by corruption, drug problems and human rights abuses.[55] In response to these perceived failings some critics argued that further steps need to be taken by Haitian leaders and the international community to secure a sustainable peace in Haiti.[56] Since that time the overall effort in Haiti has continued to be labelled as 'largely ineffectual' in that 9,000 uniformed personnel for the United Nations Stabilisation Mission in Haiti (MINUSTAH) remain in country in 2007.[57] Some argue that improvements have been forthcoming – pointing out that there have been some decreases in kidnappings, elections were carried out in early 2007, and that police are able to operate more effectively in previously impervious slum areas – but the situation in Haiti remains shaky, and a similar situation prevails in Somalia.[58]

Mandated by UNSCR 794 to use all necessary means to create a secure environment for the delivery of humanitarian aid in Somalia, Operation Restore Hope lasted from December 9 1992 to March 26 1993 and was based around the US-led United Task Force (UNITAF). Although UNITAF did not have a civilian policing component *per se*, it did get involved in trying to re-establish the Somalia National Police (SNP) force in part at least to avoid the need for UNITAF to take on policing roles. However, as Robert Perito points out, the US began to help recruit and train an Auxiliary Security Force made up of former SNP personnel, and this was significant as the US did so without a specific UN mandate though the project received UNDP funding.[59]

Then in May 1993 a CIVPOL contingent of 300 from 28 member states (300 instead of the proposed 759, with the number of nationalities causing a number of problems) arrived in Western Sahara to assist in the maintenance of law and order in the vicinity of voter registration and polling stations, and to assist UNHCR in refugee repatriation.[60] Also in Africa in that same year CIVPOL personnel were involved in the UN Assistance Mission for Rwanda (UNAMIR) that was established in October 1993. Sixty police officers were initially deployed to assist in the maintaining of public security through the monitoring and verification of the activities of the communal police and the gendarmerie that made up the Rwandese Police Force – though this number grew to 120 by late 1994 and the mandate grew to include the training of new gendarmes and their instructors too.[61]

Also in 1993, at the behest of the Macedonian government, the UN deployed the UN Preventive Deployment to Macedonia (UNPREPDEP) which quickly rose to over 1,000 personnel. UNPREPDEP demonstrated an interesting mix of both different agencies (military and police) and different multilateral institutions. Indeed, in addition to such UN deployments, other institutions began to respond to the need to secure public order in the Balkans. The Organisation for Security and Cooperation in Europe (OSCE) not only helped with municipal elections in Kosovo, but it maintained a long-running field presence in the form of the OSCE Spillover Mission (instigated in 1992 to try to prevent Macedonia from being engulfed in the conflicts that came with the breakdown of Yugoslavia), and, most importantly, it has undertaken a number of police development programmes in Croatia, Kosovo, and Macedonia where the OSCE was involved in training and integrating Albanian police.[62] The Western European Union has also done likewise in Albania with regards to police training and development too.[63]

In 1994 the UN launched a verification mission to Guatemala known as MINUGUA that involved police personnel in monitoring a ceasefire and taking part in institution-building efforts.[64] Also in 1994, following the shift from the short-lived (five months) UNITAF mission to the United Nations Operation in Somalia (UNOSOM), UNSC Resolution 814 authorised the UN Secretary General to assist Somalia in the reorganisation of the Somali police force. CIVPOL's main task was to re-organise the Somali police, and the strategy was that CIVPOL would re-engage members of the former police force; train them; equip the force with necessary logistical support; and repair police infrastructure.[65] The full complement of 54 CIVPOL personnel had arrived by July 1994, with five additional police advisers from Australia, Bangladesh, the Philippines and Zambia. US International Criminal Investigative Training Assistance Program (ICITAP) personnel also arrived in 1994 though debate raged over their possible roles as US law did not at that time allow for support for a foreign police institution.[66]

The UN mandate for the deployment to Somalia ended in March 1995 with the Somali police force having been strengthened to 6,500 officers.[67] The police force established by UNOSOM II was disadvantaged by: the ongoing armed status of conflicting factions; by a focus on keeping relatively stable areas safe rather than tackling contested areas; by a selection process that was not sensitive enough to clan politics; and by UNOSOM establishing pay rates that were unsustainable.[68] And although efforts were made to undertake broader judicial and penal reform efforts, the Justice Division plan was never actually funded nor the personnel provided, thus when UNOSOM withdrew, many of these forces and accompanying judiciaries collapsed and were often replaced by more shari'a authorities.[69] A RAND report which assessed the levels of success in terms of these nation-building efforts in Somalia argued that the mission was, overall, not a successful one.[70]

Policing efforts on Bougainville, on the other hand, have met with more robust successes to date and is notable for its grass-roots approach to building community policing at a village level The Bougainville Community Policing Project (BCPP) has been an important part of a peace process instituted after nearly a decade of secessionist violence. The BCPP began in 1999 as a joint AusAID/NZAID project. The first phase lasted from late 1999–late 2001 and was primarily focused on identifying and training suitable men and women to serve as community police. Since 2004 the BCPP recommenced some operations funded solely by NZAID and was intended to provide:

- Audit, motivation and refresher training for community auxiliary police;
- Extend community police training across the country;
- Build local capacity to enable local police to further develop community policing;

- Support improved relations between the local community, community police and the Royal Papua New Guinea Constabulary (RPNGC);
- And provide some logistical support.[71]

This project has involved outside assistance from the Participating Police Force (PPF) and local forces now include: Bougainville Police Service (BPS); RPNGC and Community Auxiliary Police (CAP). As of early 2008 the mission to Bougainville has been extended to provide additional support to the BPS to augment that support to the CAP that was provided under the initial phases outlined above.

Also more recently, British personnel have played a lead role in training the Police in Sierra Leone which has resulted in some successes.[72] And the last day of 2002 saw the conclusion of the UN Mission in Bosnia and Herzegovina (UNMIBH), the largest police reform and restructuring operation in UN history that had begun in 1995 following the adoption of UNSC Resolution 1035.[73] This was also the first time that a regional organisation (NATO) had been endorsed by the UN to lead the military part of the peace operation, and UNMIBH was later replaced in part by an ongoing EU police reform mission.[74]

The consolidation of police reform roles

The UN Secretary General's Special Representative in Bosnia and Herzegovina, Jacques Paul Klein, argued that there had been a '50 year tradition of police serving the state at the expense of the individual. In essence, it was rule by law enforcement – rather than the democratic function of police upholding the rule of law'.[75] Under the 1995 Dayton Peace Accords, the UN was given the mandate of monitoring the reform and restructuring of law enforcement institutions, while other international organisations dealt with security, refugee returns, and legal and economic reforms. The shape of the UN's International Police Task Force (IPTF) was worked out between members of the Contact Group (UK, France, Russia, Germany and the US), with the US calling for an armed, highly capable force with executive powers and with an additional ready reaction unit and European members advocating unarmed UN police monitors, the eventual result being a force that 'could operate only with the consent, cooperation, and protection of the same Bosnian police it was supposed to monitor'.[76] The IPTF did not, therefore, have executive policing powers, and indeed in the troubled times that followed in Bosnia, officers were at times taken hostage and used as human shields.[77]

Despite this apparently unpromising start, UNMBIH claims a number of accomplishments were achieved, among these:

- [Local] Police forces downsized by nearly two-thirds to 17,000 uniformed personnel – all trained to international democratic policing standards and vetted to eliminate those who had been involved in war crimes or other offences.
- Law enforcement institutions de-politicised and certified as meeting international norms of procedures and organisation.
- A new generation of police officers have been produced, with an increased proportion of them women and minorities.[78]

This deployment attempted to transform the broader organisational culture of policing in Bosnia; as evidenced by the requirement that all ten federation cantonal police and the Republika Srpska police sign a commitment to 'democratic policing' before they received assistance. However it was also dogged by problems such as those stemming from an initially slow deployment and high personnel turnover.[79] This in turn exacerbated problems of communication, as a Judicial Police Law was drafted and passed without the knowledge of many international and local officials.[80] More significantly the IPTF was, for a long time, unable to quell ongoing ethnic strife and violence.[81] Indeed, an attack on UN police and US soldiers in mid-1997 helped bring about the arrival of a Multinational Specialised Unit (MSU) charged with the protection of returnees and elected officials. This MSU was to be called on to assist in preserving public order only at the behest of the IPTF.[82] The use of Italian Carabiniere in Bosnia as the basis of the MSU therefore provided the IPTF with a formed unit for particular tasks requiring more 'muscle' that would provide a more robust response to civil disorder. This was a significant development in that it ushered in a trend towards the increased use of such formed police units in post-conflict peace operations.

In terms of the ongoing situation in Bosnia there remain some outstanding issues. EU involvement continues on in the country as ratified by UNSCR 1396, and police reform remains a key issue that is stalling Bosnia's EU membership.[83] The Bosnian situation is most significant in that it demonstrates the possibility of the EU and other actors producing some sort of division of labour, with the UN providing the initial legitimacy in a peacekeeping and peacebuilding context; NATO providing security through military deployment in NATO-led Multinational Stabilisation Force (SFOR); and then the EU stepping in to carry on longer-term police reform efforts whilst inviting along some additional non-member states too. But it also demonstrated an additional problem not yet mentioned here – that of the issue of immunity from prosecution for police deployed abroad – as the US vetoed a UNSCR extending the UN mission in 2002 as the Council had refused to grant the 46 US police officers serving in the IPTF immunity from the incoming International Criminal Court (ICC).[84]

In addition to the deployment to Bosnia, the UN was also encouraged by the successes of the United Nations Transitional Administration in Eastern Slavonia, Baranja and Western Sirmium (UNTAES). Here international police worked alongside existing local police forces, eventually replacing them with a new multi-ethnic police force. Police reform ran smoothly and to the established time frame – making UNTAES, argues Annika Hansen, the 'most immediate predecessor' for the missions in Kosovo and East Timor in that it emboldened the UNSC to approve complete legislative and executive authority for the UN in these missions.[85] International policing had begun to become a much more important part of missions around the world.

The development of international policing writ large

Gavin Brown, Barry Barker and Terry Burke have suggested in their analysis of the Australian and New Zealand contributions to the Cyprus deployment, that it is a surprise 'that it took so long for the United Nations to call on professional police from member States to facilitate peace-keeping operations'.[86] However the real surprise is that so many elements of international policing remained so underdeveloped for many years after this deployment to Cyprus. Indeed, as the narrative above clearly shows, it was only really in the 1990s that the value of international policing as an integral part of peace support (and other) operations began to be recognised. Following the experience in Namibia police began to be deployed abroad in greater numbers and with greater remits for action. But this increase in policing activity has unfolded without fanfare. The sections below therefore consider the development of international policing in a more thematic setting: pointing to the increasing roles being ascribed to police in international peace operations; to UN figures that underscore the significant increase in international police numbers; and to the increase in the capacity of different international, regional and national bodies for the provision of police professionals to any policing operation – UN or otherwise.

The development of international policing has seen a broadening and deepening of police involvement in peace operations. By the late 1990s civilian police were increasingly involved in peace operations where the criminal justice system had totally collapsed, causing police responsibilities to be broadened to include law enforcement work.[87] A shift away from the previous restriction of police 'to [only] monitor and to support the local police on training issues' in peace support operations had begun.[88] The emphasis on monitoring found in early missions through to the mid-1990s was soon joined by mandates for reform and training in El Salvador and 'police development' in Haiti. From there police deployments have increasingly been tasked with growing responsibilities.

Thus the actual institution of international policing itself has altered greatly. Up until the end of the 1990s CIVPOL focused on a 'SMART' model of civilian policing abroad – 'SMART' meaning Support, Monitoring, Administering, Reporting and Training.[89] Publications from the mid-1990s underscore this emphasis, mentioning monitoring, training and assistance as tasks for those involved in peace missions.[90] Yet, as noted, throughout the 1990s this limited policing focus was challenged as CIVPOL and other policing personnel (such as the Americans in Somalia) found themselves taking on greater responsibilities as needs and expectations changed. Gradual institutional changes in terms of the roles and mandates of the civilian police personnel involved in peace support and other operations has meant that into the new millennium such officers involved in deployments were to be tasked with the following roles:

- advisory
- mentoring
- law enforcement
- selection, recruitment, training, establishment of a credible local police force
- human rights
- humanitarian
- elections
- IDPs and returnees[91]

Further, even fairly innocuous sounding tasks like 'monitoring' have altered greatly. Here Annika Hansen points out that what was once fairly haphazard observation became far more systematic reviews that monitor compliance with internationally accepted standards of human rights and the UN Criminal Justice Standards (UNCJS).[92] Similarly, in undertaking police 'reform' in other countries it also has to be recognised that the content of such reform programmes have also changed. There has been a move away from police reform which focuses only on technical and structural issues (size, organisation, equipment etc) to that which focuses on building the public's confidence in the police as a force for public safety and security that is independent of political agendas.[93] The importance of democratic policing, in particular, has also come to the fore.[94] As we will see in the following case study chapters the emphasis now is often on capacity-building, on the support and restructuring of institutional systems in fragile or transitional states as well as in post-conflict situations, and this requires a great depth and breadth of skills.[95] Operations may require interim law enforcement and operational support as in the Cambodia case. Or, as in the Bosnia case, they can increasingly involve reform efforts based on democratic policing principles, on restructuring police forces to depoliticise them or on rebuilding indigenous forces to ensure they are capable of carrying out their policing roles.[96]

Moreover the sheer number of police professionals being involved in international policing efforts has increased dramatically. As we have seen CIVPOL numbers grew from 35 in 1988 to 1,500 during Namibia, and by February 2000 the UN had deployed a total of 9,000 CIVPOL around the world.[97] In even more recent times, numbers of UN police deployed on operations increased from 7,300 in August 2006 to 8,800 in January 2007 to 9,600 in August 2007, and projections suggest that the number will likely grow to 13,000 in 2008.[98] Others have suggested that the figure may even reach as high as 17,000 if projected deployments to Chad and elsewhere also go ahead. And these are only UN figures.

In thinking more deeply about how international policing has developed, then, it is significant that the UN has radically altered how it manages the policing part of peace operations. The Namibia case was a watershed in terms of prompting the use of a police commissioner in the field, moving the control of CIVPOL securely under the influence of police rather than pure military control. Since that time the developments in the field have been supported by corresponding shifts within UN headquarters at New York. Thus Boutros Boutros-Ghali's Agenda for Peace released in 1992 signalled a more systematic approach to CIVPOL involvement in UN peace operations and this was supported institutionally by the May 1993 creation of a separate Civilian Police Unit at the UN Department of Peacekeeping Operations (DPKO) tasked with the planning and coordination of all matters relating to CIVPOL activities in UN peacekeeping operations.[99] Yet it was not until the Brahimi Report of 2000 that the UN explicitly called on member states to 'establish a national pool of civilian police officers that would be ready for deployment to United Nations peace operations on short notice'.[100] The Report also called for a 'doctrinal shift' in the use of CIVPOL (who, since 2005, have been called UNPOL) and other personnel involved in rule of law institutions to reflect an increasing focus on strengthening human rights and the rule of law in post-conflict situations, and asserted that CIVPOL actively retrain and restructure local police, not just 'observe and scold' – thereby reinforcing the shift to executive policing.[101] The Civilian Police Unit has since been upgraded to a Civilian Police Division and the Division's head was promoted to the same level as the military adviser to the Under-Secretary General for Peacekeeping.[102] The UN Police Division remains part of the DPKO, but as of mid-2007 has become part of a new Office of the Rule of Law and Security Institutions which places the Police Division alongside Criminal Law and Judicial Advisory Section, DDR Section and Mine Action Service and which entails the Office to its own Assistant Secretary General.[103]

In addition to such developments at UN headquarters, regional UN bodies such as the OSCE and the Organisation of American States (OAS) which report back to the UN once missions are underway, have also increased their involvement in policing efforts with the OSCE having developed its own Police Academy and with OAS playing an important role in policing reform efforts in Haiti. These changes signal wider UN recognition of the growing importance of police in peace operations, but as this chapter has shown there are a number of other actors on the policing scene too.[104] Indeed, as noted above, the UN authorised NATO to undertake a Chapter VII enforcement mission in Bosnia-Herzegovina and has also mandated the International Security Assistance Force (ISAF) mission in Afghanistan. Yet regional organisations have also undertaken enforcement missions without UNSC authorisation (despite Article 53 of the UN Charter which states that this is necessary), and a division of labour is painfully being worked out between the UN, regional organisations and individual states when it comes to undertaking such policing missions.

The EU in particular is an emergent regional player in international policing efforts. In Europe both the European Council and the European Commission have become increasingly involved in international policing issues.[105] The European Council's activities are focused on the peace and security tasks assigned to it under the Second Pillar of the

EU's European Security and Defence Policy (ESDP) or Common Security and Foreign Policy (CSFP). Here a number of police training projects are offered under ESDP auspices for European Union states and/or for those aspiring to EU status. These are courses such as: civilian crisis management; training in ESDP terminology; police standards training as offered to eligible states at the European Police College (CEPOL); or more particular courses such as those intended to improve interoperability between formed police units (such as the French and Romanian gendarmerie, Spanish Guard and Italian carabiniere) for deployment on EU missions.[106] In terms of ESDP operations on the ground there have been a number of ESDP police missions ongoing in the new century in places such as Bosnia, Georgia, Former Yugoslavian Republic of Macedonia (FRYOM), Kosovo, Afghanistan, Iraq, Palestinian territories, Congo, and in Aceh, Indonesia.[107] Here there are two important points to make. The first is that not one of these has been an executive policing mission (though this is set to change in Kosovo). The second is that a working division of labour with the European Commission is starting to emerge as, for example, parts of the activity in Aceh were funded by the European Commission though monitoring was undertaken by the Council.[108] More generally there is an ambitious plan for the future of ESDP policing currently underway.[109] (Another EU institution, EUROPOL, like INTERPOL, partakes in 'policing activities' but these are predominantly intelligence gathering and information sharing institutions).

Yet this involvement of regional organisations in policing efforts is not merely the preserve of the Europeans. Far away from Europe in the vast Pacific Ocean the Pacific Islands Chiefs of Police (PICP) organisation brings together police chiefs from 21 member countries and territories throughout the region. Pushed in part by post-September 11 security demands which have placed a large manpower and budgetary burden on small island nations, at the end of 2007 the PICP released a new strategic document outlining future directions in Pacific policing beyond 2010 which encapsulates regional priorities. These focus on capacity development, increased cooperation, and ethics and integrity, and look to the issues faced in achieving such goals such as: cultural fit, stakeholder engagement, good governance, gender issues and sustainability.[110] New Zealand and Australia have also been encouraging a pooling of resources through the creation of the Pacific Regional Policing Initiative (PRPI) which was based in Fiji until the coup of January 2007, and which currently operates out of Brisbane. The five year initiative will train up to 900 Pacific police officers each year to contribute towards the fight against terrorism and organised crime.[111] Possibilities for a regional peacekeeping or policekeeping force have been mooted but these discussions have not yet resulted in any concrete initiatives.

Other regional and sub-regional initiatives, developments in information sharing and/or more general cooperation with regards to policing across borders have also been initiated or deepened in recent years. The Nordic Police and Customs Operation, the South Asian Association for Regional Cooperation (SAARC), the Southern African Regional Police Chiefs Cooperation Organisation (SARPCCO), are all examples of more general kinds of increased police cooperation. (Significantly, SARPCCO allows police from one signatory country to cross the border of another to arrest fugitives without a request and clearance from the head of the state government in which the arrest occurs).[112] The development of sub-regional bodies such as ASEANAPOL (ASEAN Police Chiefs), where the chiefs of police of members of the Association of South East Asian Nations (ASEAN) meet annually, is another example of an institution that has allowed for increased cooperation – this time focusing on information sharing.[113] Asia Pacific Economic Cooperation (APEC) and the Shanghai Cooperation Organisation (SCO) have also increasingly been involved in the security field by finding a strong *raison d'etre* in their focus on improving regional counter-terrorism capabilities and coordination, whilst the Organisation for Economic Cooperation and Development (OECD) has invested much time and resources in developing broader security sector reform guidelines too.[114]

Moreover, a number of individual states are beginning to recognise the value of sending police abroad to participate in peace support operations. Australia, for example, has increased the resources and personnel allocated to its International Deployment Group (IDG). The Australian Federal Police (AFP) has an International Division which includes a Peace Operations Unit and international law enforcement activities – and the AFP's budget appropriations have increased from $317 million in 2000–2001 to $557 million in 2003–4 (and this latter figure does not include additional monies for the Solomon Islands effort).[115] In 2007–8 the IDG is set to increase to 1,200 personnel. Nearby in New Zealand an International Service Group (ISG) was established in December 2005 and has been hard pressed to keep up with demand for its services, though it has not as of yet been able to meet those demands with a set Deployment Pool Concept.

Across the Pacific in the US the shift in official interest in policing abroad has been even more dramatic with a number of ups and downs in recent times. The US' Office of Public Safety provided police training for over one million police personnel from 34 countries in the 1960s and 70s in the areas of: criminal investigation, riot control, patrolling; interrogation; counter-insurgency and use of weapons.[116] However, due to perceived negative experiences with these foreign police forces during the first half of the Cold War, in 1974 the Foreign Assistance Act of 1961 was amended to prohibit US agencies from training or assisting foreign police (with the exception of law enforcement activity allowances for the Federal Bureau of Investigation (FBI) and Drug Enforcement Agency (DEA)). This changed with the establishment of the International Criminal Investigative Assistance Program (ICITAP) in 1986.

ICITAP was, as its name suggests, designed to improve investigative, management and training capacities in troubled countries.[117] From here, throughout the 1990s and as highlighted above, reform of foreign police forces was seen as a necessary part of democracy promotion and transnational crime prevention – and this was reflected in the numbers of US police deployed abroad (1996 an average of 154 police officers deployed each month; 1997 this average was 275, and by the end of 1999 these were up to more than 600).[118] However, there have always been difficulties in sending American police abroad to participate in overseas missions, and at least part of this trouble stems from the fact that the US has no national police force, instead the US has 18,000 state and local police departments as well as a number of highly specialised federal law enforcement agencies.[119] This has remained a problem despite attempts since 2007 to introduce a new US Civilian Reserve Corp of police professionals, and has meant that the US predominantly relies on private contractors to organise and manage 'US' policing efforts abroad.[120]

Across the Atlantic the UK has continued to increase its international policing presence too, with over 150 police deployed abroad in 2007 and with much effort going into the creation of guidelines for policing in peace operations.[121] To the north, in Canada, the Royal Canadian Mounted Police (RCMP) have also increasingly been involved in international deployments. Though some operations have a longer history, such as the deployment to Bosnia from 1996, there has been a recent surge in overseas operations, with involvement in Jordan, Ivory Coast, Haiti, Sudan, Afghanistan, Timor-Leste and the practice of an officer being based at the Geneva Centre for the Democratic Control of Armed Forces (DCAF) all being undertaken since 2004.[122]

All of the above might suggest that such missions are predominantly the domain of wealthy, western, democratic states. And indeed the more qualitative move outlined above towards the promotion of democratic policing models might also intimate this. But figures taken from the 2nd edition of the UN Police Magazine provide an instructive corrective to this assumption. Here the magazine notes that in May 2007, the top 15 police contributing countries (PCCs) for UN missions were, in order of numbers of personnel deployed: Jordan (909 deployed); Pakistan (813); Bangladesh (776); Nepal (541); Senegal (489); India (485); Nigeria (414); Portugal (292); the Philippines (288); the USA (284); Turkey (275); Ukraine (230); Malaysia (220); Romania (219); and the People's Republic of China (184).[123] States which may or may not have a strong tradition of liberal democratic processes are, therefore, now the main source of police personnel in UN peace missions.

Indeed there has been much internal institution-building within these countries to be able to support this effort. For example, Nigeria has a Peacekeeping Department in the Office of the Inspector-General, headed by an Assistant Commissioner which, amongst other things, manages a reserve pool of 500 quick-release officers for international service, runs a Language Lab to assist officers in learning international mission languages and which selects and trains officers for testing by UN Selection Assistance Teams.[124] In China, too, major changes have been forthcoming. China had first approved the sending of police to participate in UN missions such as those undertaken in Kosovo, East Timor, Bosnia-Herzegovina, and Liberia. In 2002 Chinese officials then announced that China would be establishing Asia's largest peacekeeping civil police training centre, capable of training 250 police officers at one go, in Langfang City, near Beijing.[125] Chinese People's Armed Police (PAP) had deployed 177 officers to UN missions as of October 2007, and in 2006 30 officers were sent for training courses overseas.[126] Bangladesh and Pakistan too remain strong contributing countries to UN missions, building as they do on long peacekeeping histories, whilst other newer contributors are also coming on line. Here, for example, Indonesia has also seen an increased role for the Indonesian Police Force (POLRI) both within the state itself – balancing out the traditionally very strong role of the Indonesian Army (TNI) that has recently undergone major reform efforts – and in terms of an increased capacity to deploy internationally with Indonesia potentially looking to provide 100 police to the UN mission to the Sudan. (Interestingly there has also been a transference of policing from Japan into Indonesia, with a Japanese sponsored Koban idea being trialled in

Bekasi, whilst the UNDP, World Bank and others have partaken in various police reform and training efforts (counter-terrorism and community policing focus) in Indonesia too).[127] And lastly the world's newest country East Timor, which as we shall see was itself the destination of a major UN operation, sent a contingent of civilian police to Kosovo in 2005.[128] This final deployment brings us to the start of more detailed case studies with the following chapter assessing and analysing policing deployments to Kosovo and East Timor, deployments that combined together both executive policing and major police reform programmes in confirming that international policing had reached a new level.

3
Kosovo and East Timor

This chapter and the following two further explore the emergence of the new international policing through more detailed empirical investigations of recent deployments. This chapter assesses the formative cases of the deployments to Kosovo and East Timor; formative because they challenged the international community to reassess 'its perceptions of its duties of humanitarian intervention', and because they represented acceptance of executive policing and police reform in a much more systematic and comprehensive form.[1]

Kosovo

In late 1998, following years of attempts to stem conflict arising out of the breakup of the former Yugoslavia, UNSCR 1199 called on the Federal Republic of Yugoslavia (FRY) to cease all action by its military and security forces in Kosovo. This Resolution referred to 'further possible action' by the UN, but such action was not forthcoming from this particular institution, stymied as it was by members concerned about the rise of interventionist approaches.[2] Instead NATO began to wage an air campaign in attempts to halt Yugoslav security forces carrying out ethnic cleansing against Albanian Muslims in Kosovo. Operation Allied Force began a bombing campaign in Kosovo on 23 March 1999, and the campaign lasted until 10 June. Although there was no official UNSC mandate for this initial military action, once a tenuous peace had been established the UN was later handed much of the responsibility for administering the province. Thus one senior UN official at the time stated that 'It was a NATO war, it will be a UN peace'.[3] Yet both the UN and NATO elements of the mission to Kosovo faced major problems from their inception.

NATO's military presence in Kosovo, Kosovo Force (KFOR), began operations on 12 June 1999. KFOR was originally comprised of some 50,000 personnel, reducing to 39,000 troops in 2002, 26,000 by mid-2003 and 17,500 by end of 2003 with numbers in 2006–7 hovering around the 16,000 mark.[4] UN Interim Administration Mission in Kosovo (UNMIK) was created to work alongside KFOR. Here the arrangement was that KFOR had been mandated to keep the peace by UNSCR 1244 in June 1999, whilst UNMIK's task was to rebuild a more lasting peace in Kosovo. This task meant that 'international officials took over key administrative functions, from taxation to garbage collection, in what amounted to the creation of a UN protectorate'.[5]

The transitional administration was thus to involve the assumption of the authority and functions of the state, with these tasks being divided into four broad areas: police and justice; civil administration; democratisation and institution-building; and reconstruction and economic development.[6] UNMIK consisted therefore of four main 'pillars', and their roles in rebuilding a policing capability within Kosovo is shown in the figure below:

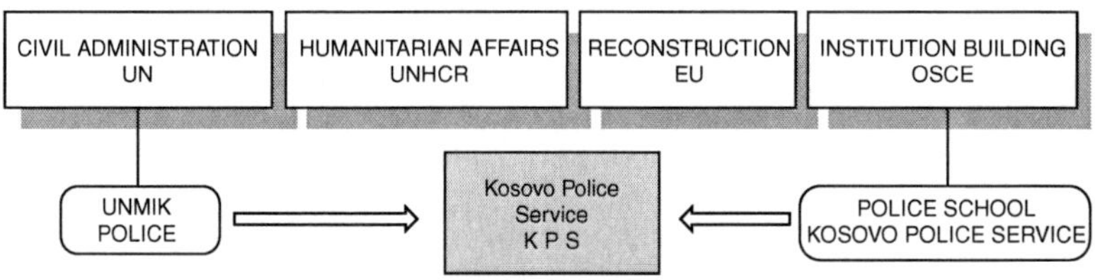

Figure 3.1 Kosovo Police Service[7]

UNMIK Police were to assist with policing and police administration, whilst (from September 1999) the OSCE was to train police officers according to international human rights and community-based policing standards.[8] The aim of these four pillars was to produce a new police service that was 'organized and functioning according to internationally recognized standard of democratic policing', and both UNMIK police and the OSCE Department of Police Education and Development were heavily involved in processing potential police recruits.[9] In terms of deployment, the mission area was divided into five regions with the UNMIK Police headquarters being located in Pristina. The five regional headquarters were located in Pristina, Pec, Gnjilane, Prizren and Mitrovica, and these were to be responsible for supervising police stations located in their area. Lastly, Border

Police were also stationed at border crossings and the airport. These arrangements, however, may well change from 2008, with the EU taking the lead.

Policing mandates and tasks

UNMIK under the leadership of the SRSG essentially operated a protectorate while overseeing development of provisional democratic self-governing institutions. Within this context there have been three main security actors, NATO's KFOR, UNMIK police and the Kosovo Police Service (KPS).

The UNMIK police operation was significantly different from previous United Nations civilian police missions, as UNMIK was a law enforcement unit with a mandate (under UNSCR 1244 of 10 June 1999):

1. To provide temporary law enforcement,
2. To establish and develop a professional, impartial and independent local police, called Kosovo Police Service (KPS).

   The mission for international police should be considered completed when the local police are able to enforce law and order according to international standards.[10]

Under this mandate UNMIK police undertook a number of tasks. In the initial phases UNMIK was to advise KFOR on policing matters. As the mission progressed and security improved, UNMIK CIVPOL were to take over normal police duties with executive law enforcement authority, and they were to be armed.[11] In case of major challenges to civil authority UNMIK also had recourse to special police units to contribute to the protection of UN staff, provide operational support and back-up to the civilian police, to deal with threats to public order in coordination with KFOR and to assist the KPS with crowd control.[12] UNMIK Special Police Units also protected UNMIK installations, and these came from India, Jordan, Argentina, Ukraine, Poland, Spain, and Pakistan.[13] (UNMIK therefore actually had three main policing components: CIVPOL (regular policing); Special or Formed Police Units (FPUs) and Border Police.) Lastly UNMIK was to transfer responsibilities for law and order and border control to the new KPS although UNMIK might still be used in an advisory or special backup capacity.[14] Specific tasks for UNMIK CIVPOL thus included: maintaining public order; investigation of crimes; preventative measures; field training for KPS; collection of criminal intelligence; border and immigration control and traffic control.[15]

At the same time UNMIK officers were undertaking this executive policing role, OSCE personnel were working to build a KPS. The rebuilding of a policing capability in Kosovo was and is no small matter. Potential KPS recruits were supposed to be at least 25, have a high school education and so on but most importantly they were supposed to demonstrate willingness to:

> work with all ethnic groups; follow the rule of law and protect human rights of all people, regardless of ethnicity, and to be intolerant of ethnic violence; and to have sufficient intellect, stability and strength of character to learn, apply and reinforce law enforcement techniques and concepts in the context of principles of democratic and community-oriented policing and internationally recognized human rights standards.[16]

Those new recruits, intentionally recruited from all minority groups including Serbs, attended the KPS school and were then assigned to a UNMIK Police station to undertake 17 weeks of field training and 80 hours of classroom work. The KPS school opened with a US director, 200 international police instructors (from 20 OSCE states), utilised a curriculum that had been developed by ICITAP but modified for the local situation, and met its initial goal of training 4,110 officers by September 2001.[17] Indeed, by mid-2005 almost 7,000 officers had graduated from the School – nearly the 7,300 estimated officers required for effective law enforcement within Kosovo.[18] In late February 2008 Kosovo became independent, and UNMIK's role in police and justice reform (in its wound down version since achieving the above) is slowly shifting to the EU under the ESDP rule of law mission though the effects of this transition are yet to be felt.

Issues and problems arising

a) Deployment and operational problems

In designing UNMIK, the UN sought to provide an all-purpose civilian police force with full executive law enforcement in Kosovo 'as soon as possible', with KFOR providing security for this to proceed.[19] Six thousand police were originally called for, though only 4,718 officers were authorised, and their arrival was notably slow; planning began in March, 156 police had arrived by August, and only 1,800 by mid-December.[20] Indeed, following the problems faced in Bosnia, a critical part of the deployment was that it was supposed to be spearheaded by ten companies of FPUs, yet the first one only arrived in April 2000 and the last in February 2002.[21] The case of Kosovo therefore clearly demonstrated the need for police forces specifically trained for international operations, and for the UN to create a package of laws to be used to avoid the emergence of a security vacuum whilst such institutions are hammered out.[22]

UNMIK also faced a number of substantial challenges with regards to the problem of penal and judiciary systems lagging behind, with early years of the operation being marred by intimidation and ethnic bias amongst local judges and prosecutors.[23] Some commentators also suggested that UNMIK's involvement was predominantly identified as having a 'police' identity as a mission, thereby making it difficult to incorporate non-police experts into the process.[24] These two issues were recognised and responded to, to some extent, with the appointing of international judges and lawyers in 2000 and with the formation in May 2001 of a new 'Police and Justice Pillar' to ensure coordination and a cohesive approach to public security.[25] These more technical matters were, as implied above, further complicated by the overarching political and social environment within which the KPS was operating.

b) Political and social context

In addition to the logistical difficulties in obtaining enough police officers, UNMIK personnel were also faced with the daunting knowledge that in this case these UN police were to have full executive law enforcement authority.[26] The reason why this was so daunting was that the particular context that UNMIK was working in was politically, socially and economically unstable. Here, then:

> The overarching problem in this area is not first and foremost an issue of models and resources, but rather an underlying, political impediment: the absence of a final settlement over Kosovo ... Simply put, the new police officers need to know which government they represent, whom they are to report to, and which law to apply, and this has fundamental consequences for those responsible for training them.[27]

Essentially Kosovo was a security vacuum with regards to domestic law and order capacity. Police had not been operating 'properly' for at least a decade as the Yugoslav police had been interested in primarily controlling rather than serving population, and the local population remained suspicious and wary both of authority figures and of each other. The fact that a number of CIVPOL were of poor quality further hampered UNMIK as noted below.[28]

Further difficulties stemmed from the fact that controlling the Kosovo Liberation Army (KLA) proved to be very difficult, with a number of retaliatory massacres, arsons and ethnic cleansing efforts being visited on Serbian populations from mid-1999 – though successes with regards to demilitarising the KLA have since been made.[29] Since that time broader regional political interests have also played into the Kosovo issue with the so-called 'Troika' of the EU, Russia and the US competing in pursuing their own agendas, with the 'Quint' of France, Germany, Italy, the US and the UK in particular weighing into the debate, creating much uncertainty in the lead up to February 2008 and continuing to feed ethnic divisions that have seen the emergence of parallel political and social institutions throughout Kosovo.[30]

Ethnic tensions have at times resulted in violence that has been difficult to contain. For example, in the March 2004 riots the KPS, UNMIK and even KFOR were hard pushed to deal with the situation effectively.[31] Indeed one of the major criticisms here was that this situation highlighted that the KPS were just not yet ready for the jobs that were being handed over to them from UNMIK.[32] And in December 2005 police again had to step up security in Kosovska Mitrovica, 45 kilometres north of the capital Pristina after violent rioting. This is a town that is divided between the Serb-dominated north and the ethnic Albanian south, and that some suggest has 'come to epitomize Kosovo's prevailing ethnic divide' where tensions remain high and clashes occur not infrequently.[33] Following Belgrade's recent encouragement of Kosovo Serbs to oppose the new EU missions Mitrovica was again the site of tension on 17 March 2008, when Serbs attacked UN and NATO forces removing protesters from a regional court, prompting the International Crisis Group to call for the EU, UN and NATO to better coordinate their activities in gradually introducing EU rule of law (EULEX) missions.[34]

These tensions are further complicated by a continuing problem with organised crime. Contraband drug smuggling, money laundering and a brisk black market in guns and weaponry continues to present significant problems for the KPS. These are problems that have not as of yet been able to be overcome by specialist UNMIK task forces against organised crime though overarching assessments claim a significant overall improvement in the security situation compared to the one during and immediately after the war.[35]

In this context, then, it is unhelpful that, perhaps like any fledgling political entity but arguably very politically sensitive nonetheless, there is a strong desire from the local populace to have a strong military capability, a focus which can overshadow the pressing need for strong domestic law and order institutions.[36] And it is also troublesome that KPS salaries remain low and that essential equipment is scarce – at the time of the riots mentioned above the KPS did not have any riot shields, protective gear, or adequate transport and they communicated by open analogue radio.[37] These issues create a vulnerable environment where temptation in the form of corruption or other misconduct may create problems for the KPS. Thus far, however, some of the more disturbing accusations of misconduct have been levelled at UNMIK personnel.

c) Misconduct

Quality not just quantity of the international police mission was also demonstrated as being an important issue in this case with some CIVPOL being arrested (by other UN and KPS police) for human trafficking in 2005. Here, according to Amnesty International as cited in a media report by Ekrem Krasniqi, international personnel make up about 20 per cent of sex trafficking customers, though its members comprise only 2 per cent of Kosovo's population.[38] Some measures have been taken to address these issues with the arrests mentioned above coming shortly after UNMIK launched a toll-free 'HelpLine' for victims of gender-based violence in Kosovo; whilst UNMIK also runs a very busy Trafficking and Prostitution Investigation Unit (TPIU).[39]

Similarly there were some difficulties in working with the Kosovo Protection Corps (KPC), a civil organisation for whom UNMIK was responsible for and who was also regularly supervised by KFOR. Here though KPC had a 'Code of Conduct' and was seen to be 'generally compliant' to this, in the early years of the new century serious concerns were expressed about illegal and extremist activity by KPC members.[40] These more specific concerns about how to incorporate particular groups into political and security processes have beleaguered efforts in Kosovo in part because an overarching strategy for Kosovo has been lacking.

d) Planning on an ad hoc basis throughout UNMIK as a whole

As Andreas Heinemann-Gruder, and Igor Grebenschikov point out, 'apart from ousting the Serb military and police presence, stabilizing and providing a basically secure environment, no master plan existed against which implementation could be measured'.[41] Indeed this has continued to be a major criticism of the entire UNMIK mission with the continued focus on ethnic distinctions as being important in the distribution of power plus the lack of any set timetable for UN withdrawal prompting a number of commentators to berate UNMIK as a disaster.[42] This overall lack of a timetable and concrete plans for the UN's exiting of Kosovo lent itself to an unnecessarily *ad hoc* approach to institution-building, training and policing.

Furthermore, the focus on administration and order as emphasised both in Kosovo and in the next case of East Timor encouraged a very technical view of the state that resulted in the people and institutions that deliver these being seen as unresponsive to local views and inputs.[43] More effort needed to have been made to increase local ownership of the whole state-building process.

Moreover, cooperation between police personnel from contributing countries has been difficult at times, with a lack of common rules of engagement and no unified command and communication structure. Similar issues arose with regards to police-military relations. In one example, in April 2002, a police unit trying to arrest wanted Serbians in north Mitrovica came under attack and could not obtain military backup as there had been a break down in communication.[44]

Yet despite some of these shortcomings there have been some successes. For example, there is more and more crossover between NATO and the EU in terms of cross-institution communication or even in terms of key personnel moving between the two institutions. Such developments may appear minor but can have major effects on the potential success of the operation at hand. Similarly an October 2007 United Nations Development Programme (UNDP) opinion poll showed a high level of public faith in the KPS. Here the KPS, together with KFOR were – with 77 per cent approval – the most trusted institution in Kosovo and were and believed to be the least corrupt, though only 29 per cent gave UNMIK approval.[45] Further improvements may be forthcoming with UNMIK's police commissioner Richard Monk concentrating on further development of the KPS, on strengthening its human resources department, and on reversing a top-heavy command structure agreed by his predecessor.[46] The absence of major violence in February 2008 and the possibility that this is a testing ground for the EU's ESDP (which brings a determination to succeed) must also be seen as a hopeful sign, though once again the momentum must be maintained in ensuring that the local population keeps faith with the ongoing changes.

Conclusions

Kosovo represented a watershed for international policing. Here international police contingents were neither just monitoring nor training, nor did they find themselves given some executive powers along the way as they had in Cambodia. Kosovo, then, followed in the footsteps of operations in Haiti and Bosnia and thereby signified an apparent acceptance that these more experimental efforts were worthy of pursuit. The notion that external agents could police others' jurisdictions in a multi faceted way was now firmly on the table. The new international policing had arrived.

UNMIK officers were therefore tasked from the very beginning with undertaking executive policing roles in another country and, alongside the OSCE, with contributing to the rebuilding of a local police force. The rebuilding of this new police force, the KPS, was set to be a difficult task because of the need to produce an impartial, 'ethnic-blind' police force with respect for democratic governance and human rights. Kosovo's recent history meant that there was both a security vacuum within which the operation had to begin, and that there had been some identification of 'sides' – making it crucial that all minority groups be included within the new force.

UNMIK's efforts have met with some successes. It was important that Kosovo was a case whereby different aspects of the mission were able to be shared out amongst various actors and institutions in an agreed division of labour. Here the UN SRSG was tasked with coordinating the activities of UN and other agencies in all areas. Thus Pillars One and Two (Police and Justice and Civil Administration) were UN-led; Pillar Three (Democratisation and Institution-Building) was led by OSCE; Pillar Four (reconstruction and economic development) was led by EU; whilst humanitarian affairs was led by the UN and European Commission Humanitarian Office (ECHO) and NATO provided secure environment within which the others could safely operate – all theoretically under the coordination of the SRSG.

From these efforts, moreover, there is now nearly the full complement of KPS officers at work within Kosovo. Recruitment rates reflect some diversity: graduating classes numbered 1–30 had approximately 84 per cent Kosovo Albanians, 10 per cent Kosovo Serbs and 6 per cent 'Other' (Kosovo Turks, Roma, Gorani, Bosniaks and Muslim Serbs) – and 15 per cent of these were women.[47] Perhaps most importantly, surveys of more than 6,000 people conducted at the end of 2003 found that 56 per cent believed that the performance of the KPS was excellent or good, 36 per cent fair and only 6 per cent poor.[48] A 2004 UNDP report argued that the reform of local policing in Kosovo had been by and large a success, and the more recent polls as mentioned above seem to confirm that the KPS is in a relatively good position at the start of a new phase in Kosovo's history.[49]

Yet as noted here deployment and misconduct problems, issues of duplication and institutional stove piping, and planning hiccups in spite of the above division of labour hampered peace efforts in Kosovo. Most fundamentally, however, the overall context within which those police have to operate remains unresolved despite the recent achievement of independence. The situation at a higher political level remains, for now, to a large extent unsettled and this case therefore highlights the limitations of policing in such situations in that it is only one piece of the puzzle in state-building efforts.[50] And a number of these issues are repeated in the case of East Timor.

East Timor

The UN's involvement in East Timor (or Timor-Leste as the country is now called) originally involved four main phases: UN Assistance Mission in East Timor (UNAMET); International Force East Timor (INTERFET); the UN Transitional Authority in East Timor (UNTAET) and the UN Mission in support of East Timor (UNMISET). In mid-2005 UN involvement was wound down to simply involve the establishment of a local UN office in

Mission	Time	Key task
UNAMET	11 June–24 October 1999	Organise and conduct public consultation on the future status of East Timor.
INTERFET	12 September 1999–23 February 2000	To restore peace and security and to protect and support UNAMET. Command of military operations transferred to UN Peacekeeping Force in February.
UNTAET	25 October 1999–20 May 2002	Peacekeeping operation responsible for administration of East Timor until independent.
UNMISET	20 May 2002–20 May 2005	Provide assistance to core administrative functions; provide interim law enforcement; contribute to maintenance of security.
UNOTIL	20 May 2005–25 August 2006	Help strengthen democratic governance.

Mission	Time	Key task
UNMIT	25 August 2006–	Support the electoral process; restore public security; support reconstitution of PNTL.
ISF	May 2006–	Provision of security.

Timor-Leste, though a new mission (UN Integrated Mission in Timor-Leste or UNMIT) was more recently created in response to recent outbreaks of civil unrest in 2006. The key dates and roles of each of these missions are outlined in the table below.

UNAMET was tasked with undertaking a major programme of voter education and facilitating a referendum in East Timor that would see the population vote on whether or not they wanted East Timor to be an autonomous province within Indonesian territory. The vote had to be postponed twice when, despite assurances, the Indonesian government failed to control the violent activity of pro-integration militia forces who aimed to intimidate and remove pro-independence voices. Despite these problems, 98 per cent of the East Timorese electorate turned out to vote on 30 August 1999, and 78.5 per cent voted against remaining an autonomous part of Indonesia.[51] Militia forces and Kopassus attacked, driving many people from their homes or over the border to West Timor, and the attacks continued despite orders to the Indonesian forces from President Habibie to maintain order.[52] The UN's unarmed policing contingent was unable to stem the attacks and a number of East Timorese and outside powers began to urge the UN to deploy a peacekeeping force.

Under pressure from a number of places, including Australia, the United States, and the World Bank, Habibie conceded to the establishment of a 7,000 strong UN-mandated peacekeeping force.[53] This force came to be known as International Force East Timor, or INTERFET. It was a combat capable force which entered East Timor on 12 September led by Australia, and, mandated as it was to create a secure environment within the territory, INTERFET managed to restore some semblance of order. Indeed, INTERFET was a multifaceted force in that it was to be combat capable to ward off the militias, but it was also clearly designed to have a humanitarian element, and it also found itself having a strong presence in terms of maintaining civil law and order.[54] Here the INTERFET force not only utilised civilian police components but military police personnel in their security and investigation tasks too.[55]

On 25 October 1999 UNAMET was replaced by the UN Transitional Administration in East Timor (UNTAET) which, under UNSC Resolution

1272, was mandated to provide security and maintain law and order throughout the territory of East Timor; to establish an effective administration; to assist in the development of civil and social services; to ensure the coordination and delivery of humanitarian assistance, rehabilitation of humanitarian assistance, rehabilitation and development assistance; to support capacity-building for self-government; and to assist in the establishment of conditions for sustainable development.[56] UNTAET consisted of governance and public administration components, a civilian police component of up to 1,640 civilian police (including five FPUs) and an armed United Nations peacekeeping force, of equivalent size to INTERFET which took over command of military operations in February 2000.[57] UN Secretary General Kofi Annan asserted that UNTAET's mandate was 'unprecedented' in that it was to 'establish a national civil administration, assist in the development of civil and social services and support capacity-building for self-government'.[58]

In working towards these goals, in mid-2000 a unit for police development was established with 50 new recruits. Then on 10 August 2001 the East Timor Police Service was formally established by the UN, though the institution was only months later handed a strategic plan for development. (During 2002 there were three name changes for this service: East Timor Police Service, then Timor Lorosa'e Police Service, then Policia Nacional de Timor-Leste (PNTL)). Nonetheless by September 2002 strong efforts were underway to expand this fledgling Police Service, to create an East Timor Defence Force (primarily drawn from the former East Timorese pro-independence guerilla force FALINTIL) and to provide a robust legal system. As the UN's own website reports; a Prosecutor General's Office and a Defender Service; three District Courts; a Court of Appeals, and prisons in three locations were established in the course of 2000.[59] Indeed, the need to hurry these facilities along was stressed by the fact that, when this building period was underway, UNTAET's own police stopped making any arrests of suspected criminals because it had no place to put them.[60]

As these institutions came online (the police academy began training its first recruits in late March too) and as local and presidential elections began to restore local ownership of government over the country, the UN mission began to downsize. On 20 May 2002 East Timor, or rather Timor-Leste, became an independent country and with this development the UN operation was therefore transformed once more to be renamed the UN Mission in Support of East Timor (UNMISET), which gave assistance to the new government until the mission wound up on 20 May 2005, leaving only 130 UN personnel behind in advisory positions for one year as agreed to under UNSCR 1599. The change in title of the UN mission to the United Nations Office in Timor-Leste (UNOTIL) reflected this downgrading of UN involvement.

However, despite this planned phased UN withdrawal, there has been a return to Timor-Leste following the civil unrest of May 2006 that broke out after the dismissal of 591 former East Timor Defence Force personnel. On 28 April 2006, a demonstration by petitioners turned violent. In the rioting that followed, at least 37 people were killed and 155,000 people fled their homes.[61] On 24 May 2006, following riots, gunfights, looting and burning in Dili which saw eight unarmed police killed by members of the F-FDTL, Timor-Leste Foreign Minister Jose Ramos Horta asked for additional help from New Zealand, Australia, Portugal and Malaysia.

The return of International Security Forces (ISF) in late May 2006 was underlined by a very detailed diplomatic effort. Here the Australian and New Zealand contingents, in particular, wanted to ensure they had the consent of the President, Prime Minister and Speaker of the House before recommitting troops and police.[62] ISF is Australian-led, and its presence was first of all underpinned by a Status of Forces Agreement and later on by paragraph 5 of UNSC Resolution 1704 of 2006 which calls for ISF to provide assistance to the UN. ISF's role was to assist in the restoration of security, aid the re-establishment of public order, and to provide additional support to UNOTIL then UNMIT.[63]

UNMIT was created in August 2006 to allow for an extended mission in-country, and as part of that extended mission the police reform process accelerated on from previous efforts such as the preliminary screening that the AFP/Australian AID (AusAID) Timor Leste Development Program had carried out in the earlier stages. UNMIT therefore reinvigorated the UN presence, with over 1,600 officers (including 90 female officers) from 41 countries. It also took the UN role beyond capacity-building and into reforming, restructuring and rebuilding of the PNTL.

Further, UNMIT also became more 'hands-on' in other ways. Here, for example, in planning to handle the upcoming April 2007 presidential and June 2007 parliamentary elections, UNPOL were to be placed in 'key locations to ensure prompt investigations into any allegations of irregularities, especially intimidation, during the elections. That is a new addition to the security plan'.[64] Despite these measures in 2007 some further violence did emerge as Fretilin (a leftist political party in East Timor) supporters clashed with government coalition supporters – Fretilin had the biggest single party majority but were not in power, and were protesting the appointment of Xanana Gusmão as Prime Minister. Given the continuing fragility of the situation, the UNSC extended the UN mission in Timor-Leste for another year.

Finally, there are other programmes which also continue on in contributing to a fairly substantial level of international involvement in East Timor. For example, an AUD$32 million AusAID-funded project has been contracted out to Hassall and Associates to take place over the period 2002–2009. This project is intended to continue to bolster the capacity of the police service in East Timor and is jointly implemented with the Australian Federal Police (AFP), and with United Kingdom contributing additional financial resources. Here the focus is on improving the East Timor's police force's capability to: develop policies; manage finances; manage human resources; implement suitable operating procedures; and to develop a community policing capability.[65] And a similar project is ongoing with regards to East Timor's law and justice sector. Here AusAID has committed around AUD$8 million for the period 2003–8 to build capacity of justice and oversight institutions – with much support going to the UNDP 'Strengthening the Justice System in East Timor' project.[66]

Policing mandate and tasks

As indicated above, INTERFET was mandated to restore peace and security. Part of this involved the deployment of military forces that were tasked with keeping militia activity dampened down, and with undertaking disarmament, demobilisation and reintegration programmes. But INTERFET also had a more civilian component in terms of broader public order tasks. For example, in order to arrest and detain people suspected of involvement in criminal activity, INTERFET created an emergency quasi-judicial regime to provide a temporary review process for those held in the Force Detention Centre. From here INTERFET authorities issued a Detainee Ordinance on 21 October 1999 establishing the Detainee Management Unit (DMU) (where Indonesian law would continue to apply within a procedural framework based on international humanitarian law principles), and efforts were made to provide legal representation and a regular review of detainee's detention by an independent review panel.[67]

UNTAET's ultimate goal was to prepare East Timor for independence and in order to help achieve this was mandated to provide security and maintain law and order throughout East Timor. UNPOL were originally given executive policing powers given that the law enforcement capabilities of East Timor had yet to be established. UNPOL and peacekeeping forces were therefore responsible for helping to provide internal as well as border security and an important part of UN capability was the inclusion of a gendarmerie element in the UN civilian police force. This force was called the Rapid Response Unit (RRU) and was comprised of 120 Portuguese and 120 Jordanian police with military status to deal with major security threats and large-scale emergencies.[68] In addition to an interim law enforcement mandate, the UN was also tasked with capacity-building within the PNTL as it was recognised by the Secretary General that an important part of this deployment included the need for rapid development of a credible, professional and impartial police service.[69]

The initial process of recruiting and training local police forces was quite successful in terms of the rapidity of the process. Indeed, on 12 July 2000 the first 50 graduates of East Timor's Police Training College officially took up their functions as police officers for the East Timorese national police, the Policia Nacional de Timor Leste or PNTL.[70] Some 1,800 officers, from a target of 2,830, had been recruited and trained by 20 May 2002.[71] By the end of 2003, then, the PNTL was officially responsible for general policing throughout the country. (Yet, as noted below, though there was much success with ensuring a good quantity of officers, there have been concerns with regards to the quality of the actual policing taking place.)

This speedy recruitment and training helped to facilitate a fairly swift UN withdrawal, leaving a moderate involvement under UNMISET from 2002–2005. UNSCR 1410 of 17 May 2002 authorised UNMISET to undertake three main tasks:

- to provide assistance to core administrative structures critical to the viability and political stability of East Timor.
- to provide interim law enforcement and public security and to assist in the development of a new law enforcement agency in East Timor, the East Timor Police Service.
- to contribute to the maintenance of external and internal security of East Timor.[72]

More specifically, UNMISET was to be responsible for continuing to provide executive policing whilst helping the development of the national police service through training, co-location and timely and coordinated handover of responsibilities. There was some reluctance on behalf of the East Timorese authorities to access this agreement but the leadership did eventually accede.[73] Under UNMISET the international policing part of these efforts involved 1,250 CIVPOL plus other civilian support elements and was structured as shown in Figure 3.2.

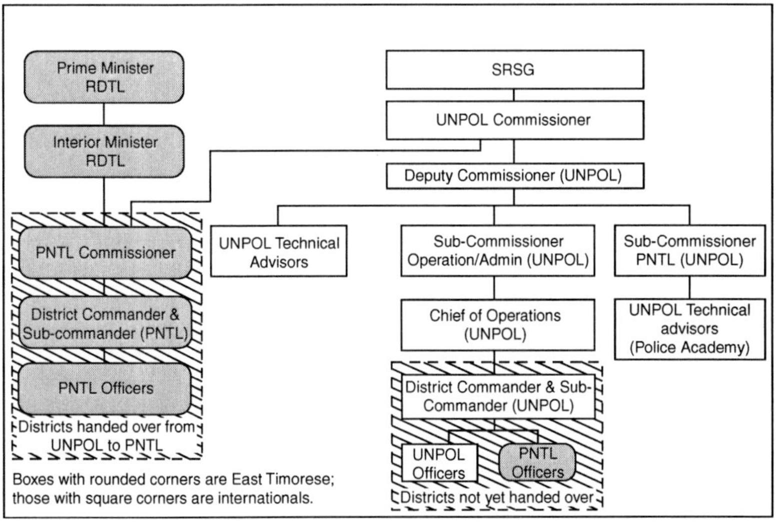

Figure 3.2 Organisational Structure of Policing Efforts in Timor-Leste[74]

This structure still theoretically exists today but, according to a number of officials, in reality there is not nearly as much cooperation and coordination between these two organisations as this figure would suggest.

In 2006, Resolution 1704 mandated UNPOL to 'assist in the planning and preparing of electoral-related security arrangements to adequately prepare the national police for performing their roles and responsibilities during the conduct of the 2007 elections'.[75] It also continued to provide a more general mandate for the restoration and maintenance of public security, institutional development, and a review of the security sector. This latter step involved the UN assisting the government to undertake a review of police, military, Ministry of Interior and Ministry of Defence, requiring the signing of a Status of UNMIT Agreement on 4 October 2006, whilst a Supplementary Agreement that laid out how public security and reform, restructuring and rebuilding tasks were to be carried out was signed on 1 December 2006.[76] The result of these agreements meant that a transfer of authority from UNPOL to PNTL began on 4 February 2008, and it is not yet certain as to whether or not this was more of a token gesture or a more comprehensive handover.

CIVPOL and later UNPOL contingents deployed to East Timor therefore had an initial mandate to undertake interim law enforcement and to build capacity within the PNTL. This was later extended under UNMIT to include reforming, restructuring and rebuilding within the PNTL given the problem of politicisation. In the very latest phase this has meant a focus on rebuilding the PNTL through processes such as screening new recruits, registering existing and newly recruited personnel, providing a basic five-day training course and then mentoring recruits for six months. More specific and or special tasks that have arisen during the course of the deployment have included riot control and the protection of static installations. At a more macro level, however, the UN has also attempted to implement a PNTL Organizational Strategic Plan for Reform, Restructuring, and Rebuilding (RRR) that focuses on operational and administrative capacities, oversight mechanisms, and coordination with other agencies involved in the security sector.[77]

Issues and problems arising

a) Planning and deployment problems

In its overall mission to East Timor, the UN has been criticised as failing to provide a comprehensive strategy for building a viable security sector, particularly with regards to establishing democratic control of the security sector, and some of these weaknesses became apparent in the events that unfolded later in 2006.[78] Overall planning has been described as 'cursory' whilst the UN policing effort has been criticised as constituting 'a story of slipshod planning, squandered opportunities and unimaginative leadership'.[79] And much has been made of the lack of coordination and cooperation between different UN agencies as well as that between UNPOL and PNTL.[80] Similarly there was often a lack of communication between the UN and major donors such as Australia and the UK who had pledged large sums of money for supporting developmental goals.[81]

The initial UNAMET mission was praised for speed of deployment, and similarly INTERFET was rolled out fairly rapidly but UNTAET was much too slow to evolve. Recruitment processes were cumbersome and, as a Human Rights Watch report pointed out, the overall quality of recruits was low, the three-month tour of duty too short (with a great loss of time and effort as each new recruit often started from scratch, re-interviewing witnesses again and again etc), less than 4 per cent of CIVPOL were female (making some sexual cases harder to investigate) and very few spoke a language intelligible to the local people. Similarly, the report stressed, a criminal procedure code was slow to develop, and a lack of institutional infrastructure, untrained CIVPOL personnel, and bureaucratic divisions within UNTAET hampered criminal investigations.[82] Moreover, even as recently as mid-2007 there were still reports of major difficulties in providing for the (mere) prescribed five days training by the UN. The Police Academy was being used as an Internally Displaced Persons (IDP) camp so there was no accommodation for police from outside of Dili and the AFP/AusAID Timor-Leste Police Development Program that was initially sub-contracted in to provide training was not at that point able to deliver training outside Dili.[83]

Most interesting, however, is the argument that one of the major difficulties for UN activities stemmed from the application of 'a traditional peacekeeping logic to address peacebuilding tasks' – and this comment will be further assessed in the concluding chapter of this book.[84] Indeed, despite the fact that 'police development' was intended to be a major part of UNTAET and UNMISET, it is notable and disappointing that in UNTAET none of the 1,270 officers were recruited to be trainers or institution-building experts, whilst in UNMISET too none of the 150 police advisors had development or capacity-building expertise.[85]

b) Contextualisation problems

In addition to these more practical issues, the question of how well the overall mission to East Timor was tailored to the needs of the local community has also been raised. Though UNAMET was lauded for its success in competently undertaking difficult electoral tasks, more interactive forms of policing that later unfolded within the missions to East Timor needed a much greater level of interest and responsiveness to the needs of the local context. To begin with, UNTAET was charged with not even engaging East Timor's political leadership in the process of establishing a new police force – resulting in a force that lacked 'strategic vision, coherent identity and institutional loyalty'.[86] A major study reviewing the work of UNPOL in East Timor found that the police focused on personnel recruitment and training, neglecting the development of the PNTL as an institution and failing to effectively work towards a handover from the UN to local control.[87] Similarly it has been argued more recently still that UNMIT's RRR report similarly did not engage enough with local officials, and indeed that it also lacked definition and detail as to how to implement the long wish-list included therein.[88]

With regards to the work of UNPOL personnel, complaints were forthcoming about a lack of cultural awareness, especially with regards to interacting with local women, and a lack of complimentary language skills or available skilled translators – the one-week UN training course was simply not enough.[89] Moreover, with regards to the establishment of the PNTL, criticism arose due to the very concentrated nature of the training programme for recruits, and due to the fact that in the recruitment process there was no consideration of whether the candidate had been pro-autonomy or pro-independence.[90] A greater awareness of the numerous social pressures (an emphasis on the connection of age with authority in certain areas and the significance of kinship and traditional hierarchies) that would face new East Timorese police officers in their work might have helped to mitigate some of the problems that later arose. With the benefit of hindsight we could say that it might have been helpful to have posted police officers out of their own local area; provided improved support networks; and to have prompted public education programmes to help bolster their standing in the community given public fears after the brutality of the previous policing regime. What was really needed, and had been called for but not achieved, was a strong working relationship to be established between the local community and both UNPOL and, thereafter, the fledgling PNTL.

Public education and public awareness programmes are essential for community policing to be effective. UNPOL efforts in East Timor have been criticised for lacking such systematic or thorough programmes although some more *ad hoc* arrangements did eventuate. Here, in a non-policing example, the New Zealand Defence Force in Cova Lima gave priority to running a local newspaper; employing and training locals as journalists to help provide much needed information in an area where rumour and misinformation was preventing successful resettlement and repatriation.[91] With regards to the implementation of community policing in general, various sources suggest that there was a lack of common understanding amongst UNPOL members as to what 'community policing' actually meant or how best to implement it. This was a problem that resulted not only from the multinational nature of the deployment but also from the fact that UNPOL contracts varied in length from a months to years, leaving little time for personnel to establish a strong relationship with the local community.

Similarly it is instructive that it has taken some time for some of the formal agreements signed between the UN and the government to be made public. As Bu Wilson has pointed out, it took considerable pressure from local NGO groups such as La'o Hamutuk to bring the details of the Supplementary Agreement signed in December 2006 out into the public domain, and there continues to be questioning as to how the UN and the government are working towards achieving the goals laid out therein.[92]

And in another more general case regarding the issue of contextualisation, some highly publicised efforts were made to connect the whole external peacebuilding effort more closely with the local population, with the World Bank and Asian Development Bank (ADB) establishing a 30-month 'Community Empowerment and Local Governance Project' (CEP) in 2000 to establish democratically accountable grass-roots structures to make decisions about how to spend community-focused grants. Yet this was not done with a strong knowledge of the local political context. Thus the CEP aimed to establish the actual local administration of the country and looked to the very local level – hamlets – to engage the population in village councils. In order to have a separation of powers between existing governance structures and the new CEPs, an arrangement was made to exclude village chiefs and other traditional leaders from being eligible for elections to the CEPs. Yet traditional beliefs held that only certain leaders can acceptably function as a political authority and, as the CEPs excluded those leaders at times locals have elected young, literate people used to dealing with foreigners whilst still continuing to look to traditional figures for leadership, or, conversely, the democratic process has been replaced by the 'acclamation' of candidates by local leaders.[93] Commentators such as Jarat Chopra and Tanja Hohe thus argue that much more could have been done to have better understood the local context before such political engineering took place.[94] These kinds of more general institution-building efforts are vitally important for thinking about the overall policing side of the mission as these set the overarching parameters within which the police will have to operate – not only in terms of determining command and control structures for national, regional and local levels of policing, but also in determining levels of social cohesion.

Lastly, a more specific example regarding context included the controversy that arose from the sending of Japan's Self-Defence Forces (JSDF). Here some East Timorese NGOs (as well as some Japanese NGOs) expressed a number of concerns about the JSDF deployment, these being that: the deployment was unconstitutional; there was a lack of closure with regards to the wartime occupation from 1942–1945 where approximately 40,000 East Timorese were killed and thousands were used as sex slaves or slave labour; and that the task allocated to the JSDF took away local jobs.[95] All of these issues have helped contribute to a working environment that was already a difficult one given the pressing rule of law needs of post-conflict societies.

c) Problems with PNTL: resources, accountability, and human rights

In the first few years of the UNMISET mission, the pressing demands of more contemporary crimes meant that investigations into the horrors of 1999 were stymied.[96] By early 2005 the Serious Crimes Unit (SCU) in Dili had convicted only 74 of 317 people indicted for the violence that racked East Timor after the 1999 vote for independence, and, disappointed by these figures, UN Secretary General Kofi Annan appointed a commission of experts to review Timor war crimes prosecutions and to improve the judicial process.[97] The process has been unpopular with successive governments as it deals with a highly sensitive and difficult matter. But out of this stems ongoing concern that these past issues have had no closure, that criminals have not had to face the law in the way that people had believed would happen with the involvement of the international community. These problems are likely to continue for some time and it is likely that many cases will never be taken through the courts for reasons of both a resource-constraint and political nature. The problems of an ill-functioning justice system may therefore cause problems for just how well a police system can hope to perform.

A number of other significant concerns about the future of the PNTL have been voiced in recent years. Specific concerns that arose in the early years of post-independence included questions over the ability of police to provide for public security and these concerns were exacerbated, in particular, by a perceived inadequacy of response to the December riots in 2002 and later by the violence in 2006. Problems in providing for adequate security were and are, however, not the only problems.

A 2006 Amnesty International report, for example, argued that the police force was suffering from a 'lack of clarity about applicable law, gaps in legislation and procedures and the existence of legislation which is inconsistent with international human rights law and standards', and expressed particular concerns about standard operating procedures in arrest rights, custody procedures and detention rights.[98] These concerns echoed those of the US State Department's Human Rights Report on East Timor for 2004 that which claimed that:

> There were numerous reports of excessive use of force and abuse of authority by police officers. Prolonged pretrial detention was a problem. The rights to due process and to an expeditious and fair trial often were denied or restricted, largely due to severe shortages

> of resources and lack of trained personnel in the legal system; there also were reports of abuse of authority by government officials.[99]

Some of these kinds of problems that surfaced within the PNTL undoubtedly arise out of the severe resource constraints being faced by the fledgling country. Food shortages are common, poverty seems endemic and the country has experienced growing social and political tensions throughout the last few years.[100] The large amount of aid coming into the country is often concentrated on paying expensive consultants rather than going towards basic and pressing issues such as poverty alleviation. For a specific example of how this relates to policing expenditure, UNMISET's two-year budget was approximately US$517 million with 22 per cent spent on personnel costs for civilian staff – yet although UNMISET had nearly twice as many East Timorese as international staff, only 0.8 per cent of the budget (3 per cent of the civilian personnel money) paid for those local staff.[101] Furthermore, an overall lack of equipment, working vehicles, and working communication devices also bedevil police forces in their attempts to provide internal order and security within this poor country.

These problems are perhaps also attributable to a capacity gap caused by a too-rapid move by the UN to downsize its UNPOL numbers from early 2002 without a 'compensating increase' in East Timorese policing numbers.[102] However, the issue of adequate numbers is not the only factor at play. UN recruitment of potential police cadets for the new police force was rushed, with critics raising objections about the inclusion of over 350 former Indonesian National Police (POLRI) and unsatisfactory 'Western' procedures for selection that was biased towards English-speakers.[103] Once established, a number of authors criticised the training provided to new PNTL recruits, both in terms of classroom and field training.

This push to get the job done quickly contributed to the UN's failure to recognise the importance of ensuring the institution of strong democratic civilian oversight and control.[104] Similarly, though, the incumbent government also demonstrated a lack of interest. In the lead up to the troubles in 2006 such institutional deficits allowed for the politicisation of the police. Indeed, the United Nations Commission of Independent Inquiry believed that the situation in 2006:

> can be explained largely by the frailty of the state institutions and the weakness of the rule of law. Governance structures and existing chains of command broke down or were bypassed; roles

> and responsibilities became blurred; solutions were sought outside the existing legal framework.[105]

Since that time there continue to be problems within the PNTL, as well as major security issues within Timor Leste as a whole, with the President and Prime Minister both coming under fire from rebel groups in February 2008. Indeed the political leadership has an ambiguous relationship with the PNTL whilst the relationship between the PNTL and the F-FDTL also remains tense. Here a number of commentators have suggested that the future security of Timor-Leste would be best served by clarifying the role and responsibilities of the police and military, by keeping the military small and out of routine policing and at the same time by building cooperative links between the police and military.[106]

Conclusion

In addition to commenting on common deployment, planning, contextualisation and resource problems, then, these two cases also speak to a number of key additional thematic issues. In Kosovo and East Timor the UN took on direct responsibility for policing. In both of these cases the SRSG was granted extraordinary powers to enact new laws, and to create new institutions including police and court systems. These operations were therefore 'formative' ones in the sense of them representing an acceptance that 'international policing' was here to stay. In these two cases international transitional administrations were set up to run the designated territory for an interim period. UN personnel were tasked with reconstructing law and order – this meant a range of tasks needed to be undertaken from day-to-day policing to long-term establishment of 'triad' of police, judiciaries and penal systems plus legal codes. Thus in his pre-departure press conference, the UN's Senior Official in Kosovo Bernard Kouchner declared that the 'lesson of Kosovo' was that:

> peacekeeping missions need to arrive with a law-and-order kit made up of trained polices, judges and prosecutors and a set of draconian security laws. This is the only way to stop criminal behaviour from flourishing in a postwar vacuum of authority.[107]

These case studies developed as part of the more general shift in international affairs towards comprehensive peacebuilding efforts that reach far and wide in reconstructing and rebuilding the various mechanisms and institutions of states, including all facets of the rule of law.

In addition to this notion of a comprehensive rule of law approach, one other issue that Kouchner could have mentioned is the need to long-term commitment to see such ambitions through to fruition. In 2008 there was still a strong external presence in both places to help with policing matters in-country. Though there remain concerns about dependency and although the aim is to police oneself out of a job, such things can also not be hurried. Although there are concerns that poverty-stricken East Timor may be too reliant on external aid, there is also much rumour that the situation that redeveloped in 2006 did so because the job was not done properly in the first place. The roll over from the UN to the EU in Kosovo in the policing sphere further underlines that this situation is a long-term commitment. In terms of more case study-specific characteristics: in Kosovo some of the most striking issues at play included the division of labour that emerged between different institutions, whilst in East Timor the concerted diplomatic wrangling that went on in 2006 ensured a strong level of commitment by those involved as well as a greater claim to legitimacy and authority on behalf of those returning to help try to achieve UNMIT's mandate.

Finally what both of these case studies highlight in particular is that policing is a vital part of internal security but that policing (as well as the rule of law and security sectors more broadly defined) is just one issue amongst many broader political and social factors at play. The underlying issue of reconciliation in Kosovo is not something that a good robust reformed police service can achieve on its own but it is nonetheless a significant part of the answer, as if the service is seen to be impartial in its service of all groups and this will help dampen tensions. Care must also be taken to ensure that bolstering police influence and capacity within the states does not unnecessarily inflame the situation, as could possibly have been the case with regards to the relationship between the PNTL and F-FDTL. Here in both cases it is also very clear that the actual or potential politicisation of security actors in politically volatile post-conflict situations is something that is difficult for outside actors to prevent. It requires attempts to ensure buy-in from political actors (as mentioned in the case of El Salvador in Chapter 2), the creation of context-specific institutional internal and external checks and balances within the political system more broadly, and by communicating a more general set of policing principles through concerted and tailored training regimes and through the creation of supporting mechanisms such as in the establishment and dissemination of professional codes of ethics.

4
RAMSI

This chapter outlines the role of the Regional Assistance Mission to Solomon Islands (RAMSI), drawing particular attention to the military-police divide as well as to the tensions arising from differences in policing styles, the need for a context-specific focus and once again highlighting the limits of policing in broader political and social contexts.

RAMSI

Solomon Islands consists of a chain of more than 900 islands located to the North-East of Australia with a fast-growing population of around half a million people. Ethnically and linguistically diverse, Solomon Islands is rich in some natural but finite resources such as forest and fisheries, and has an underdeveloped private sector. At the start of the new century Solomon Islands was a country that faced rising civil tension and strife. Increasingly unable to effectively govern the Solomon Islands since June 2000, requests for help from the Solomon Islands were first of all met with some assistance under the Townsville Agreement of 15 October 2000. A small International Peace Monitoring Team (IPMT) of 48 civilian, military and police personnel from South West Pacific countries were deployed to assist with confidence-building and monitoring in the Islands.[1] However, the situation continued to be somewhat unstable and did in fact deteriorate, leading to the Solomon Islands Prime Minister Allan Kemakeza making another formal request for help to the governments of Australia and New Zealand in 2003.[2] (In early February 2003 the EU had funded a British Police Commissioner, Bill Morrell, to be appointed to try to bring about a restoration of law and order, but Morrell soon requested increasing support from donor countries as few advances were being made). By this time public wages were in arrears; members of Parliament feared physical attack; Cabinet had been subject to intimidation and extortion; and the Royal Solomon Islands Police (RSIP, later renamed the Solomon Islands Police Force or SIPF) was becoming increasingly factionalised and corrupt. Perpetrators of such crimes included 'special constables' and their criminal associates, and renegades such as Harold Keke who stirred fighting between Malaitans and Guale populations.[3]

Eventually after much diplomatic activity at a bilateral and regional level it was decided that a regional mission, led by the Australian Federal Police (AFP), was the best solution to the problem as the Solomon Islands government was unable to reverse the problems of civil disorder and economic decline, and outside assistance was therefore seen as a vital 'circuit breaker'.[4]

The RAMSI was thus created in response to the Solomon Islands' request for help, and included personnel from Australia, New Zealand, Papua New Guinea, Fiji, Vanuatu, Tonga, Samoa, Federated States of Micronesia, Kiribati, Marshall Islands, Nauru, Niue, Palau, and Tuvalu. As the official RAMSI website suggests:

> RAMSI's mission is to help get Solomon Islands working and growing again...RAMSI does not control government nor does it make national decisions on behalf of Solomon Islands...RAMSI is not a 'quick fix' to overcome the ills that have plagued Solomon Islands. RAMSI is a long-term partnership.[5]

RAMSI's overarching organisational framework is demonstrated in Figure 4.1, showing regional input from the Pacific Islands Forum as well as how the relationship between RAMSI and the Solomon Islands government is supposed to work.

There have, however, been some tensions in the relationship, with claims of political interference by RAMSI from Solomon Islands politicians, and with counter-claims of corruption and other criminal charges being levelled at a number of prominent Solomon Island personages from the RAMSI side. This has resulted in a sensitive environment which has at times made policing a very difficult task.

Policing mandates and tasks

One of the earliest initiatives in Solomon Islands prior to the 2003 decision for a more fully-fledged response had been the provision of a

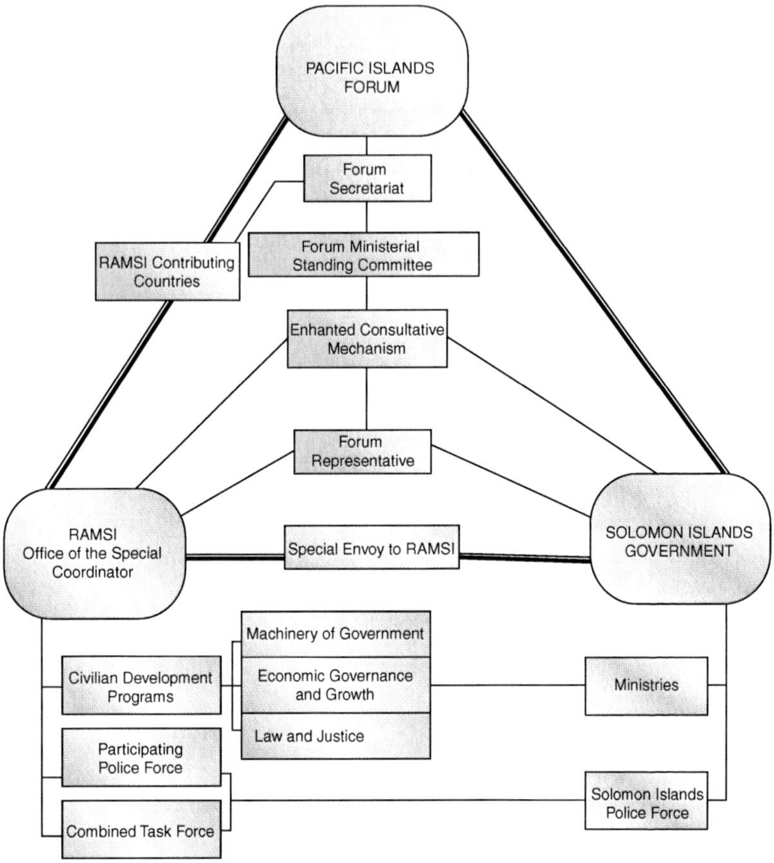

Figure 4.1 RAMSI Organisation Chart[6]

ten person police team to work in a mentoring role at the lower levels of the RSIP. However, given the situation that unfolded as mentioned above, it was felt that neither this project nor a similar Australian initiative was making enough headway in reforming the RSIP. When the situation was deemed to require a stronger response at the Cabinet level, Deputy Police Commissioner Steve Long, following a visit to Solomon Islands and discussions with Bill Morrell, argued that a policing contingent could only be effective if backed by coercive force as confronting the corrupt elements of the RSIP would be too high a risk without such backing.[7] It was from these beginnings that RAMSI was formulated.

RAMSI works on the basis of restoring three pillars – machinery of government; economic governance; and law and justice. The PPF was tasked with helping to achieve the last of those three objectives and the PPF was and is of vital significance to the mission. In terms of how the overall police part of the RAMSI deployment initially worked, the AFP played the lead agency role, and police and military contingents (predominantly from New Zealand, Vanuatu, Fiji, Samoa, Papua New Guinea, Tonga) by and large worked in with Australian requirements. Effectively this meant, for example, that the New Zealand Defence Force (NZDF) was largely integrated into the Australian Defence Force (ADF), and the Royal New Zealand Air Force (RNZAF) functioned as part of the Royal Australian Air Force (RAAF). However on the whole police officers deployed to the mission were, partly due to the greater independence vested in individuals within policing institutions, much more autonomous within the operation. Initial deployments were concentrated within the capital Honiara though this was later extended so that police were increasingly involved in villages throughout the various Solomon Islands provinces.

Sections 2 and 3 of the Facilitation of International Assistance Act 2003 outlined the tasks to be undertaken by RAMSI personnel with immunity from in-country prosecution (contributing countries were themselves to be responsible for prosecuting any alleged offences by their personnel).[8] These tasks included the provision of:

> the security and safety of persons and property, maintaining supplies and services essential to the life of the community, preventing and suppressing violence, intimidation and crime, maintaining law and order, supporting the administration of justice, supporting and developing Solomon Islands institutions and responding to natural catastrophic events.[9]

The initial phase of the deployment was intended to provide a 'security pause' to allow the Solomon Islands to regroup and this would be followed by a longer-term project to ensure ongoing stability – enabling the return to a normal state of economic affairs too. The commencement phase, Phase One, of RAMSI thus focused on restoring law and order, Phase Two began in 2004 and concentrated on the consolidation of law and order, institutional reform and reviving the economy, and Phase Three which started in 2005 then focused on further capacity-building and training – bringing the SIPF into day-to-day policing, with RAMSI PPF members concentrating on mentoring and more specialist training.[10]

Officially the mission was declared as being one of 'strengthened assistance', with the term intervention purposely avoided.[11] Similarly it was held that 'any strengthened assistance should not undermine the sovereignty of the Solomon Islands government'.[12] However this claim is a little difficult to balance against the fact that PPF officers were sworn in as 'line' members of the RSIP, thereby giving them executive powers. RAMSI was therefore to 'be police led with military support only to the extent necessary to ensure the safety of the police and others involved'.[13] Thus the police were generally mandated to restore law and order, whilst military units were mandated to help create a secure environment to enable police to operate. Police and military personnel were then assigned their particular tasks in order to achieve these respective mandates.

The policing style identified most likely to be effective in attaining RAMSI's goals was a combination of community-oriented activity that was aimed at rebuilding faith in the ability of police to maintain public safety, and more targeted law enforcement operations that identified trouble spots and the worst offenders.[14] Community policing in this particular overseas deployment meant a strong emphasis was placed on high levels of interaction with local groups and authorities to establish a strong presence on the ground in the Solomons, and to restore a broad-based secure environment within which normal life might resume.

At the beginning of the mission the PPF, in priority order, was tasked with:

- the (short-term) provision of protection to key Solomon Islands Government figures
- the arrest and prosecution of Harold Keke and his followers – here there was strong cooperation between military and police to achieve the arrest, though prosecution remained a police responsibility
- establishing law and order in Honiara
- recovering of RSIP and privately-owned firearms
- establishing law and order in the provinces

The final task included the reform of the Solomon Islands police.[15] RAMSI police contingents were instrumental in both pursuing corrupt officers within the RSIP, and in restoring the will and ability of the RSIP to resume policing themselves. Indeed, the rationale for this being a primarily police-driven mission stemmed from the fact that the Solomon Islands' police capability was lacking – in part due to high level corruption – and expatriate police involvement was believed necessary to help begin to restore this capability.[16] This process necessitated the removal of corrupt police, the dissolution of the 'Special Constable' concept that had been part of that overall corruption, the reestablishment of police outposts in villages, and the provision of retraining programmes.[17] Dismissals, enforced retirements, and redundancies provided further options for reform of the RSIP. This need to reform the RSIP meant that in practice the international police force worked alongside rather than as part of the RSIP. The PPF therefore initiated a 'vetting-before-reform' process that involved vetting, recertification and internal investigation.[18]

Military personnel working to secure the situation for police to operate were delegated their general tasks by the PPF, and these tasks remained distinct from policing functions in that they were restricted primarily to the aim of creating a secure environment to enable Police to operate.[19] Any further action would only be undertaken if the safety of police personnel required supplementation or if police resources were too stretched to cope.[20] Other tasks involved: transportation; logistical support; the provision of accommodation; catering; engineering and emergency medical facilities; a 'deterrence effect' for police to undertake searches safely; and the provision of security for the airport and Camp RAMSI.

Yet what is interesting in this case is the fact that, in addition to these general tasks, some 'special' tasks, such as the planned arrest of Harold Keke, were also thought to be best managed as discrete military tasks. Here it was thought that Keke's location, numbers of followers and weaponry put him beyond the capabilities of the police deployment.[21] Similarly the military provided an important deterrent effect following the riots of April 2006. Here the election of Prime Minister Snyder Rini resulted in general lawlessness in the capital Honiara, and the situation escalated to a riot and the burning of many buildings in the central business district. The PPF attended in riot gear, they and their vehicles became targets of the frustration of the rioters, and a number were injured. The situation quietened shortly after, and since that time in mid-2006 the numbers of personnel deployed to partake in the policing part of the mission have generally hovered around 300 police officers and 180 civilian personnel.[22]

Issues and problems arising

a) Interoperability challenges

The RAMSI deployment first of all demonstrated some of the problems typically faced in undertaking multinational operations. Here, for example, the lead AFP contingent initially had a different interpretation of what community policing entailed from the New Zealand contingent. The AFP utilised a much more force protection approach, an approach intensified following the killing of AFP Officer Adam Dunning. (This difference of opinion between police forces as to what constitutes community policing is, however, even between those ostensibly modelled on the same British tradition, a common occurrence). In another example underscored by James Watson's examination of RAMSI, RAMSI police personnel relied on their own particular internal guidelines regarding the use of force rather than referring to any external rules of engagement – highlighting a point of difference between police and military aspects of the mission too.[23] Basic issues regarding language, the speed of briefings, difficulties in understanding accented English at times led to more restricted communication between different national contingents too.[24]

RAMSI also underscored the fact that, given that this was very much a path-breaking mission in being a major police-led venture, the relationship between police and military contingents can be a little strained when it comes to reversing traditional command priorities. Prior to the mission top AFP Officer Ben McDevitt attended a military exercise where civilian police were not worked into planning phases, and indeed where the military contingents seemed to take it for granted that they could speak for the AFP and other police agencies.[25] In actually undertaking parts of the mission at times there were some disagreements over what tasks needed done first and how this should be done. For example, at times there were differences between police and military contingents in determining which items were priorities for transportation, and there were at times some differences of opinion as to whether or not set tasks did indeed fit within the primary mandate for military personnel as outlined above.[26] The ADF and other military contingents simply weren't very used to trying to operate in support of a police-led operation. Differences in planning were also apparent. Police tended to plan 'on the run' whilst military planning was much more formal and structured.[27] Future operations, James Watson recommended, should thus consider a more detailed memorandum of understanding (MOU) dealing with the handover and hand-back of emergency security control to prevent confusion about control in times of changes to the security environment.[28] And indeed much work has gone into improving ADF and AFP relations after both this deployment and ongoing involvement in East Timor.

A number of these problems outlined here have thus eased with the appointment of suitable people as military-police liasion officers, with the AFP taking over responsibility for the logistics of RAMSI in the second year, and with the *de facto* emergence of the AFP base at Majura in Canberra as a one-stop interagency shop for those deployed or deploying to RAMSI.[29]

b) Contextualisation

The issue of ownership has also been an ongoing concern. Although the 'parallel' structure presented some difficulty in promoting a sense of ownership of the new policing force within the Solomon Islands policing community, it was felt that there was little alternative in that insertion of a number of expatriate police was not enough to alter the situation. Efforts were made, therefore, to both ensure that the mission was consistent with existing internal laws and to try to ensure that this was not just seen as an Australian attempt at neo-colonialism (Australia has often been perceived as playing 'big brother' in the South Pacific).[30] In July 2003 an agreement known by the lengthy name of the 'Agreement between Solomon Islands, Australia, New Zealand, Fiji, Papua New Guinea, Samoa and Tonga concerning the operations and status of the police and armed forces and other personnel deployed to Solomon Islands to assist in the restoration of law and order and security' outlined how any action taken by Australia to put armed personnel in Solomon Islands needed to be sanctioned by the Pacific Islands Forum. This effort to ensure a regional flavour to the mission has been ongoing, though the mission is still often seen as an Australian-dominated one, and this fact has at times given politicians mileage to resist RAMSI.[31] Indeed this was a key issue that emerged in the riots of 2006 mentioned above and continued to be a bone of contention into 2007.

The 2006 riots have been put down to a number of factors: disappointment at the election of Rini who was accused by some of not presenting any change from previous corrupt regimes; manipulation of mob feeling by political actors; the influence of Chinese and Taiwanese political manoeuvring; economic stagnancy; concentration of reform in Honiara at the expense of the provinces; public perception of a double-standard on behalf of RAMSI personnel (practicing profligacy whilst preaching austerity; insisting on transparency when locals are unclear of some aspects of the mission); and, more specifically for the PPF, dissatisfaction with poor cultural engagement in policing – responses to an infamous shooting alienated many locals.[32] The riots demonstrated a lack of understanding and communication between Australian and New Zealand members of the PPF and senior RSIP officers at the scene, and served to highlight broader issues regarding cultural awareness and understanding of the local social, political and cultural context.[33] Here the determination of the AFP to buy most of their supplies from Australia so as not to create a falsely dependent economy has been seen as both an economic and cultural snub. The ways in which RAMSI convoys take over Honiara roads, the ways in which some police personnel have interacted in arrogant or patronising ways and the simple growth of gossip and rumour about insensitivity have all beleaguered policing efforts. These day-to-day issues that alienated the local community combined with other problems in reforming the RSIP (immersion techniques that overwhelmed officers, an alien management and working culture) frustrated efforts.[34]

This issue of cultural engagement, or rather lack of engagement, has, however, begun to be taken much more seriously. Here, for example, the AFP took some time to become aware of the counter-productivity of sending police who were insensitive to the local customs and lore, and have had to play catch up as best they might. Indeed, the AFP opened themselves up to academic scrutiny with engagement in the Australian Research Council funded project on 'Policing the Neighbourhood' which helped prompt a number of changes.

The AFP have therefore established much more concrete and comprehensive pre-deployment training programmes. The pre-deployment training is now a substantial five weeks, with cultural learning being integrated throughout the package and members of the SIPF travel to Canberra in order to assist in the delivery of that package. Indeed the AFP have built a state-of-the-art training facility at Majura in Canberra where police due to be deployed to RAMSI live *in situ* for eleven or so days. They take part in a number of scenarios copied or adapted from real-life situations: a traffic collision where compensation must be negotiated over a number of days; stock escape and some are run over and injured; a militia or gang raid the village at night; and all of this with no computer, break downs in electricity, basic living conditions and one shop with very limited items for purchase. This helps to ease the culture shock for those who later deploy and allows supervising trainers to assess how well officers adapt, at times resulting in personnel not being allowed to deploy abroad. It also brings together all RAMSI contributing countries (except for New Zealand personnel) for this standardised training schedule, building relationships, improving interoperability and creating some common understanding. Further language training is also now undertaken once in country.

That there is now a relatively strong relationship between locals and RAMSI is perhaps borne out in the 2006 People's Survey which suggested that, if the respondents could choose between RAMSI or RSIP to report a crime to, 44 per cent would choose RSIP and 35 per cent would still choose RAMSI.[35]

Broader initiatives such as the new civic education modules provided in primary school programmes or the 'Talking Truth' radio programme that was established early in the mission to try to inform about RAMSI's objectives and to provide a forum for local input have also been important initiatives.[36] Similarly the mention of draft principles for engagement in fragile states as part of AUSAID's strategy for Solomon Islands is significant for the overall shape of the mission as these principles begin with the need to take context as starting point.[37] However one thing that has proven very difficult to work around is the fact that Solomon Islanders have been daunted by the foreign ways in which things have at times been done, thereby discouraging them from 'stepping up' to take up roles of authority and leaving the question of 'ownership' hanging.[38] This too has begun to be addressed but this very sensitive issue has come late to the fray.

c) Image and limits of police

Lastly, RAMSI also demonstrated some of the more inherent problems with undertaking police-led missions. As the RSIP had for so long been part of the problem rather than part of the solution, the local population tended to be very wary of police. Indeed, mixed police and military patrols often found that the local people responded very positively to the approach of military personnel whilst viewing the police contingents far more warily.[39] Further, in addition to the limitations placed on police with regards to previous reputation and public image, the limitations that come with regards to the placing of policing within the broader political scene have also taken their toll on the PPF and the RSIP.

Although the police force and other law and justice sectors may be able to be reformed in terms of institutional arrangements, codes of ethics and standards of behaviour, again there remains the constraint of undertaking such reforms in a political and social context that has at times come into conflict with the aims of the mission. Here there has been dissatisfaction on the RAMSI side with the amount of money and effort being spent without what are seen as 'satisfactory' results – that is, consternation at the election and appointment of dubious characters to important political and bureaucratic positions post-2003. Although these could be seen to be political issues that should remain internal to the sovereign state, that is Solomon Islands, problems arise when politicians or senior bureaucrats are suspected, or accused of, or even sentenced with criminal convictions. There have been a number of attempts to mitigate such influences in the political arena as RAMSI has also focused on building strong accountability mechanisms. The Leadership Code Commission, the Ombudsman's Office and the Auditor-General's office as well as specialist anti-corruption training and task forces within the police themselves have all been established to try to ward off undesirable political practices.[40] But as an earlier report shows, these institutions are in themselves not necessarily enough to ensure good government and good governance and there are still ways around such institutional checks and balances.[41]

The question of where authority lies, then, when the original government has been replaced, when there have been many changes of faces and position, and when disputes later arise, remains central. This is mitigated in the case of Solomon Islands because any incumbent government, though there may be some resistance and some rhetorical sounding off against RAMSI, is still heavily reliant on some aspects of the mission. RAMSI helps to provide security, infrastructure, training, financial aid, development, education, as well as general bureaucratic and institutional support. The amount of resources devoted to RAMSI is very substantial and to lose such resources is not in the interests of any government in power.

Conclusions

Despite the critiques outlined above, RAMSI has seen a fair amount of success. The initial and subsequent deployments have both been well-timed and well-resourced, with the mission always having been talked about as a very long-term commitment.[42] And indeed phase one of RAMSI, the 'security pause', appeared to have met its objectives.[43] In terms of statistical evidence of this, the RAMSI website claims that: over 6,300 people have been arrested on more than 9,100 charges since RAMSI arrived; more than 3,600 guns have been removed from the community and crime involving firearms has decreased considerably; and that 160 former officers have been arrested for serious offences including corruption, murder, assault, rape, intimidation and robbery.[44] Other statistics similarly demonstrate some useful results. The 2005 People's Survey saw 90 per cent of respondents saying that they thought that law and order had improved or remained the same in the past year, and 59 per cent thought the situation had improved in the past year in the 2006 survey.[45] Although there is no baseline to measure this from, it is hard to gauge what the significance of such a figure is, it still talks to a perception of improvement. Further, disciplinary violations and/or charges against police for criminal activity dropped from 514 in 2003 to 340 in 2005, and investigations resolved by police action have improved to 40 per cent in 2006.[46] And in mid-2006 a Law and Justice Project was established inside the Ministry of Police, National Security, Justice and Legal Affairs.[47] Phase Two and Three have thus gone on to see RAMSI shift more into the background in policing affairs, and indeed the announcement of senior policing posts going to SIPF members was heartily welcomed in 2007 as evidence of this.

The overall picture of the law and justice part of RAMSI's three-part role is therefore a relatively good one. At the end of 2007 seven classes of new police recruits had undergone training, more senior positions were being allocated back to Solomon Islands' police personnel, and a number of new prison officers and prosecutors had also undergone formal training. Indeed, it is very significant there has been much forethought put into dealing with the three stages of law enforcement – police, courts and prisons. Moreover, it is also clear that major efforts are ongoing to try to ensure the second phase of economic development progresses. Here the sheer numbers of Australian (in particular) and other bureaucratic personnel working in-country, and the long-term commitment of the contributors augurs well for a concerted effort to help bring about the economic recovery of Solomon Islands.

In terms of assessing some of the recurring thematic issues throughout the RAMSI mission one of the most fundamental issues has been that of how to tailor the mission to the needs of Solomon Islands. Here the UNDP has called upon donors and government agencies contributing to such efforts to emphasise the importance of 'traditional structures' and the Eminent Persons Group that reviewed the work of RAMSI also recommended a return to some traditional forms of governance.[48] More broadly the gains made in the last few years need to be sustainable at the local level, and the broader economic, social and political climate remains somewhat tenuous (indeed as Mary Louise O'Callaghan pointed out in 2006 even if a strong 5 per cent annual growth rate could be maintained for the next 20 years this would still only bring the standard of living back up to 1994 figures and the 2006 People's Survey highlighted local concerns over high prices, unemployment and general prospects for the economy).[49] An ongoing improvement in public-police relationships within this broader setting is also a factor that is both desirable and achievable, as one seemingly small but undoubtedly vital issue highlighted in the 2006 Public Survey was that only 59 per cent of people who had reported a robbery or theft believed they had been treated with respect.[50]

Lastly, one of the major political issues that is somewhat out of the reach of 'just' the police force, is the fact that there is resentment, suspicion and even active undermining of RAMSI by some elites in country – and this issue that arises in the following two case studies where that local resentment is much more widespread from elite level down to grass roots.

5
Afghanistan and Iraq

In this chapter we look at two very recent operations in Afghanistan and Iraq. The US military has termed these 'Intervention, Stabilisation and Transformation' operations and they have involved the forceful removal of the leadership, the dismantling of previously existing security forces, a struggle to gain or maintain consent amongst the local populations, and a limited UN presence in the security sphere.

Afghanistan

Following the events of September 11 2001 the US threatened retributive attack against the Taliban government in Afghanistan for their role in playing host to Osama bin Laden and Al-Qaeda operatives. When negotiations failed the US, aided by the UK and other coalition partners including the local Northern Alliance, launched a military attack called Operation Enduring Freedom (OEF) to remove the Taliban from power. Much of the country fell quickly into the hands of the coalition forces and the Taliban retreated from Kabul on 12 November 2001, regrouping in the border region between Afghanistan and Pakistan and continuing to plague the situation in Afghanistan to the present day. The initial 'intervention phase' of the 'intervention, stabilisation and transformation' operation in Afghanistan was therefore relatively straightforward, but the latter two phases have been much more problematic.

Decades of internal strife preceded the overthrow of the Taliban regime, and such strife continued on in the months following the overthrow of the Taliban as warlords and criminal elements jostled for control. These highly mobile, experienced and conflicting groups presented major security problems for the fledgling Afghan Interim

Administration (AIA) and later the Afghan Transitional Authority (ATA). In light of these problems a number of efforts were made by contributors to the UN-mandated International Security Assistance Force (ISAF) to reform the security situation as agreed under the Bonn Agreement of 6 December 2001.[1] Here the overarching plan for a key part of ISAF's work – security sector reform – was launched at a G8 meeting in Geneva in 2002 and involved a lead-nation approach to five main pillars: Law Enforcement (Germany), Judiciary (Italy), Counter Narcotics (UK), Afghan National Army (US) and Disarmament, Demobilisation and Reintegration of the militia forces (Japan).[2]

With these broader strategic plans having been mapped out, ISAF deployed in January 2002. Initial tasks involved maintaining security in Kabul and surrounding areas to enable the transitional authority and the UN to operate within a secure environment (there remains a fairly small UN Assistance Mission to Afghanistan (UNAMA) which had been preceded by another UN mission that began in 1993) and to give space for the Afghan authorities to create their own rule of law institutions as this was to be a mission with a 'light international footprint'.[3] Although a Joint Coordination Committee made up of ISAF, UN, and Afghan representatives was created especially to limit confusion between the different actors involved in the security sector, there were a number of problems that arose in the early stages of the mission.[4]

US Central Command (CENTCOM) was given formal operational authority over ISAF in its first phase and effectively blocked moves to expand ISAF until October 2003, allowing for security problems to re-emerge and momentum to be lost.[5] Moreover the US-led OEF military mission continued in-country and was given precedence over ISAF operations. Since then other ISAF missions (II and III) have been led by the UK, Turkey and jointly by Germany and the Netherlands respectively. NATO took over command, control and coordination of ISAF IV on 9 August 2003 and has retained that role – extending its influence on 5 October 2006 to take command of the international forces in eastern Afghanistan from the US-led coalition. This involves the leadership of around some 35,000 troops from 37 countries that are to try to help create conditions for stabilisation by assisting Afghan authorities to extend their authority across the country, as well as the provision of a Senior Civil Representative who liaises with the Afghan government, international organisations and neighbouring countries, whilst simultaneously undertaking programmes related to security sector reform.[6]

Policing mandates and tasks

As noted above much of the policing part of the mission in Afghanistan has been carried out by Germany. Reform efforts focused first of all on the rebuilding of the National Police Academy and the training of police recruits. (Note however that the US also undertook a training role as well with both countries carrying most of the bill for police reform in Afghanistan). The Germans were quick to deploy, arriving in March 2002, and indeed in some ways the policing part of the mission had a head start with the Afghan Northern Alliance having begun training a police force as part of their long-term plans for occupying Kabul, recognising the importance of police for maintaining order in Afghanistan.[7] Germany was also building on earlier policing relationships with Afghanistan, as the national civilian police force in Afghanistan of the 1960s and 1970s was based on European models and had received training from both East and West Germany.[8]

In addition to these centralised efforts ISAF has played a minor role in policing tasks by undertaking joint patrols with the Afghan National Police (ANP), and further policing efforts have been carried out in varying forms through the work of the small numbers of police deployed in Provincial Reconstruction Teams (PRTs).[9] PRTs are authorised by UN Security Council Resolutions 1386, 1413 and 1444. These PRTs have a common objective in helping to extend the authority of the Afghan government across the length and breadth of the country through the provision of security and capacity-building roles. With regards to this latter task in particular there has been a call to ensure that governments in charge of PRTs supply those teams with good civilian expertise, and fill non-military positions on a 'priority basis'.[10] Yet these PRTs vary very widely in their composition, size, and foci as they are tailored to the needs of their allocated area. Thus:

> the German PRT in Konduz maintains a strict division of responsibility between its military and civilian components. It functions as a 'secure guest house' for civilian specialists and employs close to 375 soldiers. In contrast, the UK's PRT in Mazar-e Sharif operates with a much smaller contingent of approximately 100 personnel, and there is a very close working relationship between the military contingent and civilian PRT members from the Foreign Office, the Department for International Development (DFID), and other civilian representatives from Scandinavian countries.[11]

Germany, the US, and to a much lesser extent ISAF as a whole, have therefore had differing levels of responsibility for directing the policing effort in Afghanistan. The UN did not have a role for monitoring or training police explicitly laid out under the original Bonn Agreement of 2001, though CIVPOL did send an officer to liaise between the SRSG and the AIA on police matters, and later in May 2002 four additional police advisers were sent with the task of: advising the SRSG, Interior Ministry, and local police officials whilst also assisting German and Afghan trainers and the commander of the Kabul police (primarily with strategic planning).[12] Further UN involvement later came through the Security Unit of the UNDP Joint Electoral Management Board (JEMB) which provided operational planning, training, and equipment for the Afghan National Police prior to the elections in 2004 and 2005.[13]

Under the Bonn Compact which emphasised a 'light footprint' approach, all early police reform projects were to be advisory only.[14] The Afghanistan Compact, which came into being upon expiration of the Bonn Compact, is a five-year plan between the government of Afghanistan and the international community and it carried on with this idea of 'light' involvement. This Afghanistan Compact has no legal force. It does, however, in its declared purpose state that the Afghan government commits itself to a shared (democratic, human rights-oriented, secure) future with the international community's support.[15] The Compact therefore sets out overall goals with regards to security, governance and economic development within the country, otherwise referred to as Afghan National Development Strategy (ANDS). ISAF maintains much of the responsibility for the first of these three goals, and with regards to achieving the policing objectives of the Compact, aims to achieve by 2010 a:

> fully constituted, professional, functional and ethnically balanced Afghan National Police and Afghan Border Police with a combined force of up to 62,000 [that] will be able to meet the security needs of the country effectively and will be increasingly fiscally sustainable.[16]

Following on from the goals of the Compact, the 2005 Police Law listed police tasks in Afghanistan as being:

- ensuring and maintaining public order and security;
- ensuring individual and societal security and protecting legal rights and freedoms;
- preventive actions to stop crime;
- timely discovery of crimes and arrest of suspects;
- countering 'moral deviations, immoral social behaviour and actions that disturb public tranquillity';

- protecting public and private property and assets;
- fighting cultivation of opium poppy and marijuana;
- fighting organised crime and terrorism;
- regulating road traffic; and
- safeguarding borders.[17]

In mid-2007 the European Council took over the task of responsibility for police reform from Germany (in the European Union Police Mission to Afghanistan or EUPOL) in line with its ability to act in support of the ESDP. Security achievements touted by the Council as of June 2007 included over 60,000 ex-combatants disarmed and re-integrated;30,000 soldiers serving in the Afghan National Army (ANA); and 35,000– 40,000 officers serving in the ANP.[18] (The ANP is actually comprised of more like 70,000 personnel if we are to count day-to-day police (Afghan Uniformed Police); Afghan Border Police; Afghan National Civil Order Police (ANCOP – civil order); and the Counter Narcotics Police of Afghanistan). However critics were still arguing in 2007 that there had been no 'significant improvement in the quality of policing' in Afghanistan.[19]

The mission in Afghanistan at this point in time still faces major stumbling blocks when it comes both to the broader state-building agenda and to the more specific issue of police reform. These include resourcing issues, trying to police within a situation still plagued by major conflict, conflicting police reform programmes, and ongoing problems with respect to police culture and political interference.

Issues and problems arising

a) Too narrow an approach and too few resources

There have been a number of problems arising across the board with the efforts underway in Afghanistan – the utilisation of resources not least among them. In January 2002 over US$4.5 billion had been pledged at the International Conference on Reconstruction Assistance of Afghanistan that was held in Tokyo – and the amount was to be disbursed over a five-year period, although these pledges have been slow in coming and are also feared not to be enough to cover the costs of reconstruction efforts.[20] The establishment of a Law and Order Trust Fund in 2002 has been more useful as Tonita Murray points out, until the establishment of the Fund only 10 per cent of all estimated operational police costs could be met from the AIA.[21] Managed by the UN Development Programme (UNDP), the fund was set up to cover basic costs such as salary, equipment and facilities costs and to provide funds for training purposes too, yet it too has struggled to remain solvent in the face of delayed pledges. Even in 2007 it was estimated by the head of the Combined Security Transition Command – Afghanistan (CSTC-A) that only 40 per cent of the police had proper equipment.[22] Furthermore, in regional centres courses are eight weeks long for literate recruits, though the majority undertake a two-week Transition Integration Program for existing personnel – a course that leaves out training on basic policing functions such as in-depth study of the law, note-taking and witness statements.[23] These shortcomings have occurred despite such sizeable funds being pledged for the reconstruction of the Afghan administration and national economy. Moreover the issue of resources is only one part of the problem.

There have been criticisms of 'a slide towards expediency' where 'programmes to advance the transparency and democratic accountability of the [security] sector, while situating it within a clear legal framework, have been superseded by a singular focus on training and equipping the country's fledgling security forces'.[24] It is, therefore, not just the police training aspect of the mission that has suffered from a lack of investment of time, money and effort in Afghanistan. Of particular concern has been the lack of reform efforts directed at the judicial sector, though there is some hope that the fledgling EUPOL mission will help to address this issue given the linkages that are there to be made with the European Commission's justice programme.[25] Indeed there have been some promising signs here as in mid-2007 this oversight was at least recognised at the Rome Conference where Afghan institutions, international organisations, and donor representatives met to review progress in Afghanistan and to plan where to go next. Similarly the Afghanistan Human Development Report 2007 also called for greater focus on the whole rule of law context, and the US Institute for Peace (USIP) has had a number of reports from 2006 and 2007 urging for the development of rule of law institutions in a way that reflects the needs of the situation at hand whilst still meeting certain international legal norms. Both these USIP and UNDP reports called for a 'hybrid' model that would see two new units created within the state justice institutions: an Alternative Dispute Resolution (ADR) Unit and a Human Rights Unit.

> The ADR Unit would identify appropriate mechanisms to settle disputes outside of the courts, including referral of appropriate cases to jirgas and shuras and to Community Development Councils (CDC).

> While the ADR Unit could address minor criminal matters and all types of civil disputes, disputants would have the choice to process these cases through dispute resolution or through the courts. Serious criminal cases (including serious crimes committed in the past) would be dealt with by the formal justice system. The second element of the proposal is a Human Rights Unit (perhaps located within the Afghanistan Independent Human Rights Commission) mandated to monitor decisions made by ADR institutions (for example, jirgas, shuras and CDCs) to ensure their consistency with human rights principles and Afghan law. Once approved, the decisions could be made legally binding by the courts or other institutions of the formal justice sector.[26]

And in 2008 it is hoped that pilot projects will be unrolled in Afghanistan to see how such models will fare. Again, though, much of the success of these more technical matters rests in the hands of the political climate. Trust is difficult to achieve and, as William Maley has pointed out, 'there are considerable difficulties in rebuilding the military and police in such circumstances, for those who have little prospect of controlling the new coercive instrumentalities of the state are likely to be suspicious about those who do control them will use them'.[27] These problems, moreover, have been exacerbated further by a number of conflicting approaches in the mission to rebuild and reform Afghanistan's police service.

b) Conflicting approaches

There are a number of dualities present in police reconstruction efforts in Afghanistan with divisions in terms of the various sites of authority within the country, the issues arising from disagreements over priorities for the centralised programme for police reform, and with regards to the different roles and nature of each of the Provincial Reconstruction Teams.

Difficulties met in achieving an integrated chain of command in Afghanistan have created additional problems. Given the number of actors operating in the country combined with the rebuilding of the presidency, authority has at times been contested. One NATO official relayed to the author an example of this whereby President Karzai wanted to push a Governor out of office in the south, but the Governor was well-known for his anti-corruption stance, so the British authorities in the area argued against this and essentially helped keep the Governor in power. As of yet this has not become problematic on a large scale with regards to policing authority but indicates that this is a potential future problem.

In terms of a centralised approach to police reform in the country, in the initial phases of the mission in Afghanistan the Germans were tasked with providing police training. They were, however, soon criticised for being too academic, providing long courses with the basic training consisting of an 18 month course focusing on academics and leadership. Frustration with this and with a lack of focus on rank-and-file police brought the Americans in to help get more boots on the ground. The US therefore also started to provide police training in 2003, setting up a Central Training Centre.[28] However such provision of police came under the CSTC-A and the Department of Defense (DoD) and this training programme has had the opposing critique of being too short and too focused on a gendarmerie paramilitary style of policing.[29] There has continued to be some confusion as to how Afghan police are to take back the 'order' function from the military and ongoing confusion about military and police roles in general.[30] Emphasis on this kind of policing is also problematic as it encourages certain kinds of recruits and discourages others – women in particular.[31] Thus two approaches to police-building developed: one 'cautious and rational', building on what existed, and the other 'bold and sweeping'.[32]

In addition to this broad dualistic divide, there are other issues of mismatch arising out of the fact that there are also police from a number of different countries operating within the individual PRTs. This means that there is a parallel form of police reform and training running at a provincial level, though these efforts tend to be much smaller in scale and more tactical in focus thus their impact is 'largely local and unlikely to affect the overall reform of the Afghan National Police'.[33] This dualised system of more systematic and fundamental centralised reform of the ANP, combined with the ongoing but not necessarily identical training being undertaken by police in a PRT context is not necessarily contradictory or problematic, but there have been some difficulties arising out of this relationship. For example, in addition to issues with institutional overlap there have been more specific difficulties regarding intelligence sharing and the provision of security to police in PRTs. This is most obvious in the case of EUPOL's relationship with NATO given that Turkey asserts that Cyprus and Malta are not NATO members nor are they members of the Partnership for Peace, and that they therefore lack security clearance.[34]

Finally, in addition to the issues posed by multinational operations and the tensions that arise through differing national interests, objectives and even understandings of the local environment, one other issue *vis-à-vis* competing approaches was also made evident solely within the PRT context itself. This not insignificant issue has arguably hampered efforts in Afghanistan and stems from the cultural and organisational differences of civilian and military agencies. Within the PRT's political and civilian perceptions and priorities often differed from military ones (e.g. symbolism more important for the former with regards weapons amnesties etc. as opposed to the number of weapons yielded being more important for military mindsets and different aims and objectives in arranged and informal discussions).[35] This is evident both in terms of the political advisors role versus the military objectives of the day and in terms of the overall place of police in peacebuilding. Here Tonita Murray points out that both in the PRT context and in the overall picture that has developed in Afghanistan;

> state security and a military focus continue to dominate security sector reform and its rhetoric. This means that the range of solutions and capabilities that police can bring to peacebuilding is not fully appreciated, sometimes even by the police themselves. It is therefore not surprising that the police contribution to peacebuilding in Afghanistan has not achieved its potential.[36]

These issues relate to another major stumbling block in the efforts to provide for successful and sustainable policing in Afghanistan: that is the overarching strategic context and its unsuitability for policing roles.

c) Policing in war

As intimated above, one of the reasons for these conflicting approaches is that essentially in some provinces police are trying to police in a counter-insurgency context. There have been some successes such as the signing of a 7 December 2005 peace agreement in Faryab in the provincial police station between rival sides, proving, some commentators argued that Azadi-side had not lost its trust in the police, whose members were mainly Jumbesh-affiliated, and therefore the National Police and the governor could, and should, play the leadership role in facilitating the peace process.[37] However in a number of provinces trust is difficult to gain and maintain. The Canadians in

Khandahar, for example, are finding it difficult to undertake policing roles whilst exchanges of fire between US and Taliban troops are a frequent occurrence.[38]

There has therefore been criticism of the blurring of police and military roles in operational contexts (in addition to the confusion regarding initial training outlined above) as:

> It is counter-productive to treat police as an auxiliary fighting unit in battling the insurgency ... Afghanistan, like any other democracy, requires police service more than police force.... In countering an insurgency, the police are the first line of defence as the interface with the community. They have powers of stop and search, arrest and detention, and since they observe daily comings and goings, should be aware of the first signs of illegal activity. Yet, as the interior minister rightly said, 'it is not the responsibility of the police to fight [the insurgency]. The police are responsible for implementing the law, and we should not train our policemen with an inclination for war.'[39]

Separating out policing and military tasks and ethos should be a key objective in Afghanistan, and although attempts have been made to help clarify the roles of the ANP, there remains the potential for a confusion of roles – particularly for specialist units such as the Afghan National Civil Order Police (ANCOP) mentioned below.

d) Ethical and professionalisation issues for the ANP

Efforts to reinvent the police force in Afghanistan have been hampered by the fact that the force was largely composed of former mujahidin fighters with limited training, equipment, and who were 'prone to corruption'.[40] Some of these problems, Mark Sedra argues, could have been overcome by the instigation in 2005 of new programmes aimed at supporting further reforms and training, the provision of equipment, the rebuilding of infrastructure and the raising of salaries to commensurate with those of the armed forces.[41]

Yet in May 2006 significant riots broke out and local police were unable to control the situation, having no pepper spray, no intelligence, and no plan for dealing with such a disturbance after years of effort. And though a temporary force, the Afghanistan National Auxiliary Police (ANAP), was later born out of a presidential decree in September 2006 to further supplement the ANP, this move was controversial as these auxiliary personnel were to receive the same pay as police officers after only ten days of training, prompting the International Crisis Group to suggest that putting 11,000 men in the police uniform with even less training was not the right way to legitimise state institutions in the eyes of Afghans.[42] Such auxiliaries were also predominantly Pashtun and some Hazaras, and this was seen as a move that could potentially rearm the South and inflame tribal and militia fighters. The ANAP was then succeeded by the ANCOP force which had its first two lots of recruits move through a much more comprehensive 16 week training course in 2007. ANCOP is intended to be a multi-ethnic force especially created to deal with urban unrest and civil disorder. Recruits are trained in crowd and riot control tactics, pushing them towards the FPU end of the policing spectrum. However, though trainees are provided ethics training and training in tribal relations, there will still be some difficulties for these police with regards to the broader political and social context that prevails in Afghanistan.

Indeed though there is more of an ANP presence across Afghanistan in terms of the hardware that is visible in places like Kabul, there remains an ongoing problem with cross-cutting loyalties, with corruption, political interference and with a lack of ethnic and gender balance within the ANP.[43] Here the International Crisis Group says that hearts and minds are being lost not won, and has called for the political authorities in Kabul to improve the institutional mechanisms to support an uncorrupted, literate (estimates suggest that almost 70 percent of the ANP are not fully literate) efficient, loyal and depoliticised police force that is: accountable to the public (by having clearly displayed ID cards for public complaints etc.) as well as to official oversight mechanisms (for example by having a police commissioner and clear lines of authority down to district level, sothat the police service is at operational arm's length from the executive); well paid and rewarded for good service; not subject to conflicting legal codes (a new criminal code is underway for 2008); and immune from damaging political interference.[44] This last issue is an ongoing problem, with cases of interference either at the Presidential or Governor level being well-known both in-country and by the international community. Two final problems that are as yet to be tackled fully are the narcotics issue, as this remains one of the few sources of income for many inhabitants, as well as how to work with the question of gender.[45]

Conclusions

The policing part of the mission in Afghanistan has had some successes. There have been improvements in infrastructure, training, and equipment, uniforms have been provided as has training in human rights, and courses have more recently been offered in specialist skills such as traffic control, computerised immigration and passport examination.[46] There is also hope that the mission will improve through the adaptation of hybrid rule of law systems. Here there has been talk of taking on board aspects of local justice systems, whilst the US is also looking to the possible adoption of an Arban strategy – finding local tribes willing to undertake a security role with US blessing, and potentially making police answerable to local governors.

Yet to date the mission still struggles as the broader political and social context remains unsettled, and as resources deployed to tackle this are still spread too thinly. Though this may help avoid too much in the way of accusations of neo-colonialism, a 'light footprint' also risks failing simply because the efforts made are potentially not far-reaching enough or are unsustainable. Lastly, one issue not yet raised here that has been problematic and that is also a common issue with regards the following case study of Iraq, is the question of the place and suitability of private security firms. In October 2007 the Afghan government began to crackdown on private security actors following a number of unsavoury incidents. In 2004 one DynCorp employee provoked outrage by slapping the Minister of Transport in the face while protecting President Hamid Karzai, but it was the 2007 scandals involving Blackwater in Iraq that helped prompt the Afghan government to pursue further reform activities in their own country.[47]

Iraq

Iraq is an interesting case not in the least because in the early days of the outbreak of conflict in 2003 two academics argued that 'policekeeping' would be the key to ensuring the reestablishment of security and governance in Iraq. Graham Day and Christopher Freeman called for the creation of a large 'blue force' of (primarily Muslim) gendarmerie from surrounding nations to avoid what they saw as the precariousness of military peacekeeping in that particular situation. They believed that such policekeeping would act to prevent and combat ethnic, religious and political violence as well as economic crime and usual public order threats – and that this combined with judicial efforts would make the formulation and execution of an exit strategy a much easier task for the international mission.[48] However, astonishingly little planning for a policing role in Iraq was in fact undertaken by US and other authorities, and this lack of preparation resulted in major security problems as military proved unable to deal with the disorder that followed.

As has been commonly noted elsewhere, it seemed as if officials in the US believed that it would be capturing a state that had all of its major institutions intact. Initial assumptions were that the Iraqi police would be an important and cooperative part of the rebuilding process, with then-National Security Adviser Rice stating that: 'the concept was that we would defeat the army, but the institutions would hold, everything from ministries to police forces'.[49] However, as Robert Perito has argued, the 60 or so thousand members of the Iraqi police forces were at the very bottom of a complex security system and the national force was:

> composed of an academy-educated officer corps and a thuggish, uneducated, and largely untrained rank and file. Poorly equipped, badly led, and underpaid, the police were known for their brutality and petty corruption. Police did not patrol but remained in their stations until ordered to make arrests.[50]

Moreover, this force did not, as had been assumed, remain as a cohesive entity to help maintain public security, instead it rapidly dissolved following the US-led invasion in early 2003.

The decision that was made to then disband Iraqi security services contradicted lessons learned in rebuilding Japan and Germany after World War II, and although some Iraqis may have viewed the security forces as representatives of a 'hostile ethnic minority actively oppressing them', Thomas Mockaitis suggests that had the Sunni-dominated police and military been restricted to the Sunni triangle, then they could have helped reduce general lawlessness.[51] Instead, a major security vacuum arose as the US military had not been tasked with managing civil disorder of this ilk and there had been no provision for a policing mission *per se*.[52] Brigadier General Vincent Brooks, US Central Command spokesman said 'At no time do we see [the US military] becoming a police force'.[53] Yet when the violence became more entrenched in the early phases of the occupation, US Central Command (CENTCOM) sent more military police and assigned infantry to police duties.[54]

Understanding this was not a long-term solution to the problem, by April 2003 the US authorities made a public appeal for Iraqi police to return to duty, though this caused public outrage, and such police forces that did return were unarmed, ill-equipped and still lacking in leadership.[55] A small Iraqi Civil Defence Corps (later renamed the Iraqi National Guard) was created as a readily deployable constabulary force whilst longer term recruitment and training plans were put into place. Such efforts were, however, hampered by the emergence of a security vacuum that was promptly filled by militias who portrayed those employed in the security sector as traitors or collaborators, and these personnel were prime targets for politically-motivated attacks.[56] Major efforts were made in 2004 to exponentially increase the number of police recruits though this lowered recruitment standards and recruitment and retention have continued to be difficult tasks, not least because of the risks of working as an Iraqi police officer, with an estimated 12,000 killed in the months from end 2003 to the end of 2006.[57] Indeed a new recruit referred to himself and other police officers in Iraq as 'walking dead men'.[58]

Problems with attacks on police continued into 2006 and additional training for police operating in a 'non-permissive' environment was approved that year.[59] Some advances were subsequently made by the end of that year. At this stage the Multi-National Security Transition Command (MNSTC) had trained and equipped 135,000 members of the Iraqi Police Service (IPS), as well as 24,400 Iraq National Police (INP) and 28,360 members of the Border Police.[60] The IPS functions as a crime control service, the INP are 'harder' police units that have recently been implicated in atrocities leading to some to call for their disbandment, the Border Police provide for border control, and the Facilities Protection Service provide static guards for buildings and personal security guards for VIPs. Though such numbers do not indicate what kind of quality of police officer is being produced, they do indicate the scale of involvement in police training underway in Iraq.

At the end of 2006 external reviews such as that carried out by the Iraq Study Group began to assess where the policing effort should go from here. This particular group was comprised of members from both parties in Congress. It was co-chaired by James Baker III and Lee Hamilton, and was created in March 2006 to undertake what eventuated into an eight month review of the situation on the ground. In addition to other broader political, social and economically focused recommendations the members of the group commented on the issue of police and criminal justice, finding five key recommendations for the Iraq government and six for the US which, in summarised form, called for:

- The INP and Border Police to be transferred to the Ministry of Defense where the police commando units will become part of the Army and the Border Police to have total responsibility for border control;
- The IPS to be given greater responsibility to conduct criminal investigations and to increase cooperation with other elements of the judicial system, and the Iraqi government to provide funds to improve communications equipment and motor vehicles for the IPS;
- The Iraqi Ministry of Interior to expand the capability of the major crime unit and to exert more authority over local police forces – including being the sole authority to pay police salaries and to disburse financial support to the local police – and to identify, register and control Facilities Protection Service;
- The US DoD to continue to train the INP and the Border Police, with the US Department of Justice to direct the training of police forces under the Ministry of Interior;
- Embed US civilian police officers to cover all levels of the IPS and to replace the military police personnel currently assigned to training teams;
- FBI to expand its investigative and forensic training and facilities within Iraq to cover terrorism as well as crime;
- And, the US Department of Justice to lead the organisational transformation of the Iraqi Ministry of Interior and the US Department of Justice to establish training programmes for judges, prosecutors, investigators, to create anti-corruption mechanisms and to provide courthouses, secure housing for judicial staff and witness protection facilities.[61]

In mid-2007 it was apparent that the need to reform and adequately support the Iraqi police effort was still very pressing, with one Coalition military commander asserting that 'the failure of local police forces to provide a permanent security presence was the biggest obstacle to stability in Iraq.'[62] And a number of problems continue on in the policing sector into 2008 as noted below. The following sections therefore outline official objectives for the policing role in Iraq before pulling apart some of the key issues faced in attempts to carry out those objectives in a very challenging security environment.

Policing mandates and tasks

Following initial efforts whereby a short-term security pause was achieved mainly through military means, there have since been two main avenues for securing internal order in Iraq. The first is the more centralised effort to help provide for an effective domestic Iraqi policing capability, and the second has been a move towards more localised security and development efforts as evidenced by the expansion of the PRT concept – mirroring to some extent the pattern outlined in the Afghanistan case above.

Also noted above there was too little in the way of forethought and planning with regards 'what to do' post the immediate invasion phase in 2003. Further, as noted in Chapter 2, and Haiti and Somalia aside, there has long been a concern within the US not to get directly involved in internal policing reform efforts. It was therefore not until March 2004 that President George W. Bush finally signed a new National Security Presidential Directive which assigned responsibility for 'train and equip' police program. What is most significant here is that this responsibility was signed over to the DoD. In previous times the US State and Justice Departments had responsibility for any police efforts abroad, but in this instance it was thought that only the US military had enough resources for this project.[63] (The Department of Justice still had input into the rule of law sector; however, it was to be responsible for upgrading Iraqi courts, the prison system and in training Marshals to protect members of the judiciary).[64] This decision to hand over police efforts to Defense has had a number of ramifications as outlined below.

In terms of more localised security and developmental efforts, PRTs have, since 2005, been an important part of US strategy in Iraq. The emphasis of such PRTs on security and development goals entails that they engage in aspects of security sector reform, thereby extending the more centralised efforts undertaken by ISAF headquarters in Kabul. Though these PRTs differ in terms of their make-up and the type of environment within which they operate, the objectives of PRTs in Iraq are said to have one common objective: to expand the central Iraqi government's authority to all areas of the country and improve the ability of provincial authorities to deliver essential services.[65] At the end of 2006 there were ten PRTs operating in Iraq. The United States led seven, and coalition partners Britain, Italy, and South Korea led three. These provincial level PRTs are predominantly focused on assisting local governments to develop budgets, implement development strategies and provide essential services.

In bolstering this initial PRT set-up, in January 2007 President Bush called for a 'New Way Forward' which included plans for the number of PRTs to double, and for these new PRTs to be embedded with Brigade (Army) and Regimental (Marine) Combat Teams (otherwise known as B/RCTs). Plans were originally made for six new Embedded Provincial Reconstruction Teams (ePRTs) to be based in Baghdad, three in Anbar Province, and one in Babil. These new PRTs were to be created to work at the city, district, and neighbourhood level to essentially allow moderates to have political space to operate, to bring violent extremists under control, and therefore the focus was intended to be on shaping the political environment rather than building infrastructure.[66]

At the beginning of 2008 there were 13 of these ePRTs. They began their operations with four person teams that initially drew on Defence Department staff and from the US National Guard or Reserves but the State Department has, since March 2007, begun recruiting civilian contractors and most ePRTs now have eight to 12 personnel.[67] These ePRTs have focused on building relationships with local officials and civil society, undertaking reconciliation work, rebuilding more specialist forms of infrastructure, and disbursing smaller grants for economic development.

Issues arising

a) Planning, deployment and resourcing issues

It is clear that the mission in Iraq has been bedevilled by a lack of comprehensive planning. As a number of commentators have pointed out, the combat operation was conducted successfully but that the pre-combat diplomacy and post-combat reconstruction phases have thus far failed to impress.[68] Moreover early efforts to put into place the little post-combat planning that had been undertaken were not at all well executed.

Of the 6,600 police personnel that had been recommended by US Justice Department (2,500 of which were to be gendarme) only 50 arrived in the first nine months and their tasks were massive, with one trainer potentially being responsible for more than 50 police stations and attendant personnel.[69] One year later there were still only 375 police advisors on the ground.[70] Further delays were to be found throughout the mission with training programme for Iraqi police beginning in Jordan in December 2003 but not reaching capacity until spring 2004 and, though the curriculum in Jordan was based on the one NATO had utilised in Kosovo, the Iraqi course was cut down from four months of classroom instruction and 12 weeks of field training to ten weeks of class work only.[71]

Similar shortcomings can be found in the broader rule of law context with only 870 judges out of a needed 1,500 in place in Iraq by January 2007, and with only 99 trained judicial investigators.[72] The issue with regards to the difficulties in recruiting suitable personnel into the policing and justice sectors continue, and are further complicated by high numbers of casualties and attacks on such figures of government authority.

b) Blurring of military and police

A confusion of military and policing roles has further hampered efforts in Iraq. In March 2004 the Civilian Police Advisory Training Team (CPATT) with both military and civilian personnel was established under the Multi-National Security Transition Command (MNSTC-I) with an Army general and a civilian from the Justice Department in lead roles. However, as Robert Perito has noted, this resulted in a lack of common goals and a lack of agreement as to the desired character and mission of the police.[73] Justice Department officials sought to create a lightly-armed police force with an emphasis on community policing, whilst at the same time the US military were creating 'heavy police units' made up of former soldiers (Public Order Battalion, Mechanised Police Unit and Emergency Response Unit composed of unvetted Sunnis with military weapons and counter-insurgency training) that were merged in 2006 to create the Iraqi National Police (INP) and which was engaged in death squad activities.[74] Indeed an Iraqi official who helped create these special units warned then Defense Secretary Donald Rumsfeld that they could potentially become a source of problems rather than a solution to the insecurity being experienced in Iraq.[75] In response to such developments, the Iraq Study Group Report, as noted above, argued that the INP police commando units and the Border Police should come under DoD not Interior and should become part of the new Iraqi army.[76] The Group Report further argues that in line with these changes DoD should fund the INP and Border Police, and Department of Justice should pick up the responsibility for training the Iraqi Police Service.[77]

As Iraqi police are accustomed to a centralised chain of command and that they practice more military-oriented traditions than those in the West, and given the previous history of Iraq's security sector agencies, it is vital that the police-military divide be clearly circumscribed.[78] This has not as of yet been achieved within the Iraq context, and although the activities described here have not all gone unpunished, they serve to highlight the difficulties in having a 'Police' force undertaking what is essentially a military role in a counter-insurgency context as well as ongoing difficulties with the ongoing sectarian divide, and such abuses have undoubtedly caused major setbacks for the overall mission in Iraq.

c) Coordination issues

The situation in Iraq has also highlighted a lack of coordination and cooperation between American agencies tasked with different roles in rebuilding Iraq. In one example, the Department of State had undertaken a 'Future of Iraq' project that set out options for security sector reform as written with the help of exiled Iraqis but this report was ignored or simply not circulated to other departments.[79]

In Iraq proper too there are a number of different coordination problems. One is simply a factor of limited time in that the rotation of personnel can result in a continuity problem with US civilians usually serving one year in PRT, for example.[80] Another general problem is in the recruitment field. As Robert Perito notes there have been some issues with recruitment (sending six Colonels to one PRT where they outranked the commander of the B/RCT or the hiring of contractors with a lack of field experience or cultural awareness); with the fact that ePRTs operate with a lot of autonomy and though they coordinate with provincial-level PRTs, the latter do not always know what the PRTs are doing nor do they necessarily agree with their evaluations.[81] Thus here further problems stem from the dualised system which sees again a centralised effort run through the Multi-National Security Transition Command – Iraq (MNSTC-I), which manages training and assistance for police, courts, and prisons but does so without reference to the PRTs.[82] There is therefore confusion as to the role of provincial police and the centralised system with the Ministry of Interior, leading to uncertainty as to who to follow in what circumstances.[83]

d) Standards and status of policing

Further, the task of developing Iraq's police service has been beset with problems regarding the varying quality and loyalty of recruits – on both sides of the fence. There have been problems with both those recruited at home to lead the reform and rebuilding effort, and those recruited locally in Iraq.

The issue of private contractors has been a particularly problematic one for the effort in Iraq. Contractors have played significant roles in rebuilding Iraq. DynCorp, for example, was selected to undertake criminal justice reform programmes; providing police, corrections and judicial advisors who would work at national, provincial and municipal levels.[84] In June 2004 shortly before the US handed over sovereignty to the new Iraqi administration, a decree was issued that gave some levels of immunity from Iraqi legal processes to private security contractors operating in Iraq for any actions carried out as part of their work. This decree has recently been challenged, however, in large part due to an incident in September 2007 when Blackwater employees, contracted to protect those undertaking work for the US State Department, became embroiled in a scandal following the death of 17 people.

In late 2007, then, the Iraqi government was looking to pass law that would see immunity of private contractors removed, it was approved by cabinet and was due to come before parliament.[85] There remains for the present time a legal loophole that makes it difficult to hold US contractors accountable for their actions in places such as Iraq, but such personnel problems are also to be found amongst local recruits too. Indeed additional accountability problems were also headline news in late 2007 when DynCorp was unable to account for claimed expenditure in Iraq.[86] Yet there are also distinctions between such contractors. DynCorp sub-contracts US police, they are all US citizens, carry arms provided by the US government and therefore differ from the many fully private companies that provide 'security' in Iraq on a much more *ad hoc* and less visible basis.[87]

In terms of the development of a domestic policing capacity part of the ongoing problems faced in the policing sector stem from an overwhelming emphasis on recruiting large numbers of police at the cost of good quality police. This has been further exacerbated by inadequate training regimes. Those who had served under Saddam were enrolled in a three week Transition Integration Programme (TIP) adapted from Balkans training regimes which emphasised basic human rights principles, providing firearms, patrolling and search training, whilst new recruits were send to an eight week course in Jordan where it was hoped 32,000 police would graduate from the college each year but where some estimate only 30 per cent had undergone training (and training that was questionable in terms of relevance) when sovereignty was handed back in mid-2004.[88]

The quality of the fledgling Iraqi police force has since been found wanting. In 2005 Human Rights Watch claimed that arbitrary arrest, torture and ill treatment of suspects was commonplace, that extortion was rife and that given such occurrences the rebuilding of a good relationship between the new police service and the public was going to be a difficult task.[89]

Since then the Study Group Report of 2006 has pointed out that there needed to be 'substantial reforms to purge bad elements and highlight best practices' within the Ministry of Interior – not only is there huge variation in police standards but there is also the problem of politicisation of Iraq's guiding bureaucratic and governmental arm.[90] Once that process is completed the Report then recommended the Ministry of Interior be the sole entity responsible for the police budget, and that it should make efforts to extend the authority of the Criminal Investigative Division over local police forces.[91]

Tony Pfaff further argued that in 2007 the Iraqi police were still locked in a 'culture of crisis'. Here he suggested that corruption emerged domestically within the Iraqi policing situation despite such activity being unacceptable to Iraqi cultural norms because of the very low pay rate and resources allocated to the police, and – perhaps even more significantly – further claimed that professional policing roles and identity have been undermined by hiring and promotional practices that favoured some family, tribal or political affiliations over others.[92] He reports many instances of cases whereby, when the two twin imperatives of maintaining a cohesive group and obeying the law come into conflict, the needs of the group win and therefore:

> despite understanding the right thing, and desiring to do the right thing, a strong culturally informed disposition to submit to authority, can conflict with this understanding and desire to make reform difficult.[93]

These issues, combined with the negative press emerging from the abuses perpetrated by some Iraqi police as noted above, has resulted in a situation whereby police are frequently isolated from the public they are intended to serve. When senior police officers are accused of vigilante killings, when journalists reporting on corruption and criminal activity within the police are killed, and when even police chiefs complain that they cannot trust their officers then there are major systemic problems of abuse to be overcome.[94] Similarly the problems faced with non-performance or desertion of police personnel in the face of more significant fighting in April 2008 has further acted to weaken the fledgling national police service.[95] Pfaff hoped that the introduction of new laws outlining procedures to discipline and prosecute police misconduct and criminal activity would help to mitigate the problems seemingly endemic in the police services. Additional hopes are held for the launching of new training missions for the INP unit as part of an increased involvement by NATO, led by the Italian Carabiniere.[96] However, the effects of such laws and such training have not as of yet taken hold.

This issue once again points to the limits of policing too. In more general terms the question of political settlement and the resolution of the tension and intra-state conflict currently ongoing in Iraq and in the other cases assessed here is something beyond the reach of policing *per se*, but it is at the same time a phenomenon that successful professional and ethical policing can help to bring about. More specifically, one feature that has been most prominent in this particular case *vis-á-vis* how to successfully carry out policing and all other ongoing operations on the ground is the question of legitimacy. The situation in Iraq therefore brings us back to the 'big questions' regarding intervention, sovereignty and whether or not international policing in whatever form can be a legitimate objective.[97]

The tumultuous situation in Iraq also raises the question as to whom may police whom and why, with commentators suggesting that there needs to be a bigger role for the UN in order to bring about peace.[98] This has echoes of the very first case study analysed in this book. NATO was to conduct the military campaign and the UN was to secure the peace in that case. The rise of the UN as a policing actor as mentioned in Chapter 2 may see international policing efforts centralised with that particular body though such a scenario, should it occur, is currently very far off. And such a scenario would indeed bring about its own issues such as questions of organised hypocrisy, the normative desirability of peacebuilding efforts, accountability issues, and resource issues – questions that are raised in the following final chapter.

Conclusions

The two cases here demonstrate a number of similarities. Both have problems with the blurring of police-military divide, a feature that seems endemic in situations where authority remains highly contested. They also face dualities of authority and sources of information within the coalition efforts themselves given the dual set-up of a centralised reform effort with more minor efforts being undertaken through the PRT system. Private contractors have been both necessary (due to the US' predominance in these missions and its lack of expeditionary policing ability) and often problematic. The recent histories of policing forces in these two countries are also of an ilk. These histories have typically been those of repressive forces that served the autocratic political agenda of the day though there is an older history of more service-oriented policing in Afghanistan in particular. Both of the cases presented here therefore express the vast problems faced in attempts to undertake policing in war, in attempting to introduce democratic policing to areas where such a concept is a very foreign one, and the need to try to establish the role of police as an accepted authority.

6
The New International Policing in Theory

The relevance and fundamental roles of police in international peace operations have grown dramatically. This has brought police professionals into a new sphere of action. After all, police forces are intended to maintain internal order, military forces to provide an external protection and expeditionary capability. This chapter now assesses the current status of the police-military divide given the suggestion that policing and military spheres have increasingly converged. It therefore asks how the rise of police in international situations may be seen to be qualitatively different from military involvement, and points to how this phenomenon relates to the changing nature of the domestic/international divide in international relations.

This chapter begins with a general assessment of the traditional nature of police and military forces in liberal democratic states. It then outlines a number of recent challenges to this police-military divide – both from the police and from the military ends of the spectrum as well as from developments in the post-September 11 era which have acted to further blur the distinction between these two disciplined services. The chapter then returns to a discussion that asks what fundamental differences remain, concluding that, though the police-military divide has undoubtedly changed it remains as relevant as ever, particularly given the different roles and functions of these agencies in peace operations. Given this importance of policing as distinct from military roles the following chapter then assesses what the new international policing means both in operational and broader political terms.

The police-military divide in theory

The traditional distinction between the police and military was fundamental to the rise of the modern state and the modern state system.

Historical sociologists have asserted that modern states are defined by a number of features – most notably claiming a legitimate right to a monopoly over internal and external violence. This monopoly is expressed in internal affairs through the creation of national policing institutions and other regulatory mechanisms, and, once internal pacification is complete, with the development of standing armed forces which assert state monopoly over the means for external violence.[1] This division between forces for the maintenance of internal law and order versus forces that defend against outside forces has thus traditionally formed the most basic division between police and military forces.

Military forces have therefore traditionally been identified as the bearers of externally-focused force on behalf of the state. Soldiers engage in armed violence on behalf of the state, but in order to do this they must wear uniform, obey state authorities, and to obey strict laws that regulate the use of military force.[2] Theoretically at least, then, there are different rules for the conduct of soldiers in war than mere civilians – the ability for someone to kill and for it to not be called murder requires that soldiers be something extraordinary.[3] And here the extraordinary functions that help define a soldiering role include the maintenance of defensive capabilities, the potential use of maximum force and the pursuit of 'victory' in war should it be required. All of these have long been the traditional touchstones of modern standing armed forces. Most notable in the military doctrine that underpins all of this, however, has been the notion of the 'enemy' who must be incapacitated or destroyed. This focus on the 'enemy' presents a particular ethos that shapes broader notions of the requirements of defence, and that legitimises the maxim of maximum force. Moreover, it has also been interpreted as requiring the values of hierarchy, discipline, and teamwork to permeate military institutions and culture in order to enable military forces to respond as effectively as possible to potential challenges to national security.[4]

Despite these very general commonalities there are a number of different ways in which today's military forces operate. Some countries like the US have pursued a force protection model that emphasises deterrence and that limits interaction with local people during operations, thereby theoretically limiting risks to soldiers.[5] Force protection approaches for ground troops are also often combined with an emphasis on 'shock and awe' tactics that serve to further maintain distance between those military forces and the local population. Other countries, particularly those with a long tradition of peacekeeping, or those who have emphasised the importance of human security or nation-building in their security policies, may interact much more closely with the local population. (Of course even here it must be said that military forces may undertake peacekeeping operations in very different ways – with some UN forces in Lebanon, such as the French or Fijian, being seen as more 'aggressive' in not wanting to allow any armed groups in their area of operations and being seen to be tough with everyone, whilst others in the mission were less stringent).[6] These differences in military approaches to operations more closely reflect similar differences between countries that have a greater community focus in policing institutions versus more paramilitary approaches too.[7]

Modern policing institutions are said to be the creation of nineteenth century nation-states and empires, though similar social control mechanisms can be found throughout other times in history in the form of parish constables and suchlike.[8] Early theories of punishment focused on the individual and the significance of individual choice and autonomy, but at the end of the nineteenth century these theories were soon replaced with personality-based theories which looked for certain character traits as determining criminality. Post-war approaches saw a new focus on social control, and this focus on re-education, improving living standards of the lower classes and alternative detainment strategies prevailed until the 1970s. Since then policies have predominantly focused on general prevention. Thus 'instead of the police simply trying to punish crimes after they have been committed, they should prevent them "by protecting order"'.[9] This aim is thought to be able to be achieved by police acting in roles such as: crime-fighter; emergency operator; social enforcer or social peacekeeper.[10] Tasks traditionally focus on the prevention of, response to and punishment of crime in order to maintain law and order and to support the civil power. Much police work involves tasks such as patrolling, criminal investigation and traffic work (the three of which generally occupy up to 85 per cent of police time in modern democratic states), as well as other administrative duties, riot or other special tactics group work and so on.[11] Skills that are valued in police work include general powers of observation, negotiating skills, knowledge of the law, good morals, and an ability and willingness to use coercive force if necessary. Theories of policing have tended to be normative, that is, identifying what the ends of policing should be – and these ends include the maintenance of law and order, the pursuit of the social good, increasing domestic harmony, and the preservation of human life.[12] In more recent years this focus on ends has been joined by a new emphasis on means, most notably the use or threat of coercive force, as similarly important in identifying the defining principles of police work.

Yet there are a number of ways that police forces can be constructed in order to pursue these objectives. David Bayley suggests that attempts to catagorise policing styles (such as 'Anglo-Saxon', 'Continental' and 'Communist') are 'unsatisfactory' due to the complexity of police institutions.[13] Yet for the purpose of beginning to try to make sense of the kinds of methods and principles contemporary police forces draw on today, we can make some very broad generalisations. Policing in general is divided into an axis of force and control versus service and care. The force/control end emphasises crime control and the maintenance of order, the service/care end is associated with models of 'community policing' where the emphasis is on services to the public and the protection of citizen's rights.[14] And despite Bayley's warning it is useful to first of all remind the reader that this discussion pertains to liberal models of policing, and thence to point to the 'Ango-Saxon' and 'Continental' traditions to highlight how the nature or organisation of police forces differs between modern liberal democracies today.

Policing in the British tradition focuses on law enforcement, the upholding of laws that protect basic rights, on the provision of broader social order and, more recently, on the principle of 'community policing'. Here individual officers are very autonomous, can act independently if required, and function in a less hierarchical atmosphere. Policing foci in states influenced by this tradition have moved towards a 'service'-oriented function, with community policing being described as a philosophy that seeks to make policing community-oriented, problem-oriented and proactive or preventive in focus.[15] It requires increased cooperation between police and others, has a problem-solving focus, looks to decentralise police operations, and looks to shift attention to the root causes of illegal behaviour.[16]

In contrast to this tradition which insists on a clear separation of policing as a much more civilian, community-focused model, some European models often utilise the notion of the 'third force' (riot squad roles, or more militarised gendarmerie police units that are often called 'constabulary forces' or 'formed police units').[17] Here, militaristic elements in police strategy are incompatible with the notion of community policing and indeed the rise of 'formed police units' has been seen as evidence of an increased 'militarisation of the police'.[18]

New challenges to the police-military divide: the militarisation of the police?

These 'third force' kinds of police units, as represented by European paramilitary police and the like and as increasingly used in peace operations, are units that are much more self-sufficient in terms of dedicated logistical capabilities. These are cohesive units rather than just collections of individual police officers and they are commonly referred to as Formed Police Units (FPUs – the main term used in this book), Integrated Police Units (IPUs) or Stability Police Units (SPUs).

As Michael Dziedzic and Christine Stark note, such FPUs are valuable in providing an interim force between military and community police responses in peace support operations because they are:

> robust, armed police units that are capable of performing specialized law enforcement and public order functions that require disciplined group action. They are trained in and have the flexibility to use either less-than-lethal or lethal force, as circumstances dictate.[19]

Dziedzic and Stark further outline how FPUs are 'rapidly deployable, logistically self-sustainable' and are better suited to 'survive in the anarchic conditions that often prevail during the early stages of most missions' thereby filling a gap in capabilities between 'military contingents that are proficient in the use of lethal force and individual international police, who have very limited force options and may even be unarmed.'[20] These forces therefore specialise in the 'harder' edge of policing: riot control; protection roles; organised crime, CT and counter-insurgency; border patrol; and intelligence collection. (Interestingly, FPUs are also cheaper than their individual counterparts. Unlike the provision of individual officers to the UN which do not qualify for reimbursement, but who receive a mission subsistence allowance of from $2,400 to $4,500 per month, governments providing these FPUs do get reimbursement (albeit less at around $1,400 per month) which makes recruitment of FPU's an easier task.[21] FPUs are therefore 50 per cent less costly than individual police personnel, and are even slightly less expensive than their military counterparts and are thought to be even more cost effective in terms of their ability to perform daily mission requirements that are mandated to them).[22]

The greatest difference between European style policing and British policing traditions therefore rests on greater caution of the latter towards militaristic policing styles, culture and organisation.[23] In contrast to the image of the local British bobby who undertakes to serve the local community through crime prevention and problem-solving, the French gendarmerie are para-military in the limited sense of the term – they are accountable to the Minister of Defence rather than Interior, and in times of war have a military role as a light infantry division.[24] However, despite this, it must also be said that they are predominantly located in rural areas and along main highways and although more heavily armed they are very rarely called upon to act with stronger force within times of peace.[25] Similarly the MSU used in Bosnia made up of Italian Carabiniere was primarily drawn from the more elite airborne battalions, most of whose recruits are drawn from those leaving military service, and could therefore be said to be more military in nature.[26] These MSU also lived in military barracks and their equipment was as good as if not better than other infantry forces.[27] At home the Carabiniere are seen as both military police and an internal security force.[28] Given such confusion of terms (can a force that is essentially light infantry with some additional training be labelled police?) these kinds of forces create major difficulties in efforts to demarcate police and military.

The very existence of FPUs highlights that there are some undeniable similarities between police and military forces. Indeed they have explicitly been called forces that:

> straddle the line between military and police and have characteristics and capabilities of both types of forces ... they can deploy rapidly to respond to situations that require greater force and firepower that can be provided by civil police, but that do not require the firepower of infantry or armoured units ... [they] are trained to deal with civilians and are skilled at using the minimum amount of force necessary to control the situation.[29]

Moreover no matter what model of policing is pursued it is quite clear that 'most police forces are still organised along military lines, with uniforms, chains of command, progression through the ranks, strong disciplinary rules and formalised training'.[30] There is, therefore, at times some cross over at the tactical and operational levels. Similarly there is often a shared sense of purpose in the tasks that such agencies undertake. The notion that 'a central feature of cop culture is a sense of mission. This is the feeling that policing is not just a job but a way of life with a worthwhile purpose, at least in principle', is highly compatible with the way in which military personnel feel about their chosen profession.[31] There are also claims as to more specific instances of increased militarisation of police forces in particular cities or countries in terms of the types of weapons used or the organisational culture of local police forces. Similarly the role of military police in moving from military to civilian policing as demonstrated in places such as Haiti further blurs the military-police divide.[32] In addition to these developments, a number of shifts for military forces in recent years have also created further confusion as to the difference between police and military forces.

New challenges to the police-military divide: the 'police-ification' of the military?

There was a perceptible change for military institutions in the post-Cold War era, with personnel finding their niche in a new and uncertain world. The post-Cold War era was identified either as one of a 'democratic peace' where there was a growing 'obsolescence of major war', or as a 'coming anarchy' whereby a 'clash of civilisations' constituted one potential future for the world.[33] 'New wars' were seen by some to be the new major challenge to security – wars defined by lawlessness, war-lordism, war economies, protection rackets and the end of order.[34] State sovereignty was increasingly seen as involving responsibilities as well as rights, and the theoretical inviolability of a state's boundaries was challenged.[35] Further, states were often pressured by publics influenced by the CNN effect and unprecedented human rights activity to intervene in the affairs of others who were seen to be failing to protect their citizens from genocide or other humanitarian disasters.[36] Western states in particular were inspired by the immediate post-Cold War Enlightenment notion that we were at the end of history where liberal democratic values were said to have triumphed, and where it was believed that peace prevails between mature liberal democratic states.[37] These states were similarly influenced by the rise of the human security paradigm that called for individuals not states to be the referent for security efforts. Such states were thus at times also motivated to try to transplant liberal democratic values abroad, including the democratisation of other police forces, with varying levels of success. 'International security' therefore became a much more broadly focused phenomenon that was no longer necessarily restricted to the politico-military aspect of inter-state relations and this, amongst other factors noted below, helped provide the environment within which military roles came closer to policing roles than ever before.[38]

The nature of soldiering was thus revisited in light of these dramatic changes in the international security field. Arguments as to what the key roles of military forces should be in this post-Cold War era were often made in either technical terms (the rise of the network force and 'risk-free' warfare) or with respect to just what the role of soldiering should entail. Here Gustav Daniker's Guardian soldier concept echoed

Morris Janowitz's much older notion of soldiering that argued for a strong constabulary ethic amongst soldiers (though we must also remember that Janowitz was aware of the reluctance of the military to undertake policing tasks).[39] Janowitz claimed that 'the military establishment becomes a constabulary force when it is continuously prepared to act, committed to the minimum use of force, and seeks viable international relations rather than victory because it has incorporated a protective military posture'.[40]

The move towards a constabulary ethic could be said to have been aided by the increased involvement (in terms of overall numbers of personnel, dollars and the increasing numbers of countries involved) in peace support operations where civil-military cooperation within missions is increasingly necessary, and which requires the undertaking of diverse tasks such as the monitoring of borders, patrolling of cease-fires, and the protection of electoral processes. In particular, the emergence of second generation peacekeeping involving aspects of state-building and a stronger hearts and minds approach has required the development of particular skills in increasingly multi-purpose forces.[41] Peace enforcement and humanitarian intervention operations similarly presented new challenges. Peace enforcement missions (admittedly rare since Somalia) are played much more along the traditional military lines of identifying an enemy, whilst deployments in instances where humanitarian needs are extraordinarily pressing might necessitate involvement in the protection and distribution of humanitarian aid, the defending of UN safe havens, the halting of ethnic cleansing policies and aiding the implementation of peace plans. All of these military operations other than war (MOOTW) have, a major RAND study has claimed, meant that MOOTW may come to resemble police work.[42]

Moreover, in addition to these new roles come other changes too. In the edited collection 'The Postmodern Military: Armed Forces After the Cold War', the various authors were interested in exploring many recent developments that were occurring within the military forces of certain 'postmodern' liberal democracies. Developments that were identified in these cases included the increasing permeability of civilian and military spheres; the reduction in differences in the armed services based on service branch, rank and combat versus non-combat roles; a change in military purpose from fighting wars to conducting missions not traditionally considered military; a more extensive use of multinational military forces legitimated by supranational institutions; and the internationalisation of military forces themselves.[43] Social and economic trends have helped promote an increased civilianisation and out-sourcing of non-key soldiering roles such as catering or even transportation – increasing the crossover between civilian and military spheres in terms of tasks, time and culture too.[44] The roles accorded to militaries have therefore multiplied, whilst military culture and institutional structures have been increasingly exposed to forces of a civilian, humanitarian or legal nature. And this brings us to the specific question of law.

International law has increasingly been seen as a means to legitimate and regulate international military deployments.[45] Though this has been especially apparent in the case of forceful military deployments, Kosovo being the most prominent example, there has also been a greater stress laid on the need for strong legal frameworks for all peace support missions and, indeed, for the role played by civilians in international settings.[46] This has signalled to some authors that the use of force has increasingly become a form of 'regulation' with states focusing on 'non-lethal techniques of social control' both for external and domestic affairs.[47] This focus on law also means that soldiering now involves greater levels of responsibility, and by inference increased autonomy and accountability – bringing policing and military spheres a little closer in some areas of action. The effects of these more operationally-oriented post-Cold War developments, moreover, have been further compounded by strategies that seek to minimise risk and build order in a post-September 11 world.

Challenges in the post-September 11 world

The advent of the terrorist attacks of September 11 prompted a US-led war on terror, ignoring traditional definitions that identify terrorism as a crime to be dealt with by law enforcement agents. Motivated by concerns that more static counter-terrorist measures needed to be bolstered by assertive and pre-emptive activities, the US's shift away from dealing with terrorism through an overall reliance on law enforcement means has been met with great concern. This concern stems from a desire to avoid imbuing terrorists with any sense of legitimacy that the term war brings, and to retain the higher moral and legal ground to distinguish the actions of governments challenged by terrorism from those terrorists themselves.[48] This latest development of a 'war on terror', though more of a slogan than a doctrine that saturates all approaches to security, still serves to blur the conceptual lines between policing and military affairs.

It no longer seems clear in an era of a 'war on terror' and in a situation where a new category of 'illegal combatant' has entered into the jargon of international law, as to where the boundaries of war, crime and terrorism begin and end.[49] Here, in addition to the issue of legal decision-making processes constituting a central part of modern military operations (mentioned above), we must also recognise the wider significance of the growth of international humanitarian law and pay heed to the institutional and normative shift that has seen the creation of the International Criminal Court (ICC). Now in addition to the ability to take states to court at the International Court of Justice, individuals may be taken to court at the ICC to face war crimes charges or charges of crimes against humanity. Though a long time in the making, the ICC is a very young institution that has indicted only a few high profile individuals thus far; yet it is of important symbolic significance in furthering the strength of international law.

The ability to bring soldiers to court as criminals not prisoners of war again presents some challenges for categorising war and crime. These categories may have been somewhat unclear in previous times too, but these last few years have witnessed unprecedented challenges to these theoretical bounds. Indeed, although there has always been a place for a military response to terrorist emergencies, such responses have involved complicated emergency powers legislation that sees the situation handed over to military forces for a short period of time in a military aid to the civil power (MACP) role. Police still often retain overall control of the operation and indeed will conduct a police investigation into the situation once the immediate emergency is resolved. The assigning of counter-terrorist roles to military agents is therefore not unheard of, but the institutional emphasis that post-September 11 has been placed on the potential military response to counter terrorism is unprecedented. For example, NATO had acknowledged the threat of terrorism in the 1990s in its 1991 and 1999 Strategic Concepts documents, but it was essentially sidelined as more of an internal issue for member states to deal with individually. Post-September 11, NATO released a document entitled 'NATO's Response to Terrorism' which laid out some key principles for NATO counter-terrorist strategy and which led to the creation of NATO's Military Concept for Defence Against Terrorism which suggests that military roles in defending against terrorism might encompass: anti-terrorism and counter-terrorism (essentially defensive and offensive measures); military cooperation and consequence management in dealing with the effects of a terrorist attack.

Further, the argument that failing or failed states are sources of such terrorist activity has increasingly dominated international security concerns in the post-September 11 era.[50] Here, again, both terrorism and issues pertaining to the creation and maintenance of law and order within state bounds have traditionally been dealt with by policing, not military, establishments. Thus with the declaration of an oxymoronic 'war on terror' and subsequent use of military force to pursue anti-terrorist campaigns combined with interventions into failing states that require major state-building exercises that need both military and policing roles, it is no wonder that there is much confusion as to appropriate roles for military and policing personnel in addressing security problems. If we are emphasising terrorism and law and order as the new major international security issues, how might we use the military to respond to these issues? Or do we need to revisit the balance of policing and military capabilities as we begin to reassess their roles in this new international security environment? Such questions are further compounded by counter-insurgency operations, such as those conducted in Iraq and Afghanistan which pose further challenges to the police-military divide. This challenge is not a new one, with Thomas Mockaitis claiming that 'the British Army for much of its history has been more of an imperial police force tasked with maintaining order and later combating insurgency within a global empire'.[51] Indeed even more recently in 2007 US General David Petraeus, in charge of the war in Iraq, has suggested that counter-insurgency is more like 'armed social work' requiring a more intellectual approach.[52]

Lastly, then, this concern that there may be a connection between terrorism and failed states has acted to push the state-building and peacebuilding agenda to unprecedented levels. Though this notion of state-building began in the 1990s with the evolution of peacekeeping as discussed prior, the idea that weak or failing states may be hosts to major terrorist activity has been part and parcel of a new security-development nexus.[53] As noted in the RAMSI case study amongst others, police play a vital role in this new agenda that sees the need to move beyond just the provision of a 'security pause'. International actors have increasingly recognised that there also needs to be a more sustainable peacebuilding and state-building effort that promotes broader development goals if a more positive and enduring form of peace and security is to be achieved. The notion of state-building does, in this sense seem quite instrumental in terms of removing the potential for threats arising from a security vacuum. However the concomitant emergence of a 'peacebuilding consensus' has acted to provide ethical argument for such institution-building exercises too.

Peacebuilding has seen a greater role ascribed to actors that can engage in both security and developmental roles as the objectives of peace missions have moved from the simpler act of the separation and monitoring of warring parties, to the much more complex and difficult aim of establishing a self-sustaining positive peace.[54] Yet such state- and peacebuilding activities have not been 'neutral'. Peacebuilding has been associated with both democratisation and marketisation and thus is a 'specific kind of social engineering, based on a particular set of assumptions about how best to establish durable domestic peace'.[55]

In light of all of these developments, then, law enforcement issues, suggest Peter Andreas and Richard Price, are being transfigured into security issues. Indeed they claim that:

> One of the most important blurrings of traditional boundaries occurring in the post-Cold War era is that between an internally oriented domestic police sphere and an externally oriented military sphere.[56]

Their claim appears to be made evident by the developments described above, by increasing police interest in quasi-military tactics and equipment for specialist response units, and by the fact there has been an increased interest in the deployment of police forces abroad. Here, in the US case at least, Michael Hardt and Antonio Negri also claim that 'the separation of tasks between the external and the internal arms of power (between the army and the police, the Central Intelligence Agency (CIA) and the FBI) is increasingly vague and indeterminate.'[57] Others have spoken of a troubling elision occurring between, first, military and police and, second, between 'police as the intrastate building of civil order and police as international aggression'.[58] There has, therefore, been a process of blurring at work which has served to make policing and military spheres less distinguishable in various fields since the end of the Cold War, and this has been compounded by events after September 11, but what are the limits and what is the exact nature of this convergence?

A convergence of sorts

There is convergence of the police-military spheres at a meta-level. This is evident not only in the fact that police are increasingly being deployed abroad, but also through the kinds of military and police doctrines that are emerging. This may become less noticeable if police are increasingly deployed abroad in significant numbers – thereby relieving the military of tasks they are often loathe or ill-prepared to perform and freeing them to return to more traditional tasks – but at the present time there appears to be a significant convergence between the two when it comes to the overarching blurring of internal/external security spheres in world affairs. Yet there remain a number of significant divergences between the two forces.

First of all in terms of more conceptual differences, the military are very much agents of the government whilst police are primarily agents of the courts and the law. Thus although the military is an instrument for furthering the external political and strategic goals of the day, police forces are in and of themselves an actual physical and conceptual embodiment of the political and social values of each society. Hence the repeated notion that policing is political. To extend this notion, as Otwin Marenin notes:

> the police are a political institution, symbolically and in practice. In democracies they should not be partisan in their work (that is, support the interests of specific sub-national groupings, including themselves, in their society) but they cannot be a-political. Their work will always have differentiated political consequences, and will be seen to have by the state and civic society, even when they enforce law, maintain order and carry out all ancillary tasks effectively and according to rules, for social order is never neutral in its impacts on the life chances of individuals and groups. The work of the police will force them to take sides in societal disputes and will affect the distribution of resources and rewards among groups and individuals. This is true for western democracies as it was for South Africa under apartheid.[59]

Military forces are, or should be, much more isolated from the political and social spheres of life, at least in liberal democracies. This also reminds us that the police bring certain fundamental values to their posts that go beyond those of the military. The military may embody certain values (honour, bravery, service to country and so on) but in general their status as removed, extraordinary parts of society mean that these values may not necessarily be disseminated into the wider community. Police, on the other hand, are often tasked with being the bearers of law, justice, and rights. They can, in the very way that they operate within societies, shape these societies within which they function. This is a point that is returned to throughout this book too as it bears on the dissemination of certain (liberal) norms at the international level through this 'new international policing'. Indeed, although the question of which agent (i.e. UN, regional, individual states) is to give international policing authority at the global level remains open and contested in contemporary times, the following chapter discusses how the rise of international policing suggests we have more in common as an international society, and that there is a form of authority to be found in the very embodiment of liberal policing practices themselves.

Indeed, for policing to occur there is a locus of authority in control. Police are there to reinforce a legal authority that is in existence, whilst military forces operate at times when that authority is being contested.[60] Policing in the modern era relates to the maintenance of civil order, 'the civil police is a social organisation created and sustained by political processes to enforce dominant conceptions of public order'.[61] Here it is instructive to heed the words of Jacques Rancière for whom the notion 'police' means an established consensual social order.[62] Indeed, in all commentary about the role of police in contemporary international peace support operations there is much reference to the notion that 'building rule of law institutions must begin as soon as the fighting stops' – suggesting there must be some sort of agreed social order that is represented by the ability of police and policing to exist.[63] Moreover, this notion that rule of law institutions can only operate once the fighting stops because of such reasons regarding the need for political and legal authority is further buttressed by the difference in actual function between the police and military.

Military and policing ethos, ideas about force and coercion, their levels of autonomy and notions of individual responsibility, whether or not they can really operate in times of war and the very kinds of roles they perform in their service of governments or law remain distinct. Major differences between military and police functions include: different ideas about the use of deadly force; the concept of arrest and the discretion to deprive someone of their liberty; the prevention of crime and disorder; and the disparity in operating principles and command (organisational) structures.[64] John McFarlane further identifies the most important of these as those relating to the personal responsibilities of a police officer, how these are affected by notions of discretion, and how this results in the graduated use of force.[65] The policing minimum use of force rule is mirrored to some extent in the military notion of proportionality, but a strong distinction still remains, buttressed by the notion of 'the enemy' that exclusively underpins military doctrine that necessitates the use of maximum force. This helps to demarcate the example given above regarding the role of the carabiniere in Bosnia, where though similarly housed and armed, were nonetheless separated out from regular army by their culture and particularly their training in riot control methods.[66] Here, in particular, experiences in Bosnia brought home:

> the limitations of military personnel in terms of equipment, training, policing and mediation skills in transitional phases of conflict. The US conclusion was that international constabulary forces were required to take responsibility for tasks such as crowd control, election security and returnee protection.[67]

Therefore although in earlier peace operations military forces have at times had to act as '*de facto* police officers' they do not have the relevant experience in performing civilian police tasks.[68] In the words of former Supreme Allied Commander in Europe, General Wesley Clark, modern war requires policing capabilities and 'most militaries are simply not capable of performing such functions effectively'.[69] The statement that 'the aftermath of the Iraq war has shown us that good soldiers are not always good cops' might therefore seem a little facile.[70] Military personnel have tried hard to avoid such roles and as noted in the case studies where in Iraq the US Department of Defence has attempted to lead policing efforts with very mixed results and where policing in a situation where the military operation has taken precedent has proven very difficult for police efforts in Afghanistan, military personnel are not police despite finding themselves at times necessarily picking up similar-sounding tasks. Thus once again for reasons related more to function and capability, policing may be impossible in times of war. Here, for example, in a confidential conversation one senior policeman once commented that 'you don't send the mice to play with the cats' when referring to his delay in agreeing to send police to what essentially amounted to a war zone when the situation in East Timor erupted in 2006. Lastly, military forces also remain much more hierarchical in most respects, as opposed to the more horizontal layout of policing institutions and culture where levels of individual autonomy are much higher, and where debate between different ranking individuals over appropriate courses of actions is more acceptable.

In summarising how the military-police divide might give greater insight into the changing nature of contemporary international operations, the traditional difference in the level and nature of interaction between military and police forces and the community within which they are operating is key. These differences in interaction emerge from the kinds of objectives that each force is primarily directed towards achieving. These primary objectives are, in the case of military forces, either those of defence, attrition of an enemy, or the provision of 'security' in terms of the immediate quelling of violence. In policing, those primary objectives are either the achievement of law enforcement, public order, or the provision of a public regulation service that supports civic institutions.[71] Police everywhere are there to 'serve and protect'.[72] Though the military may act as a protection force, they do not necessarily have such an overarching emphasis on serving the community in the same way. Thus even when deployed abroad side by side the two forces conduct themselves in quite distinct ways, and though military personnel are useful for separating, monitoring and demilitarising two combatants they are ill-suited to most public order tasks.[73]

However, Andreas and Price are clearly onto something with their claim that 'one of the most important blurrings of traditional boundaries ... is that between an internally oriented domestic police sphere and an externally oriented military sphere', and it is a matter that is much broader than issues of just a tactical or operational nature. There is a blurring of spheres of operation currently occurring, true, and the clue lies in their mention of 'internally-oriented' and 'externally-oriented' spheres as, as shown above, such boundary-drawing exercises have increasingly been challenged in the post-Cold War era. By the start of the new millennium, then, involvement in international security affairs had potentially begun to mean involvement in others' internal affairs to a much greater extent than ever before. All manner of security agents, including police, from one jurisdiction were and are increasingly concerned with and able to act in response to events outside of their traditional bounds. If these agents are police rather than any other agents, however, then they bring particular elements to bear that impact upon the overall tenor and trajectory of the operation.

Conclusions

The rise of international policing has come about through a confluence of various events and agendas. The reconceptualisation of international security, the blurring of the military/police and internal/external divide, the rise of law in international affairs, the failed states-terrorism thesis, the state-building agenda and the peacebuilding consensus have all acted to help facilitate or in turn be facilitated by the rise of international policing.

As this chapter has discussed, externally-oriented and internally-oriented spheres are, at the meta-level, overlapping to an unprecedented degree. But this chapter has also demonstrated that military and policing roles, tasks, ethos and mandates are still distinct phenomena in terms of their overall defining characteristics. Policing, when done well, remains more of a 'fundamental' or 'positive' force than military action in that policing aims not only to enforce the law but to foster wider notions of justice and community in the name of the law. Police act in support of the very fundamental basis of the state itself, whilst military forces (unless resisting their role or constituting the government themselves) act at the behest of the political demands of the incumbent government. The term 'positive', moreover, is not intended to denigrate the role played by contemporary military forces, but rather to indicate the so-far unmatched ability of police to potentially improve state-society relations by increasing community support for domestic political and social institutions and *vice versa*. It is also not to suggest that the outcomes of policing actions will always be rosy or 'good', but rather has connotations like that associated with the term 'positive peace' in that, in this example, it suggests something more than just a lack of war. Policing can therefore be 'positive' in this way in terms of not just meaning a stemming of violence or conflict but a potentially very real source of state-society engagement and capacity-building too as 'policing goes to the very heart of state-building, since a credible national institution that helps provide security and justice for the population is central to government legitimacy'.[74]

This remains the key difference in terms of the kinds of contributions that military versus police forces can make, policing is to a certain extent risk management (particularly in law enforcement rather than community policing focused models), but this is still a different kind of risk management to that undertaken by the military. Police engage with communities daily and, in desiring public order and security, aim to achieve greater social cohesion in general. As such, the deployment of such agents fits well with the shift from management of conflict in the peacekeeping era towards the desire to go further to resolve conflict at a time where we are experiencing something of a 'peacebuilding consensus'.[75] And this remains true despite the challenges posed by the events and aftermath of September 11. In fact this will remain true as 'the aim is to enhance the capability of local institutions so that they can do the job themselves' – an aim undeniably also commensurate with the narrower goal of risk management in that any risk is transferred back to the re-vitalised indigenous police forces.[76]

The 'new international policing' therefore constitutes an under-utilised instrument that may well present states with an invaluable resource for responding to crises abroad. This new international policing may come to replace military forces in a number of areas if this resource is given greater priority. Indeed, as complementary institutional developments have indicated, there does appear to be an unprecedented interest and a greater willingness to utilise police in international affairs.

The 'new international policing' is thus a term that, at a more operational level, refers to an increased ability and willingness of states to undertake international policing efforts that may entail assertive roles in the name of humanitarian aid, risk management, or the preservation of order. Police now simply have much more of a role to play in meeting contemporary security challenges and in addressing previous 'gaps' in international security operations. This policing remains distinct from military action, but its emergence underlines the constantly changing nature of international relations – especially the shifting notion of what constitutes an international security issue and how best to respond to those security issues. Thus the new international policing also seems to signify that, in order for this operational shift to have occurred, a concomitant political shift has also occurred. There is therefore a much broader interpretation that we must consider in attempts to define the new international policing. This is the notion that the concept of 'policing' others in the world has become more acceptable. Military interventionism may seem heavy-handed but in some ways always remains one step removed from social control. This is because militaries operate in times and places where a contest for authority is ongoing, whilst policing occurs in times outside of war where there is a legal authority to uphold. This question of authority is key, and it and other key themes are now further explored in the following and final chapter.

7
The New International Policing

Although its roots can be traced back to Cyprus, Namibia, the move to reform in El Salvador and the use of executive powers in Cambodia and Haiti, the 'new international policing' truly arrived with the ambitious policing mandates undertaken in Kosovo and East Timor. It was then further consolidated by the deployments in the Pacific – particularly RAMSI – and its efficacy is currently being sorely tested in Iraq and Afghanistan. As far as operational considerations are concerned this new international policing involves the increased willingness, capability and ability of actors to police within others' jurisdictions in certain situations, both in terms of the provision of temporary policing forces and in terms of longer-term developmental programmes. This operational shift has been sketched out in part by the previous chapters but is summarised in more thematic terms in the section below on the challenges that policing brings to international relations.

In addition to these operational considerations a number of broader political ramifications are at stake. After all, the move to reforming, restructuring and rebuilding police forces means that this approach is not merely a temporary security provision but may also be a form of political and social engineering. The first major political ramification of the new international policing, then, is that the rise of international policing efforts have both contributed to and act to reinforce recent changes to sovereignty and intervention norms that have seen the non-intervention principle being placed under increasing stress, whilst at the same time seeking to restore sovereignty to a local source of authority. Furthermore, this process is not an ideologically neutral. As Andreas and Nadelmann have argued, 'states internationalize policing efforts not only to better control transnational interactions but also to promote their own ethical and social norms'.[1] At the present time the dominant norms that are being promoted are those that push a liberal, democratic and human rights agenda and the dissemination of these norms through international policing efforts – with missions effectively using international policing as a 'transmission belt' of liberal democratic values – can potentially shape and reshape the global scene in very fundamental ways. This shift is analysed below in the section on the political aspects of the new international policing.

International policing: operational considerations

In the case study chapters we saw that since the watershed deployments in Kosovo and East Timor the new international policing has arisen as states have continued to acquire:

1. An increased ability (capacity and capability) to police others' jurisdictions narrowly defined in operational terms.

This in turn has created:

2. A growing division of labour between police and military, and an increase in status and importance for policing and related institutions as international actors.

These developments show that, as police have become an increasingly important part of the international security scene, this has given rise to a range of operational challenges, and has redefined the roles of international security actors. These claims will be discussed in turn.

a) Operational challenges

In peace operations one of the most important functions of the police is to help provide populations with 'security, stability, safety, and the assurance that transparent law enforcement and judicial processes provide the same protection and penalties for all citizens'.[2] According to the UN Police Division, policing activities undertaken to help provide for this can be grouped into three main categories, categories which provide useful mechanisms for highlighting the depth and breadth of international policing in contemporary times. The first of these categories is interim law enforcement. This includes arrests, detentions, and patrolling in country, as well as confidence-building, on the job mentoring, advising, training, transition and support to the host police service. The second is operational support: public order; crowd control; anti-riot; capability-building; mentoring; training and protection of UN facilities and personnel. The last is reform, restructuring and (re)building. Here police connect with other rule of law agencies in helping to provide legislation, systems, procedures, codes, values, organisation, management, vetting, training, basic material, logistics and communications.[3] Although such activities are the bread and butter of police at home, what is significant is that these activities are occurring at an 'internationalised' level in certain situations – whether those situations are UN mandated peace support operations, regional missions or unilaterally driven operations and so on as shown in the case study chapters here.

The first operational issue that arises from such forms of international policing is that of police gaining increased status as international actors. Much emphasis has tended to rest with planning the military part of peace missions, with not enough thought given to what will happen after the immediate security pause. This was shown most recently in the Iraq case, and the aftermath of such operations has led commentators to argue that strategic planners must 'give as much attention to planning post-conflict policing as to planning combat operations'.[4] The neglect of police as vital international actors is due to the relatively limited use of police in international situations until recent times, and the significance of police is only just now being recognised due to states developing an increased willingness and capacity to utilise their police force abroad.

International policing therefore provides an alternative agent for international action. This has two possible effects, either it will allow for militaries to redefine their core roles, and provide for a renewed division of labour, or it may result in the creation of a single force with specialised arms; military, FPU and individual community policing. As noted in the previous chapter, in 1960 Morris Janowitz claimed that 'the military establishment becomes a constabulary force when it is continuously prepared to act, committed to the minimum use of force, and seeks viable international relations rather than victory because it has incorporated a protective military posture'.[5] Yet there will be no need for transformation of the military if police continue along their current trajectory as they are set to be an increasingly important part of international affairs as long as there remains a commitment to increasing standing police capacities and attendant logistical capacities.

Police, unlike military forces, are not usually waiting to deploy for missions abroad. In the late 1990s Michael Berkow identified two major issues facing proponents of international policing – personnel and logistics. With regards to personnel issues, if police are always actively engaged in their primary domestic mission, this makes it very difficult to find enough trained personnel to deploy, whilst civilian police also lack the logistical support required to operate in remote and often hostile locations around the world.[6] The notion of a standing police capacity has therefore recently started to be taken on board by some states (as noted in Chapter 2), and is demonstrated most strongly in the Pacific where the Australian Federal Police have used their International Deployment Group (IDG). However even in this case it can be difficult to justify to publics and those who hold the purse strings as to why police are an increasingly important part of international as well as domestic security. Increasing public awareness as to the value of international policing in the domestic arena will therefore be a key component in resolving these ongoing personnel issues.

The logistical issue at hand here is that police do not have an expeditionary capability. This combines with the heightened security demands of the early phases of post-conflict peace missions to create a reliance on military capabilities. This was clearly demonstrated in RAMSI and in Afghanistan where military forces both protect and assist policing missions. The issues that arise from these factors – lack of standing capacity with no expeditionary capability etc. – are often talked about in terms of the 'gaps' they engender.

First of all the notion of a 'deployment gap' refers to the fact noted above that given the lack of standing capacity it may take a very long time to deploy policing forces. This means that it can be difficult to take advantage of the 'golden hour' in complex post-conflict situations. Here there is often difficulty in achieving a timely police response to situations as there will often be a temporal delay between the deployment of military forces and the delivery of police forces. The functional differences between these two disciplined forces can also lead to an 'enforcement gap' in that there is often a need for military to provide muscle to provide a secure environment for the policing part of the mission to unfold. The increased use of FPU's, which are very cohesive, mobile and have specialised training, has gone some way to bridging this gap. However, as Annika Hansen and Alice Hill both argue, the problems that have arisen from the use of such forces – specifically the potential militarisation of the police and the impact of this on public trust and faith in the police – have tended to diminish the promise of such specialised units.[7] The situations in Iraq and Afghanistan where military and policing roles have been blurred serve as cases in point here. Thus in areas where there is a lack of trust in the police or where the point is to demilitarise and civilianise police forces, the use of FPU's can potentially be counter-productive. There remains a dilemma here as there may be an operational need for FPU abilities but as the Iraq case shows, in situations where police are overwhelmed in capability and numbers, this can all too easily result in the creation of units that are over-militarised and over-reactive.

The ability to deploy enough numbers of police is important. In considering nine case studies of attempts to rebuild security after conflict, a major RAND report judged Kosovo and East Timor most successful in terms of limiting violence due in part to the fact that these cases had the highest levels of international police forces.[8] This underscores the fact that numbers matter, and the recent input into standing police capacities is necessary to generate these numbers. This issue of quantity is further complicated by the issue of the dispersal of those police (particularly in terms of the rural-urban divide), as well as by temporal issues – the overall length of the mission and the length of rotation of personnel.[9]

In addition to such quantitative issues, there are also concerns relating to the quality of police personnel that are available to deploy. Given the domestic politicking required to release police into overseas posts, those posts may not always be filled by the best and brightest. In reviewing past operations, Chuck Call and Michael Barnett noted that certain core police qualifications were often missing: such as those relating to language or to driving ability (in Mozambique over half of the 1,000 CIVPOL could not drive), and indeed they noted how such police can often create problems themselves (some Bulgarian police in UNTAC had a penchant for frequenting brothels and attempting to smuggle exotic snakes).[10] And as seen in the case studies, a number of the problems faced in Kosovo, Iraq and Afghanistan have stemmed from such issues of the varying quality of personnel deployed. Indeed the issue of the quality both of international police on deployment abroad and those being recruited into fledgling police services in the host country emerged time and time again.

A further issue also raised in Chapter 3 relates to the problem of ensuring that the skill sets of personnel are appropriate to the tasks mandated. The comment during UNTAET that the UN was trying to undertake peacebuilding with a peacekeeping mindset underscores the fact that police in peace missions could well be mandated to undertake a variety of tasks. This not only means that police may find themselves undertaking executive policing roles in another country that has a different language or culture and so on, but also that there may well be a need for such police personnel to be able to help rebuild policing institutions from the bottom up, a task that requires specific skill sets.

The key issue of quality control also arises when we consider the role of private police. Although DynCorp recruits police officers for and on behalf of the US State Department, unsuitable candidates still get through the screening process yet little has been done to improve national standards.[11] What is more, other companies have even fewer external quality controls and accountability mechanisms. The accountability problems with Dyncorp and other private security companies have been amply demonstrated in the case studies here, but the issue of private policing is a major topic in its own right.[12] For present purposes it is simply important to note that the rise of private police serves to counterpoint the fact that peace support operations involve a number of different security actors.

b) Redefining roles

As we have seen, a new division of labour has arisen within international affairs when it comes to the roles of different private, national, regional and international security actors. This has occurred in all cases in terms of a division of labour regarding police and military forces, in Afghanistan in the lead country concept and in Kosovo in the roles taken up by the UN, the EU, the European Commission Humanitarian Office the OSCE and NATO. With regards to policing and judicial reform capabilities here James Dobbin has suggested that NATO will begin to look to the EU for help in peace operations in future and not the other way round given the EU's greater strength in the rule of law sphere.[13] Different actors may be more useful or seen to be more legitimate in certain areas than others: thus the European Commission was able to continue on with policing reform efforts in Georgia at a point when the European Council was seen as too intrusive, whilst the Pacific Islands Forum ensured a regional flavour to an Australian-led mission in Solomon Islands. The most important issue here will be the maintenance of good communication and a solid working relationship between whichever actors are involved in such operations. The mix of actors involved in international policing efforts should therefore be tailored to suit the local context.

This need to contextualise missions is a vital one. When it comes to undertaking international policing missions, there are different models of policing, different understandings of how to make an arrest, of how to respond to the command 'clear the area' or to 'subdue' someone resisting arrest and so on that can be put into practice. There is ongoing debate over the nature of police – should they be seen as simply enforcers of the law, as agents of development, or as community problem-solvers – and any combination of such models may prevail in different situations. In some cases, such as in Kosovo and East Timor it was 'considered inevitable that the civilian police carry arms'.[14] However, it was considered vital that arms not be carried by both military and police in Bougainville. Moreover, the organisational structure and so on must suit the context and be sustainable. Here Kaplan has expressed some concern about the over-reliance of western systems on material aspects of police work and the sheer complexity and size of supporting agencies (courts and prison systems) will mean too much focus on the material aspects of policing versus the all-important practise of policing.[15]

Policing is part of a wider approach that encompasses other parts of the law and justice sector and broader political and developmental goals. Any police reform is therefore also necessarily bound up with broader legal reform where justice and penal reform are part and parcel of any approach taken.[16] One clear historical example as noted in Chapter 2 as to why this is so vital is highlighted in the case of Haiti as where penal and judicial reform did not take place, contributing to problems with the Haitian police force.[17] Indeed RAMSI's success to date arguably owes much to the effort that was put into planning just what to do with those arrested in this 'strengthened assistance' operation.

More broadly, a preoccupation with policing when only narrowly defined as the immediate provision of law and order, can have a detrimental effect on more macro-level developmental goals. This was a critique of the earlier years in East Timor and continues to be an ongoing issue with the appointment of Judges and Prosecutors in Iraq. An emphasis on the provision of public order over the need to consider why people are rioting may lead to too narrow a focus on what policing is. An emphasis only on law enforcement may paint civil society as dangerous as much of the discourse on 'public security' suggests that civil society can be viewed as potentially hostile or, in the least, 'far from a partner'.[18] Similarly the way in which a mission is associated with different partners may also have an impact on overall effectiveness as highlighted by the identification of UNMIK's involvement as having a 'police' identity as a mission that made it difficult to incorporate non-police experts into the process.[19]

In addition to an understanding of just what types of 'policing' are being undertaken in different contexts, a clear understanding of the mandate is also vital as the type of policing used will be shaped by just what the focus of the mission is. At times police personnel have undertaken activities outside their remit. Annika Hansen gives the example of the IPTF in Bosnia where they began investigating human rights abuses by the Bosnian police and aiding local authorities in their investigations despite no clear executive policing mandate.[20] Indeed a major critique of peacekeeping and other missions in general is that mandates may often be extended or enlarged without much in the way of input from key host country stakeholders during this process. This brings us to the final point, that is, the limitations of policing.

As policing is not made in a vacuum at a domestic level – constrained as it is with regards to the quality and quantity of recruits, the relationship with justice and penal institutions, the social, economic and political context – it should be of no surprise that there are a number of limitations for policing at the international level. Here there is a key issue at stake, which relates to what are those core values being espoused through instances of international policing that cannot be done away with. For example, if there is a clash between democratic or human rights values and local values, which is to win out? This is particularly pressing in an executive mission. Here as Mobekk points out, police may risk offending the population by intervening in traditional practices, yet if they do not do so, they might tacitly be supporting a system of justice that may contravene international human rights standards.[21] There is also a seductive tendency for strong Western states to want to build others' institutions in their own image, or there is a tendency in nation-building to return to institutions that might actually be the problem not the solution.[22] And there is often 'an apparent clash between the pursuit of *security* versus *democratic* and *human rights* agendas'.[23] International policing therefore takes part in an international order that places a number of demands upon it beyond the technical and into the political and normative realm.

International policing: political considerations

In the introductory chapter it was suggested that at a higher political level the new international policing phenomenon presents:

3. The potential for states to police world order more broadly defined.
4. A challenge to, and at the same time a reinforcing of, the concept of statehood – a challenge because a state may be required to relinquish aspects of sovereignty to allow others to police it, yet

at the same time a reinforcement as it can lead to improving security of that state by contributing to the strength of the state (plus contributors increase the external security of their own state by improving the internal security of others).

5. The opportunity to make use of the police/society interface in others' countries to both disseminate one's state's own norms and to take a better understanding of the policed state's norms back to one's own. Thus this contributes to a broader agenda of standardisation, the pursuit of common policing principles and norms at a global level. This also thereby feeds into a transmission belt for liberal agendas at a fundamental level. In liberal societies it is the police who uphold the rule of law and protect democratic values such as individual human rights. Though police are only part of the puzzle they are nonetheless a very important one, representing as they do the guardians of public welfare and acting as the public face of authority. The new international policing is not, therefore, a neutral phenomenon but rather part of a larger normative project that seeks to spread liberal values across the globe.

The rest of this chapter will explain and defend these claims in greater detail, beginning with the final point that the new international policing is a transmission belt for liberal agendas.

a) Dissemination of liberal values

An interesting feature of the move towards policing or police-led missions, is that it assumes that the question of right authority has been settled in advance – that there is a significant level of agreement as to who has the authority to police society. Thus far, however, agential authority has been negotiated on a case by case basis or, as shown in Kosovo and East Timor, may potentially default to bodies such as the UN in cases where there is a lack of local source of governance and where consent has been achieved. Further, the example of East Timor, where Australian and New Zealand diplomats worked hard to ensure that the authority and legitimacy of any return to East Timor would not be questioned by other sources of authority (President, Speaker of the House etc) shows how potential contests over that question of authority can be pre-empted. However where that agential source of authority is highly contested policing is nigh impossible. Thus Mathieu Deflem and Suzanne Sutphin claim 'a society that has not attained a degree of pacification cannot afford a civilian police' – a claim which appears borne out by the fact that civilian police in Iraq and Afghanistan are hard pressed to undertake 'policing' at all.[24] Moreover the current difficulties in Iraq and Afghanistan are in large part due to the fact that not only is the authority of the agents attempting to undertake policing in these situations contested, but that the kinds of values that are being espoused though these efforts are contested too.

Hence the claim that 'no global sovereign claims universal policing authority' is true in one sense of the term.[25] There is no one universally accepted agential source of policing authority, no supreme sovereign global authority in a corporeal sense. Yet in a broader usage of the term this claim is false. Police are agents of the court and of law. And with all international policing deployments thus far, there has been a remarkable level of agreement as to the locus of universal policing authority when understood in a normative sense.

To see this, note that one of the most important developments in international relations in recent times has been the rise of legalism. International law has become much less *ad hoc* with a number of institutional and normative developments ongoing. Thus far the rise of legalism has not been matched by the consolidation of a matching permanent international policing capacity.[26] Yet this is changing. We are clearly moving towards more systematic forms of international policing and this suggests that firstly, there is an absence of competing claims to authority of a sort and secondly, that we may be moving towards agreement as to where the locus of international policing authority exists. As noted, however, the relevant international authority is not as of yet found in the corpus of any particular agent, but rather is a more fluid kind of authority that currently stems from the types of principles being espoused; the rule of law which upholds, protects and promotes liberal values. This is the normative authority at play here.

> Democratization, human rights observances, development, and free market economic reform have been adopted as the pillars of new settlements by the leading states and organizations which constitute the liberal, cosmopolitan international community. ... The sustainable resolution of conflict therefore implies deep and multi-dimensional forms of intervention, and a liberal and cosmopolitan faith on the part of the interveners in the infallibility of their approach...[and] the installation of a liberal democracy resting on human rights, humanitarianism, an agreement on what constitutes development, and a globally integrated economy is

> the only governance formula the international community will invest in.[27]

The kind of centralised policing authority that we currently have, then, rests for now in that police are deployed to further the liberalisation agenda. Policing at a global level is set to become more uniform along democratic, human rights and liberal models, albeit with some adjustment to suit local contexts as noted above. As of yet this theme of international policing as being a liberal international policing agenda remains dominant and does not face significant challenge in the form of a similarly strong alternative political agenda. Indeed, even more recent police reform efforts like the recently proposed trilateral effort in Tonga, a monarchical society, which see Australia and New Zealand looking to provide support for a democratic policing reform programme for the Tongan police service, or that of continuing bilateral attempts by Australia to encourage a de-politicised transparent police service in Papua New Guinea, demonstrate how central this liberalisation agenda is.[28]

Policing is intricately bound up with the development of societies and *vice versa*. The consistent pursuit in all cases to achieve liberal democratic models of authority as the end result of these policing efforts indicates there is a normative authority at play here and this has major ramifications for norm dissemination. This leads us down the route of the promotion of international policing norms not only in terms of the dissemination of these kinds of political and social values within the societies that are being policed in post-conflict and other operations, but this may also be a two-way street in terms of the experiences of those undertaking the policing.

In particular, the new international policing offers a means by which key liberal values can be disseminated both to those doing the policing and to those being policed; to encourage these values amongst those that contribute police to such missions as well as within those countries that are the recipients of international policing efforts. As to the first of these points, consider the UNPOL figures presented in Chapter 2, which demonstrate that the major providers of police personnel come from countries not necessarily associated with democratic policing or with strong human rights records. Yet the missions undertaken thus far with the help of such police forces – including all of the case studies covered here – have been done with the aim of creating liberal democratic states with institutions conducive to the protection and promotion of human rights.

Moreover the UN Police Division is currently seeking to develop doctrines and pre-deployment training curricula for all UNPOL personnel that will see such values being promoted as key guiding principles for action.[29] Only 65 per cent of UNPOL officers generally receive any form of pre-deployment training to prepare them for international deployments and only 35 per cent receive training and information on matters relevant to their duties in the international context.[30] It is hoped that pre-deployment training for all UNPOL will be standardised along liberal democratic lines with additional modules being created on a case by case basis as tailored for imparting knowledge about particular missions. The training and inculcation of such police forces with these kinds of values for missions abroad could potentially see these police forces return to their own countries with different expectations and understandings of their role as police.

Thus although the 1979 UN Code of Conduct for Enforcement Personnel, which encapsulates many of these key liberal values, has not as of yet achieved the acceptance that was sought for it amongst UN member states, this renewed focus on creating more comprehensive doctrine and curricula provides UNPOL with much more concrete guidelines for action.[31] The aim is to ensure that those undertaking policing roles in peace operations, under UN auspices at least, have had some common training in issues such as human rights, due legal processes, ideal relationships between police, society and government in democratic societies and so on. UNPOL will therefore have to become familiar with and act in accordance with these values. Thus 'policing' may follow what has happened more narrowly in criminal justice where 'the rising tide of international collaboration on crime control has involved both the homogenization of criminal justice systems (and particularly criminal laws) towards a common norm and the regularization of criminal justice relationships across borders'.[32] This is already underway in one sense as the UN is beginning to accreditate national training centres and pre-deployment training packages.

As far as those who are being policed are concerned, police efforts are part of a much broader agenda that has both security and development-focused aspects, which both seek to foster liberal values. International policing at the present time is closely associated with democratic policing, with the spread of liberal democratic values. Police can support democratic development but they are only a means to that end if they: give top priority to individual citizens and private groups; are accountable to the law rather than the government; protect human rights; and are transparent in their activities.[33] Democratic policing is characterised by:

> an orientation to service for civic society, rather than the state; transparency and accountability; the representativeness of personnel as measured by the distribution of salient identities in society;

> integrity management as a central function of police administration; a semi-autonomous status of the police organization and system; the treatment of police as citizens; and the possession of skills needed to perform their tasks efficiently and effectively, as indicated by the degree of professionalism at all ranks of the organization and across specific functional tasks (e.g., managerial skills at the higher ranks, technical skills in investigations, or people skills by street level police in encounters with citizens).... One important aspect of democratic police organizations is that they are capable of frequent, critical and informed self-reflection, the analysis and evaluation of adopted practices, and the capacity to adapt to changing circumstances. There has to be an institutional capacity for self-examination and organizational change – and not by necessity, for self-protection when events go wrong or when forced to – but as part of the normal operating philosophy and organizational culture of the police.[34]

In terms of the effects upon those being policed, then, Roland Paris has succinctly summarised the liberal objectives of the overarching modern peacebuilding agenda as incorporating four key mechanisms: the insertion of political and economic liberalism into peace settlements; providing expert advice during implementation; conditionality attached to economic assistance; and proxy governance.[35] Policing is a key state function that is directly targeted in these liberalisation projects. Policing roles focus most directly on specific liberal values such as the promotion of civilian democratic oversight of the agency that enforces law and order, the promotion of the rule of law and human rights, the emphasis on the criminal responsibility of individuals, and also with regards to the representative nature of those police forces being reformed – particularly with regards to gender, ethnic or religious composition.

The case studies analysed here do, admittedly, demonstrate that these ideals of democratic policing may be difficult to realise in practice. Kosovo shows the limits of this agenda in that, although it may help temper the political and social environment, it is still subject to those broader currents too. East Timor shows how even a newly created police service can become politicised. Indeed, 'any effort to create a more apolitical and human police force will depend on whether other features of society – including political parties, elections, the judiciary and the like – are subjected to similar changes. This is a tall order'.[36] There are also numerous instances of police behaving badly in international mission, thereby serving to undermine these key values through contradictory actions, corrupt practices, human rights violations and the like. But despite the behaviour of individuals, the point remains that the new international policing embodies an institutional commitment to the promotion of liberal norms. This opens up the possibility of policing world order in a responsible and responsive manner that could potentially be to the benefit of all parties.

b) States, statehood and policing the world order

Nevertheless the new international policing phenomenon might be seen to lend itself to a far more disquieting way of policing world order. Changing conceptions of international security – of what constitutes a matter for international security and ideas as to what response to take with which kind of actor – have quietly contributed to major shifts at the meta-level of global politics. In particular the inside-outside divide that constituted the international system as we know it is increasingly challenged by the blurring of internal and external security spheres which opens up the possibility of policing the world order in a way that does not look to be consistent with the kinds of liberal principles being espoused.

The rise of the modern state and the modern state system was intricately bound up with the initial pacification of subjects to establish internal forms of state sovereignty and the turning outward of the use of force to allow for the maintenance of external forms of state sovereignty. However norms regarding sovereignty and intervention have changed dramatically in recent years, from the controversy surrounding the rise of 'humanitarian interventions' in the 1990s, through the political fallout from 'preventive regime changes' in the first few years of the twenty-first century, to the UN World Leaders' Summit of 2005 witnessing representatives of states accepting, in theory at least, that sovereignty is a responsibility as well as a right.[37] These changing ideas as to what kind of world we live in and what constitutes matter for international interest and action, has impacted upon conceptualisations of security.

Deploying domestic agents abroad suggests both instances of extraterritoriality in some cases and the lending or sharing of sovereign power in others. This situation is thus one of fluidity in the interpretation of sovereignty and intervention in contemporary times. Immunities and executive powers in particular highlight how the rules of sovereignty have altered.[38] Though, as Stephen Krasner and others note, sovereignty has always been conditional, the rise of international policing and the development of these kinds of accompanying characteristics has created precedent for more systematic and regular breaches or alterations to concepts of sovereignty and intervention.[39]

The use of police in international operations is a strategy aimed at reconstructing one of the very core parts of statehood in order to rebuild functioning states, albeit in very different forms from those that were in place prior to these efforts. International policing is, therefore, for the moment an activity that impinges on state sovereignty in order to later resurrect that sovereignty in the liberal democratic model. However, whilst the new international policing undoubtedly has this potential, there is a concern that this agenda also has the potential to lead to a new division of the policed versus those who police.

The end of the Cold War was said to herald in a new world order. This notion was soon replaced with commentary that this era, one reeling from events in places such as the former Yugoslavia, Somalia, and Rwanda, was now an era of world disorder. In response to this the post-Cold War years witnessed the emergence of a discourse about 'risk' – both in terms of the notion of global risks, and in terms of the formulation of risk management strategies at global, local and personal levels. At a domestic level, then, it is claimed that we are seeing a 'reconceptualisation of criminals: no longer are they either "individuals inherently at risk" or "in need of rehabilitation", they have become "risk creating agents"'.[40] And as security has become a much more global concept – in that peace and security require global responses – these new security emphases have further lent themselves to the globalisation of risk.[41] This has led commentators such as Christopher Coker to argue that:

> the only option to governments is to police the world. And in a globalised age we see the emergence of a new concept of policing, which takes its cue from the domestic model, where people have moved away from 'community policing' to 'policing communities of risk'.[42]

Given concerns about the security effects of failed states, the domestic notion of 'policing communities of risk' could potentially see an ongoing, unceasing and much more active 'policing' of states and or territory deemed to be sources of risk. This in a way is reminiscent of Robert Kaplan's mid-1990s thesis on the 'Coming Anarchy' where he presented the world of the future as divided into failing, poverty-stricken anarchical areas versus those states that were 'well fed and pampered', or Robert Cooper's notion of modern versus post-modern states.[43] Wealthier states may begin to pay contractors or poorer states to police these areas of risk, reinforcing that division and leading to garrison states on the one hand and territory characterised by a lack of law and order on the other.

To date policing missions have all had the central goal of policing oneself out of a job, though this could be replaced by a continuous rolling deployment of police to maintain international order that is less obvious than military action but in fact much more intrusive. Although the prohibitive cost of such missions and the continuing theme of the importance of development and self-governance count against this, there is some food for thought to be found in the comments of those critical of the concept of UN peacekeeping, particularly in discussing the issue of consent. Here, for example:

> In several cases, as in Central America and Mozambique, comprehensive peace plans and agreements ... extracted parties' consent not only for the initial UN deployment, but also for subsequent UN activities in the field. By carefully placing the peacekeeping mandate on peace accords, international actors increasingly downplayed the requirement of seeking consent at every stage of the operation.[44]

Indeed, as noted in Chapter 2, the US did not have an explicit mandate for policing in Somalia but undertook such tasks anyway because of the demands on the ground, and a similar situation unfolded in Cambodia.[45] The case studies covered more comprehensively here, moreover, cover a wide range of mandates that were either negotiated to some extent in the UN, through regional arrangements, or unilaterally decided in the wake of more aggressive interventions such as those in Afghanistan and Iraq.

Furthermore, in all of these situations there arguably remains a lack of accountability, albeit on a sliding scale with Iraq at one end of the spectrum and RAMSI at another. This is because in such situations accountability is a very difficult objective to achieve. If consent and political responsiveness are not consistently revisited and re-earned then accountability during the mission is much more tenuous. Onc interesting development in the RAMSI case, then, was the ongoing use of an annual People's Survey to assess levels of satisfaction with RAMSI's performance. Though this does not in and of itself constitute accountability *per se*, it does provide some public measure for expressing dissatisfaction and thereby provides a prompt for appropriate responses.

These two key notions of consent and accountability then bring us back full circle to the notion of local ownership. Given that, as mentioned above, the current aim is for international police to police themselves out of a job by rebuilding local capacity so that it is self-sustaining, this issue of ownership is key and must remain so to avoid slipping into neo-colonial forms of global policing. Sovereignty after all relates to the notion of control and an ability to act in an autonomous fashion (with a number of limits naturally). Three possibilities for effecting local ownership have been identified: consultations; shared authority (interim governments; shared control and command systems; hybrid courts); and the use of local personnel in key positions of authority.[46]

The case studies assessed here show some of these various strategies in action. The initial UNMISET deployment to East Timor and the return in 2006 under the UNMIT mandate demonstrate the importance of consultation in smoothing the way for successful operations, just as the lack of consultation formed a key weakness in the UNTAET part of the UN's involvement. Interim governments have been a popular choice in recent years, whilst the possible adoption of a hybrid model which sees the transference of core democratic policing values, with these being tempered by local context has been mooted in Afghanistan at the beginning of 2008 where new hybrid justice systems may be piloted. Lastly, the more recent placement of Solomon Islanders to key positions within different parts of RAMSI has helped to ease relations.

This question of ownership can be a difficult one, however, as good intentions which recognise the importance of participation of the local population do not necessarily translate into an understanding as to how that participation might be best facilitated. This has been seen in East Timor with the creation of the CEPs by outside donors not really fitting in with local notions of legitimate political leadership. Indeed a number of critics such as Jarat Chopra and Tanja Hohe suggest most recent UN peacebuilding missions from Afghanistan to East Timor have often excluded local input.[47] It can also be difficult to ensure that the ownership promoted is the 'right ownership', not empowering those that caused much of the trouble in the first place – and this is one concern that remains an issue in Kosovo as elsewhere.[48] In Kosovo macro-level issues dominate, there is overdependence upon external governance and local consensus is very weak.[49] Further as shown in the RAMSI case there can be difficulty in encouraging and supporting responsible local leaders to actually take on that ownership role. Handing over ownership is always desirable but not always possible. Similarly the case of Iraq shows how the local police service simply disintegrated after the invasion and how post-2003 recruitment and retention has been very difficult as Iraqi police have, amongst other things, become too closely associated with the foreign intervention thereby making police a popular target for insurgents. And though there may be a desire to build on local models and to take local ownership seriously, any situation where police reform is on the agenda is one where there is immediately a presumption that what exists is inadequate and therefore in need of change.[50] Yet ongoing attempts at local ownership are still necessary as peace cannot 'be imposed from the outside but needs to be nurtured internally through patient, flexible, responsive strategies that are in tune with domestic political realities', and such strategies require that local ownership be enabled not stymied by external policing efforts.[51]

Conclusion

If we are to truly 'police' world order in the spirit of liberal democratic community policing models rather than simply managing communities in a more risk-management, law enforcement style, then, the whole point is that such policing efforts must act to serve the society within which they are operating. Yet, as Richmond points out, a number of studies appear to indicate that, 'peacebuilding, despite being couched in the language of a liberal peace, has overlooked the social and human consequences of the process of constructing that peace'.[52] And indeed, it could easily seem that the new international policing is just a new form of liberal imperialism: as Zolo wonders, could any such cosmopolitan project 'ever be anything other than an inherently hegemonic and violent undertaking?'.[53] This raises the question of whether the rise of international policing is a desirable phenomenon. This question undoubtedly requires deeper exploration, but, as a starting point, I end this book by suggesting that there is promise in the more 'positive' possibilities of international policing efforts proceeding along liberal democratic lines.

The new international policing presents a new opportunity for a more 'softly, softly' and longer-term commitment to resolving security woes. Military operations generally begin with an exit strategy in mind, whereas police deployments are, from the very beginning, an admission of a need for long-term involvement. As military and policing missions are qualitatively different, those 'policing' missions which are subsumed within an overbearing military context such as those ongoing in Iraq and Afghanistan struggle to even be policing missions. Although there may be some operational need to utilise a more law enforcement approach in post-conflict societies until 'mature democratic political governance, a legitimate, stable and effective police organisation, and a high level of community stability and consensus' are in place such that community policing models can be pursued, such professional policing still creates a very different operation and begets different responses from military-led deployments.[54]

Deploying a police-led mission like that in RAMSI instead signals very clearly that the nature of the deployment is law-enforcement focused, and removes the possibility of that deployment being interpreted as potentially signalling a state of hostility. The deployment of civilian police in leading international operations assumes questions of legitimate authority have been settled in advance, and immediately indicates that the mission will have different objectives and will rely on different methods to achieve those objectives. Creating peace operations that not only involve police but that give them priority within the mission alters the overall trajectory of that deployment from the very beginning. But questions as to whom is doing the policing, who is being policed and why must be assessed on a case by case basis to ensure that international policing efforts are serving and protecting 'the people', just as domestic policing efforts are intended to do. And although this particular agenda is being pursued as a quiet revolution to consolidate liberal democratic norms at an international level, there is also a need to tailor such general themes to the local context. Democratic reform should focus on elements critical to democratic policing (not replicate whole or part of existing systems and procedures simply because they come from police forces in democratic countries) and it should be sensitive to local policing traditions and cultural values in order to truly 'protect and serve'.[55] If this is achieved then the notion of international policing writ large will also have been achieved in form, function and spirit of that term.

Notes

Chapter 1 Introduction

1 UN Secretary General U Thant as cited in Gavin Brown, Barry Barker and Terry Burke, *Police as Peacekeepers: The History of the Australian and New Zealand Police serving with the United Nations Force in Cyprus 1964–1984* (Victoria Australia: UNCIVPOL, 1984), p6.
2 The use of the term 'police' will be used to refer to civilian police not military police unless noted in the text.
3 Chuck Call and Michael Barnett, 'Looking for a Few Good Cops: Peacekeeping, Peacebuilding and CIVPOL', *Peacebuilding and Police Reform*, eds. Tor Tanke Holm and Espen Barth Eide (London and Portland OR: Frank Cass, 2000), p64.
4 See: J.W.E. Sheptycki, 'Transnational policing and the makings of the postmodern state', *British Journal of Criminology*, 35 (4), Autumn 1995, pp613–35 for a good analysis of some of these developments in Europe – he particularly points to the growth of intelligence sharing and improved cooperation overall in the region.
5 Graham Day and Christopher Freeman, 'Policekeeping is the Key: Rebuilding the Internal Security Architecture of Postwar Iraq', *International Affairs* 2 (79), March 2003, pp299–313.
6 Annika S. Hansen, *From Congo to Kosovo: Civilian Police in Peace Operations*, Adelphi Paper 343 (Oxford: IISS, 2002), p33.
7 David H. Bayley, 'Policing: The World Stage', *Policing Across the World: Issues for the Twenty-First Century*, ed. R.I. Mawby (London: University College London Press, 1999), p4. Bayley went on to use the term 'international' to refer to research that was cross-national in approach (comparing police institutions in different states), whilst 'transnational' research was used to refer to studies such as analyses of police cooperation across borders.
8 Erwin A. Schmidl, 'Police Functions in Peace Operations: An Historical Overview', *Policing the New World Disorder: Peace Operations and Public Security*, eds. Robert Oakley et al. (Washington DC: National Defense University Press, 1998), p26.
9 J. Benyon, 'Policing the European Union: the changing basis of cooperation on law enforcement', *International Affairs*, 70 (3), 1994, p504.
10 Otwin Marenin, *Restoring Policing Systems in Conflict Torn Nations: Process, Problems, Prospects* (Geneva: Geneva Centre for the Democratic Control of Armed Forces, 2005), p6.
11 Andrew Goldsmith, 'Police Accountability Reform in Colombia: The Civilian Oversight Experiment', *Civilian Oversight of Policing: Governance, Democracy and Human Rights*, eds. Andrew J. Goldsmith and Colleen Lewis (Oxford and Portland OR: Hart Publishing, 2000), p169.
12 Note here, however, that the term 'police' may be a rather slippery concept as in its strictest definition it denotes uniformed sworn police officers, how-

ever non-sworn civilian personnel may also be closely involved in policing efforts – trainers advising on human rights standards, medical specialists providing psychological training in dealing with post-traumatic stress disorder, management, human resources and employment law experts and so on – and I therefore refer to 'police professionals' in the text when more than uniformed sworn officers may be involved.

13 Annika S. Hansen, *From Congo to Kosovo: Civilian Police in Peace Operations*, Adelphi Paper 343 (Oxford: IISS, 2002), p25.

14 Michael J. Dziedzic, 'Introduction', *Policing the New World Disorder: Peace Operations and Public Security* eds. Robert Oakley et al. (Washington DC: National Defense University Press, 1998), p12. David H. Bayley, 'The Contemporary Practices of Policing: A Comparative View', *Civilian Police and Multinational Peacekeeping – A Workshop Series: A Role for Democratic Policing*, National Institute of Justice (Washington DC: US Department of Justice, 1999), p6, also argues that 'policing cannot be separated from politics'.

15 Sandra Whitworth, 'Where is the politics in peacekeeping?', *International Journal*, 50 (Spring 1995), p435.

16 Robert Perito, *Where is the Lone Ranger When We Need Him? America's Search for a Post-Conflict Stability Force* (Washington DC: USIP, 2004), p5. The case study of Solomon Islands highlights how military personnel were at times seen as being less threatening and more trustworthy to the population as the RSIP had been implicated in of much of the difficulties being faced at that time.

Chapter 2 A Brief History of International Policing

1 Police programmes in Latin America have predominantly been US bilateral efforts that focus on technical or technological matters but some have included demilitarisation and human rights training efforts too. For more information on this see: Ethan Nadelmann, *Cops Across Borders: Transnational Crime and International Law Enforcement* (University Park: Pennsylvania State University Press, 1993); Washington Office on Latin America (WOLA), *Demilitarising Public Order: The International Community, Police Reform and Human Rights in Central America and Haiti* (Washington DC: WOLA, 1995).

2 Erwin A. Schmidl, 'Police Functions in Peace Operations: An Historical Overview', *Policing the New World Disorder: Peace Operations and Public Security* (Washington DC: National Defense University Press, 1998), p27.

3 Espen Barth Eide and Tor Tanke Holm, 'Postscript: Towards Executive Authority Policing? The Lessons of Kosovo', *Peacebuilding and Police Reform*, eds. Tor Tanke Holm and Espen Barth Eide (London and Portland OR: Frank Cass, 2000), p214.

4 Robert Perito, *Where is the Lone Ranger When We Need Him? America's Search for a Post-Conflict Stability Force* (Washington DC: USIP, 2004), p69.

5 David H. Bayley, 'The Contemporary Practices of Policing: A Comparative View', *Civilian Police and Multinational Peacekeeping – A Workshop Series: A Role for Democratic Policing*, National Institute of Justice (Washington DC: US Department of Justice, 1999), p5. See also: David H. Bayley, 'A Foreign Policy for Democratic Policing', *Policing and Society*, 5 (2), 1995, pp79–94.

6 Erwin A. Schmidl, 'Police Functions in Peace Operations: An Historical Overview', *Policing the New World Disorder: Peace Operations and Public*

Security, eds. Robert Oakley et al. (Washington DC: National Defense University Press, 1998), pp30–1.

7 Alex Morrison, 'Methodology, Contents and Structure of UN Civilian Police Training Programmes', *The Role and Functions of Civilian Police in United Nations Peace-keeping Operations: Debriefing and Lessons*, ed. Nassrine Azimi, Report and Recommendations of the International Conference Singapore December 1995 (London: Kluwer Law International, 1996), p143.

8 Annika S. Hansen, *From Congo to Kosovo: Civilian Police in Peace Operations*, Adelphi Paper 343 (Oxford: IISS, 2002), p26.

9 Erwin A. Schmidl, 'Police Functions in Peace Operations: An Historical Overview', *Policing the New World Disorder: Peace Operations and Public Security*, eds. Robert Oakley et al. (Washington DC: National Defense University Press, 1998), p21. For both of these deployments to the Middle East these 'policing' labels often caused concern as 'police' in the Middle East often had negative connotations.

10 Gavin Brown, Barry Barker and Terry Burke, *Police as Peace-keepers: The History of the Australian and New Zealand Police Serving with the United Nations Force in Cyprus 1964–1984* (Victoria, Australia: UNCIVPOL, 1984).

11 Robert Perito, *Where is the Lone Ranger When We Need Him? America's Search for a Post-Conflict Stability Force* (Washington: USIP, 2004), p84.

12 For an overview of these developments see: Cedric Thornberry, 'Namibia', *The UN Security Council: From the Cold War to the 21st Century*, ed. David Malone (Boulder CO and London: Lynne Reinner, 2004). In particular Thornberry traces UN efforts to remove South Africa from Namibian territory and (p414) highlights the stalling tactics deployed by some actors against the determination of the non-aligned movement to ensure that UNTAG was well-funded and well-armed.

13 UNSC Resolution 435 as cited in Roger Hearn, *UN Peacekeeping in Action: The Namibian Experience* (New York: Nova Science Publishers Inc, 1999), p58.

14 Roger Hearn, *UN Peacekeeping in Action: The Namibian Experience* (New York: Nova Science Publishers Inc, 1999), p69.

15 Stephen Fannin, 'UN Peace Settlement Plan for Namibia (UNTAG)', *The Role and Functions of Civilian Police in United Nations Peace-keeping Operations: Debriefing and Lessons*, Report and Recommendations of the International Conference Singapore December 1995 (London: Kluwer Law International, 1995), p114.

16 The 'Australian Plan' as outlined in The Commonwealth of Australia, *Cambodia: An Australian Police Proposal*, Working papers prepared for the Informal Meeting on Cambodia, held at Jakarta 26–28 February 1990 (Canberra: R.D. Rubie Commonwealth Government Printer, 1990), p36.

17 Alex Morrison, 'Methodology, Contents and Structure of UN Civilian Police Training Programmes', *The Role and Functions of Civilian Police in United Nations Peacekeeping Operations: Debriefing and Lessons*, ed. Nassrine Azimi (London: Kluwer Law International, 1996), p144.

18 Roger Hearn, *UN Peacekeeping in Action: The Namibian Experience* (New York: Nova Science Publishers Inc, 1999), p73.

19 Roger Hearn, *UN Peacekeeping in Action: The Namibian Experience* (New York: Nova Science Publishers Inc, 1999), pp147–55.

20 Chuck Call and Michael Barnett, 'Looking for a Few Good Cops: Peacekeeping, Peacebuilding and CIVPOL', *Peacebuilding and Police Reform*, eds. Tor Tanke Holm and Espen Barth Eide (London and Portland OR: Frank Cass, 2000), p43.

21 For an overview of these US policing and military operations in Panama see: Anthony Gray and Maxwell Manwaring, 'Panama: Operation *Just Cause*', *Policing the New World Disorder: Peace Operations and Public Security*, eds. Robert Oakley et al. (Washington DC: National Defense University Press, 1998).

22 Sinclair Dinnen, Abby McLeod and Gordon Peake, 'Police-building in Weak States: Australian Approaches in Papua New Guinea and Solomon Islands', *Civil Wars*, 8 (2), June 2006, p92.

23 James Sheptycki, 'The Constabulary Ethic and the Transnational Condition', *Crafting Transnational Policing: Police Capacity-Building and Global Policing Reform*, eds. Andrew Goldsmith and James Sheptycki (Oxford and Portland OR: Hart Publishing, 2007), p50, notes that the US Office of Public Safety provided police training for over one million police personnel from 34 countries in the 1960s and 70s in the areas of: criminal investigation, riot control, patrolling, interrogation, counter-insurgency and use of weapons.

24 Muhammad Anwarul Iqbal, 'An Overview of the CIVPOL Operations in Angola (UNAVEM)', *The Role and Functions of Civilian Police in United Nations Peace-keeping Operations: Debriefing and Lessons*, Report and Recommendations of the International Conference Singapore December 1995 (London: Kluwer Law International, 1995), pp95–6.

25 As noted by Abraham K. Klobodu, 'A Perspective from Ghana', *International Police Cooperation: A World Perspective*, eds. Daniel J. Koenig and Dilip K. Das (Lanham MD: Lexington Books, 2001), p162 such personnel assisted in escorting food aid to areas hit by the allied forces.

26 Peter Gastrow, Special Advisor to the Ministry of Safety and Security in South Africa, cited in a *PeaceWatch* report on the conference entitled 'Police Are Critical to the Peace Process', as found at http://www.usip.org/peacewatch/1996/696/Police.htm, accessed on 02/02/2005.

27 S/25264, *Further Report of the Secretary General Pursuant to SC Resolution 743*, 10 February 1993, as cited in John Hillen, *Blue Helmets: The Strategy of UN Military Operations*, 2nd edn (Washington DC: Brassey's, 2000), pp168–9.

28 Mats Berdal, 'United Nations Peacekeeping in the Former Yugoslavia', *Beyond Traditional Peacekeeping*, eds. Donald C.F. Daniel and Bradd C. Hayes (London: Macmillan, 1995), pp229–30. There was never any mandate for those CIVPOL to have executive powers to preserve public order.

29 Ali Mahmoud, 'UN Operation in Mozambique (ONUMOZ)', *The Role and Functions of Civilian Police in United Nations Peace-keeping Operations: Debriefing and Lessons*, Report and Recommendations of the International Conference Singapore December 1995 (London: Kluwer Law International, 1995), pp43–4.

30 Annika S. Hansen, *From Congo to Kosovo: Civilian Police in Peace Operations*, Adelphi Paper 343 (Oxford: IISS, 2002), p17.

31 Aldo Ajello and Patrick Wittman, 'Mozambique', *The UN Security Council: From the Cold War to the 21st Century*, ed. David Malone (Boulder CO and London: Lynne Reinner, 2004), p437.

32 Aldo Ajello and Patrick Wittman, 'Mozambique', *The UN Security Council: From the Cold War to the 21st Century*, ed. David Malone (Boulder CO and London: Lynne Reinner, 2004), pp448–9.
33 Ali Mahmoud, 'UN Operation in Mozambique (ONUMOZ)', *The Role and Functions of Civilian Police in United Nation's Peace-keeping Operations: Debriefing and Lessons*, Report and Recommendations of the International Conference Singapore December 1995 (London: Kluwer Law International, 1995).
34 Annika S. Hansen, *From Congo to Kosovo: Civilian Police in Peace Operations*, Adelphi Paper 343 (Oxford: IISS, 2002), p21. Though it must be recognised that some police reform efforts followed the UN peace operations in Namibia and Mozambique, these were all bilateral efforts only – undertaken by the Spanish in Mozambique for example.
35 Rama Mani, 'Contextualizing Police Reform: Security, the Rule of Law and Post-Conflict Peacebuilding', *Peacebuilding and Police Reform*, eds. Tor Tanke Holm and Espen Barth Eide (London and Portland OR: Frank Cass, 2000), pp12–13.
36 Interestingly, and as noted later in this chapter, the El Salvadorean police have since seen international policing as a role that, having seen the results of a more successful example of reform and rebuilding, they willingly contribute to.
37 Otwin Marenin, *Restoring Policing Systems in Conflict Torn Nations: Process, Problems, Prospects* (Geneva: Geneva Centre for the Democratic Control of Armed Forces, 2005), p53.
38 Michael J. Dziedzic, 'Introduction', *Policing the New World Disorder: Peace Operations and Public Security* eds. Robert Oakley et al. (Washington DC: National Defense University Press, 1998), p8.
39 Robert Perito, *Where is the Lone Ranger When We Need Him? America's Search for a Post Conflict Stability Force* (Washington DC: USIP, 2004), p99.
40 Cheryl M. Lee Kim and Mark Metrikas, 'Holding a Fragile Peace: The Military and Civilian Components of UNTAC', *Keeping the Peace: Multidimensional UN Operations in Cambodia and El Salvador*, eds. Michael W. Doyle et al. (Cambridge: Cambridge University Press, 1997), p107.
41 Cheryl M. Lee Kim and Mark Metrikas, 'Holding a Fragile Peace: The Military and Civilian Components of UNTAC', *Keeping the Peace: Multidimensional UN Operations in Cambodia and El Salvador*, eds. Michael W. Doyle et al. (Cambridge: Cambridge University Press, 1997), p108.
42 Cheryl M. Lee Kim and Mark Metrikas, 'Holding a Fragile Peace: The Military and Civilian Components of UNTAC', *Keeping the Peace: Multidimensional UN Operations in Cambodia and El Salvador*, eds. Michael W. Doyle et al. (Cambridge: Cambridge University Press, 1997), p113 footnote.
43 William Maley, 'International force and political reconstruction: Cambodia, East Timor and Afghanistan', *Security Sector Reform and Post-Conflict Peacebuilding*, eds. Albrecht Schnabel and Hans-Georg Ehrhart (Tokyo: UN University Press, 2005), p300.
44 Michael Doyle, 'Peacebuilding in Cambodia: Legitimacy and Power', *Peacebuilding as Politics: Cultivating Peace in Fragile Societies*, eds. Elizabeth Cousens et al. (Boulder CO and London: Lynne Reinner, 2001), p101.
45 Annika S. Hansen, *From Congo to Kosovo: Civilian Police in Peace Operations*, Adelphi Paper 343 (Oxford: IISS, 2002), p26.

46 James Schear and Karl Farris, 'Policing Cambodia: The Public Security Dimensions of UN Peace Operations', *Policing the New World Disorder: Peace Operations and Public Security*, eds. Robert Oakley et al. (Washington DC: National Defense University Press, 1998), pp82–3.
47 United Nations Crime Prevention and Criminal Justice Branch, *United Nations Criminal Justice Standards for Peace-keeping Police* (Vienna: UN Office at Vienna, 1994), p3.
48 Chetan Kumar, 'Peacebuilding in Haiti', *Peacebuilding as Politics: Cultivating Peace in Fragile Societies*, eds. Elizabeth Cousens et al. (Boulder CO and London: Lynne Reinner, 2001), p21.
49 Robert Perito, 'US Police in Peace and Stability Operations', *USIP Special Report*, #191, August 2007, p6.
50 Sebastian von Einsiedel and David M. Malone, 'Haiti', *The UN Security Council: From the Cold War to the 21st Century*, ed. David Malone (Boulder CO and London: Lynne Reinner, 2004), p470 and p474.
51 Rama Mani, 'Contextualizing Police Reform: Security, the Rule of Law and Post-Conflict Peacebuilding', *Peacebuilding and Police Reform*, eds. Tor Tanke Holm and Espen Barth Eide (London and Portland OR: Frank Cass, 2000), p14.
52 Chuck Call and Michael Barnett, 'Looking for a Few Good Cops: Peacekeeping, Peacebuilding and CIVPOL', *Peacebuilding and Police Reform*, eds. Tor Tanke Holm and Espen Barth Eide (London and Portland OR: Frank Cass, 2000), p49.
53 See: Michael Bailey et al., 'Haiti: Military-Police Partnership for Public Security', *Policing the New World Disorder: Peace Operations and Public Security*, eds. Robert Oakley et al. (Washington DC: National Defense University Press, 1998).
54 David H. Bayley, *Democratizing the Police Abroad: What to Do and How to Do It* (Washington DC: US Department of Justice, 2001), p53.
55 Sebastian von Einsiedel and David M. Malone, 'Haiti', *The UN Security Council: From the Cold War to the 21st Century*, ed. David Malone (Boulder CO and London: Lynne Reinner, 2004), p476. They cite a US Information Service poll that suggested that 70 per cent of Haitians had confidence in the police in early 1998 and also highlight the problems brought by a 'lamentable' local judicial system.
56 Chetan Kumar, 'Peacebuilding in Haiti', *Peacebuilding as Politics: Cultivating Peace in Fragile Societies*, eds. Elizabeth Cousens et al. (Boulder CO and London: Lynne Reinner, 2001), p24.
57 See: David M. Law, 'Conclusion: Security Sector (Re)Construction in Post-Conflict Settings', *International Peacekeeping* 13 (1), March 2006, p111 for mention of this perceived ongoing ineffectiveness.
58 Commentary on the contemporary situation in Haiti has been relayed to the author in a number of settings.
59 Robert Perito, *Where is the Lone Ranger When We Need Him? America's Search for a Post Conflict Stability Force* (Washington DC: USIP, 2004), p103.
60 Jurgen Reimann, 'Debriefing on CIVPOL Experiences: United Nations Mission for the Referendum in Western Sahara (MINURSO)', *The Role and Functions of Civilian Police in United Nations Peace-keeping Operations: Debriefing and Lessons*, Report and Recommendations of the International

Conference Singapore December 1995 (London: Kluwer Law International, 1995), pp107–10.

61 Cheik Oumar Diarra, 'United Nations Assistance Mission for Rwanda (UNAMIR)', *The Role and Functions of Civilian Police in United Nations Peace-keeping Operations: Debriefing and Lessons*, Report and Recommendations of the International Conference Singapore December 1995 (London: Kluwer Law International, 1995), pp101–2.

62 Robert Barry, *The OSCE: A Forgotten Transatlantic Security Organisation?*, BASIC Research Report, July 2002 (London: British American Security Information Council, 2002), p18.

63 Chuck Call and Michael Barnett, 'Looking for a Few Good Cops: Peace-keeping, Peacebuilding and CIVPOL', *Peacebuilding and Police Reform*, eds. Tor Tanke Holm and Espen Barth Eide (London and Portland OR: Frank Cass, 2000), p48.

64 The mission was originally known as United Nations Mission for the Verification of Human Rights and of Compliance with the Commitments of the Comprehensive Agreement on Human Rights in Guatemala, though from 1997 the mission – expanded by a small military and medical contingent – became known as the UN Verification Mission in Guatemala.

65 Selwyn Mettle, 'Operation in Somalia (UNOSOM)', *The Role and Functions of Civilian Police in United Nations Peace-keeping Operations: Debriefing and Lessons*, Report and Recommendations of the International Conference Singapore December 1995 (London: Kluwer Law International, 1995), p54.

66 Lynn M. Thomas, 'Peace Operations and the Need to Prioritize the Rule of Law through Legal System Reform: Lessons from Somalia and Bosnia', *Small Wars and Insurgencies*, 15 (2), Autumn 2004, p74.

67 Selwyn Mettle, 'Operation in Somalia (UNOSOM)', *The Role and Functions of Civilian Police in United Nations Peace-keeping Operations: Debriefing and Lessons*, Report and Recommendations of the International Conference Singapore December 1995 (London: Kluwer Law International, 1995), pp54–5.

68 Ameen Jan, 'Somalia: Building Sovereignty or Restoring Peace?', *Peace-building as Politics: Cultivating Peace in Fragile Societies*, eds. Elizabeth Cousens et al. (Boulder CO and London: Lynne Reinner, 2001), pp69–70.

69 For details on the planned judicial and penal reforms see Robert Perito, *Where is the Lone Ranger When We Need Him? America's Search for a Post Conflict Stability Force* (Washington DC: USIP, 2004), p107.

70 James Dobbin et al., *America's Role in Nation-building from Germany to Iraq* (Santa Monica CA: RAND, 2003), ppxxi and p68.

71 NZAID, *Bougainville Community Policing Project Phase 3 2004–6* (Wellington: MFAT, 2005).

72 Otwin Marenin, *Restoring Policing Systems in Conflict Torn Nations: Process, Problems, Prospects* (Geneva: Geneva Centre for the Democratic Control of Armed Forces, 2005), p56 puts this down to three things. One, that the government was willing to be politically incorrect and accept outsiders as executive leaders; two, that there was one major donor which minimised coordination problems etc; and three, that the implementers on the ground were familiar with policing and recent thinking about democratic policing.

73 See: Adekeye Adebajo, 'West Africa's Tragic Twins; Building Peace in Liberia and Sierra Leone', *Building Sustainable Peace*, eds. Tom Keating and W. Andy

Knight (Saskatchewan: UN University Press and The University of Alberta Press, 2004), pp167–88.

74 Lynn M. Thomas, 'Peace Operations and the Need to Prioritize the Rule of Law through Legal System Reform: Lessons from Somalia and Bosnia', *Small Wars and Insurgencies*, 15 (2), Autumn 2004, p74.

75 UN Secretary General's Special Representative in Bosnia and Herzegovina Jacques Paul Klein as cited in 'Police Reform in Bosnia and Herzegovina Signals a Mandate Completed', http://www.un.org/Depts/dpko/yir/english/page5.html, accessed on 01/02/2005.

76 Robert Perito, 'US Police in Peace and Stability Operations', *USIP Special Report*, #191, August 2007, p7.

77 Robert Perito, *Where is the Lone Ranger When We Need Him? America's Search for a Post-Conflict Stability Force* (Washington: USIP, 2004), p31.

78 UN Secretary General's Special Representative in Bosnia and Herzegovina Jacques Paul Klein as cited in 'Police Reform in Bosnia and Herzegovina Signals a Mandate Completed', http://www.un.org/Depts/dpko/yir/english/page5.html, accessed on 01/02/2005.

79 Chuck Call and Michael Barnett, 'Looking for a Few Good Cops: Peacekeeping, Peacebuilding and CIVPOL', *Peacebuilding and Police Reform*, eds. Tor Tanke Holm and Espen Barth Eide (London and Portland OR: Frank Cass, 2000), p59.

80 Lynn M. Thomas, 'Peace Operations and the Need to Prioritize the Rule of Law through Legal System Reform: Lessons from Somalia and Bosnia', *Small Wars and Insurgencies*, 15 (2), Autumn 2004, p75.

81 James Dobbin et al., *America's Role in Nation-building from Germany to Iraq* (Santa Monica CA: RAND, 2003), pxxi notes that despite democratic elections and some improvements in terms of inter-ethnic relationships, concerns have been expressed that the government may be constitutionally weak and vulnerable to organised crime and political extremism (See also the chapter on Bosnia in his text).

82 Annika S. Hansen, *From Congo to Kosovo: Civilian Police in Peace Operations*, Adelphi Paper 343 (Oxford: IISS, 2002), p71. See Chapter One in Robert Perito, *Where is the Lone Ranger When We Need Him? America's Search for a Post-Conflict Stability Force* (Washington: USIP, 2004), for more details on what happened in that situation in 1997.

83 'Bosnian Politics: Cracking Up', *The Economist*, 27 October 2007, p43.

84 Robert Perito, *Where is the Lone Ranger When We Need Him? America's Search for a Post-Conflict Stability Force* (Washington: USIP, 2004), p295.

85 Annika S. Hansen, *From Congo to Kosovo: Civilian Police in Peace Operations*, Adelphi Paper 343 (Oxford: IISS, 2002), pp27–8.

86 Gavin Brown, Barry Barker and Terry Burke, *Police as Peacekeepers: The History of the Australian and New Zealand Police serving with the United Nations Force in Cyprus 1964–1984* (Victoria Australia: UNCIVPOL, 1984), p2.

87 As argued by Michael Emery, UN Department of Peacekeeping Operations, and Erwin A. Schmidl, Austrian Ministry of Defence, in their papers given to the 'Police Functions in Peace Operations', UN Workshop, May 10 1996, as cited in a *PeaceWatch* report on the conference entitled 'Police Are Critical to the Peace Process', as found at http://www.usip.org/peacewatch/1996/696/Police.htm, accessed on 02/02/2005.

88 Leif Ahlquist et al., 'The Command and Control of UN Peace Support Operations', *The Human in Command: Peace Support Operations*, eds. Peter Essens et al. (Breda: KMA Royal Netherlands Academy, 2001), p150.

89 Halvor Hartz, 'CIVPOL: The UN Instrument for Police Reform', *building and Police Reform*, eds. Tor Tanke Holm and Espen Barth Eide (London and Portland OR: Frank Cass, 2000), p31.

90 Alex Morrison, 'Methodology, Contents and Structure of UN Civilian Police Training Programmes', *The Role and Functions of Civilian Police in United Nations Peacekeeping Operations: Debriefing and Lessons*, ed. Nassrine Azimi (London: Kluwer Law International, 1996), p143.

91 UNPKO, 'CIVPol Division and Police Force Generation Powerpoint Slideshow', as found at http://www.un.org/depts.dpko.training/MCPAS/MCPAS/CivPol_files/slide0341.htm, accessed on 09/02/2005.

92 Annika S. Hansen, *From Congo to Kosovo: Civilian Police in Peace Operations*, Adelphi Paper 343 (Oxford: IISS, 2002), p18.

93 Annika S. Hansen, *From Congo to Kosovo: Civilian Police in Peace Operations*, Adelphi Paper 343 (Oxford: IISS, 2002), p13.

94 See, for example: National Institute of Justice, *Civilian Police and Multinational Peacekeeping – A Workshop Series: A Role for Democratic Policing* (Washington DC: US Department of Justice, 1999).

95 Interview with Andrew Carpenter, Strategic Policy and Development Section, Police Division, UN Department of Peacekeeping Operations, November 2007.

96 Joshua G. Smith, Victoria K. Holt and William J. Durch, 'From Timor-Leste to Darfur: New Initiatives for Enhancing UN Civilian Policing Capacity', *The Henry L. Stimson Center Issue Brief*, August 2007, p3.

97 David H. Bayley, *Democratizing the Police Abroad: What to Do and How to Do It* (Washington DC: US Department of Justice, 2001), p4.

98 UN Police Presentation, Third Meeting of the International Policing Advisory Council, 30–31 August 2007, National Museum of Australia, Canberra.

99 CIVPOL emerged out of the deployment to Cyprus, and it is important to note that CIVPOL efforts are typically supported by bilateral law enforcement assistance programmes, multilateral activities, and non-governmental organisations – all requiring major personnel contributions and other forms of investment. Michael J. Dziedzic, 'Introduction', *Policing the New World Disorder: Peace Operations and Public Security*, eds. Robert Oakley et al. (Washington DC: National Defense University Press, 1998), p7 gives the examples of, respectively, the US Justice Department International Criminal Justice Division (ICITAP); the UN Crime Prevention and Criminal Justice Division; and the American Bar Association. Annika S. Hansen, *From Congo to Kosovo: Civilian Police in Peace Operations*, Adelphi Paper 343 (Oxford: IISS, 2002), p21.

100 See Recommendation 10, Summary of Recommendations, United Nations Secretariat, *Report of the Panel on United Nations Peace Operations*, UN Doc. A/ff/305, S/2000/809 (August 21 2000), p7, as found at http://www.un.org/peace/report/peace_operations, accessed 8/10/2005.

101 United Nations Secretariat, *Report of the Panel on United Nations Peace Operations*, UN Doc. A/ff/305, S/2000/809 (August 21 2000), p7, as found at http://www.un.org/peace/report/peace_operations, accessed 8/10/2005.

102 Annika S. Hansen, *From Congo to Kosovo: Civilian Police in Peace Operations*, Adelphi Paper 343 (Oxford: IISS, 2002), p22.

103 This raises the profile of this Office substantially, improving its status relative to the other agencies within UN DPKO – the Office of Operations, Office of Military Affairs, and the Policy, Evaluation and Training Division. Complementary to such in-house reshuffling, the UN Police Division has also been making concerted efforts in other fields. It has created: a Rule of Law Index (ROLIX) to assess a cross section of rule of law factors in a mission area; Doctrine Development Groups to work on the development of doctrine and policy in areas such as policy relating to FPU's and Pre-Deployment Training; and has developed a Standing Police Capacity (SPC) that consists of 27 personnel to be 'always ready to go' to start up new operations or to assist existing ones with expert services; and has enlisted the help of an International Policing Advisory Council (IPAC) to help provide strategic advice and a 'specialised and dedicated high-level forum for critical discussion and policy-level input on international policing matters' made up of prominent policy-makers, experts and specialists in the field – see UN DPKO, Government of the United Kingdom, of Great Britain and Northern Ireland and Government of Norway, *International Policing Advisory Council (IPAC) Summary Meeting Report*, 16–17 August 2006, Wilton Park, United Kingdom, p6 and p1.

104 This trend mirrors the more general debate surrounding how to manage security issues in international affairs – with the suggestion now being that the UN should look to 'subcontract' missions out to regional bodies. Dating back to 1993, if not before, to a time when the UN was heavily overstretched and essentially incapable of meeting the demands of peace-keeping across the world, there has been an uneasy working out of how and when the UN may *authorise* a regional body to undertake peace missions.

105 Under the Maastricht Treaty Europe has a three 'pillar' system: Pillar One (which involves a strong role for supranational bodies such as European Commission; Parliament; European Court of Justice); Pillar Two which outlines a Common Security and Foreign Policy (CSFP); and Pillar Three – which refers to internal security, justice and home affairs (the latter two are predominantly intergovernmental with the strongest role being played by the Council as representing member states).

106 European Council, *EU Training Programme in ESDP 2007–9 Handout* (Brussels: EC, 2007).

107 *ESDP civilian, police and military operations*, The Council of the European Union, as found at http://www.consilium.europa.eu/uedocs/cmsUpload/ESDPoperations.jpg, accessed on 6/10/2007 and *European Security and Defence Policy Operations*, The Council of the European Union, http://www.consilium.europa.eu/cms3_fo/showPage.asp?id=268&lang=en, accessed on 6/10/2007.

108 For example those states aspiring to EU status to be held to certain EU standards developed predominantly through the European Courts of Justice and Commission projects have also at times worked in places where a European Council or ESDP presence was less desirable, such as in the case of the Georgia border mission, and a number of police reform efforts have been

undertaken, though admittedly here for the Commission the emphasis is usually more on judicial reform. Thanks to members of the European Commission for discussions about the nature of these and where the division of labour lies with the Council. See the website of the European Court of Justice for more information on these expected common standards. For example those states aspiring to EU status to be held to certain EU standards developed predominantly through the European Courts of Justice and Commission projects have also at times worked in places where a European Council or ESDP presence was less desirable, such as in the case of the Georgia border mission, and a number of police reform efforts have been undertaken, though admittedly here for the Commission the emphasis is usually more on judicial reform.

109 As Graham Day and Christopher Freeman, 'Policekeeping is the Key: Rebuilding the Internal Security Architecture of Postwar Iraq', *International Affairs*, 2 (79), March 2003, p313 note, The EU's Rapid Reaction Force (ERRF) was intended to have a European Security and Intelligence Force (ESIF) of 5,000 special purpose police in place by the end of 2003. This had been decided at the 2000 Santa Maria de Feira European Council under the principles of the Third Pillar of the Maastricht Treaty, and that force was to have at least 1,000 police officers deployable within 30 days. Here gendarmerie-type police from four countries – France, Italy, Spain and Portugal – potentially make up 25 per cent of the 5,000. This follows on from France, Italy, Portugal, Netherlands and Spain committing themselves to the creation of European Gendarmerie in 2004. (The EU therefore has Integrated Police Units (IPUs) capable of performing executive law enforcement, though this is yet to be tested in practice, whilst NATO too has Multinational Specialized Units (MSUs) with a unit strength ranging from 250–600 personnel. However, again the issue of military versus police arises here with NATO seeing units such as the *carbinieri* as one such example of these police units – a point that is elaborated on in following chapters.) Michael Dziedzic and Colonel Christine Stark, 'Bridging the Security Gap: The Role of the Center of Excellence for Stability Police Units (CoESPU) in Contemporary Peace Operations', *USIPeace Briefing*, June 2006, as found at http://www.usip.org/pubs/usipeace_briefings/2006/0616_coespu.html, accessed on 8/10/2007.

110 Pacific Islands Chiefs of Police, *Future Directions in Pacific Policing: Beyond 2010*, vols 1 and 2 (Wellington: PICP, 2007).

111 Allan Hawke, 'Regional Co-operation in the Pacific: An Australian('s) Perspective', paper presented to Redefining the Pacific? Regionalism, Past, Present and Future, Dunedin, 26 June 2004, p10.

112 Obi N.I. Ebbe, 'International Police Cooperation in Africa', *International Police Cooperation: A World Perspective*, eds. Daniel J. Koenig and Dilip K. Das (Lanham MD: Lexington Books, 2001).

113 Teo Kian Teck, 'Singapore's Experience with International Police Cooperation', *International Police Cooperation: A World Perspective*, eds. Daniel J. Koenig and Dilip K. Das (Lanham MD: Lexington Books, 2001), p247.

114 See: OECD DAC, *Security System Reform and Governance: Policy and Good Practice*, A DAC Reference Document (Paris: OECD, 2004). Also see the official

Shanghai Cooperation Organisation website at http://www.sectsco.org/, and that of APEC at http://www.apec.org/.

115 Elsina Wainwright (with contributions from John McFarlane), 'Police Join the Front Line: Building Australia's International Policing Capability', *ASPI Strategic Insights* (Canberra: Australian Strategic Policy Institute, 2004), p4.

116 James Sheptycki, 'The Constabulary Ethic and the Transnational Condition', *Crafting Transnational Policing; Police Capacity-Building and Global Policing Reform*, eds. Andrew Goldsmith and James Sheptycki (Oxford and Portland OR: Hart Publishing, 2007), p50.

117 Thanks to discussions with Robert Perito 5/11/2007 for pointing out that ICITAP was originally brought in as a temporary measure and was sited within the Department of Justice though funded out of the State Department.

118 David H. Bayley, *Democratizing the Police Abroad: What to Do and How to Do It* (Washington DC: US Department of Justice, 2001), pp3–4.

119 William Lewis, Edward Marks and Robert Perito, 'Enhancing International Civilian Police in Peace Operations', *USIP Special Report*, 22 April 2002, p3.

120 As noted by Robert Perito, 'US Police in Peace and Stability Operations', *USIP Special Report*, #191, August 2007, pp2–3, the implementation of a US Civilian Reserve Corp concept was approved in 2007. This Corp was to be made up of three tiers. The first tier was to consist of 100–150 current employees (Active Reserve Corp deployable in 24 hours); the second was to see the creation of 1,000 new jobs (Standby Reserve Corps in 60 days); and the third tier (initially 500 up to 4,000 in Civil Response Corp) was to involve personnel that are not all necessarily police officers but that are somehow involved in rule of law institutions. However, at the end of 2007 this initiative had been stalled in Congress, the budget for the project continues to diminish and it is unlikely to be carried through with as intended though a more watered down version may come into being. ICITAP too has been pushed out of post-conflict policing as the US State Department has moved to take on such responsibilities though, as is demonstrated in Chapter 6, such efforts are still facing major problems at this point in time. David H. Bayley, *Democratizing the Police Abroad: What to Do and How to Do It* (Washington DC: US Department of Justice, 2001), p5 notes that Clinton's Presidential Decision Directive 71 (PDD-71) of February 2000 was formulated to try to improve American participation in international policing. For an outline of this earlier PDD and the difficulties faced in implementing it see: William Lewis, Edward Marks and Robert Perito, 'Enhancing International Civilian Police in Peace Operations', *USIP Special Report*, 22 April 2002 – these included the fact that funding was done on an annual basis, that police were recruited by a contractor, by a lack of support and profile in the Congress and White House and so on. Further commentary is also to be found in Robert Perito, *Where is the Long Ranger When We Need Him? America's Search for a Post Conflict Stability Force* (Washington: USIP, 2004), pp278–80.

121 See for example Police and Justice Team, *Peace Support Operations: Information and Guidance for UK Personnel*, April 2007 (London: Foreign and Commonwealth Office, 2007).

122 For more detailed information on recent and current deployments see the RCMP website at http://www.rcmp-grc.gc.ca/intpolicing/intpolicing_e.htm. Benoit Dupont and Samuel Tanner, 'Not always a happy ending: The organisational challenges of deploying and reintegrating civilian police peacekeepers: A Canadian perspective', paper presented to *Community Policing in Three Dimensions Workshop*, 12–14 December 2007, Canberra, Australia, co-sponsored by the Regulatory Institutions Network, ANU and the Berkeley Centre for International Justice note that when requested to deploy to such missions, the Foreign Affairs and International Trade Canada (FAC) ministry appoints a special committee made up of members from the Canadian International Development Agency (CIDA), Public Safety Canada (PSC) and the RCMP which assesses the feasibility of the request, coordinates involvement and designs the policy framework and guidelines for deployment.

123 UN News Service, 'Top Contributing Countries Graph May 2007', *UN Police Magazine*, 2nd edn., June 2007, p11.

124 *Summary Meeting Report of the Second Meeting of the International Policing Advisory Council (IPAC)*, Transcorp Hilton, Abuja, Nigeria, 22–23 January 2007, p6.

125 *Peoples Daily Online*, 'China to Build Asia's Largest UN Police Training Center', as found at http://english1.people.com.cn/200208/20/print20020820_101732.html, accessed on 08/02/2005. For more details on the growth of Chinese involvement in UN peace missions (police and military), see Pang Zhongying, 'China's Changing Attitude to UN Peacekeeping', *International Peacekeeping*, 12 (1), Spring 2005, pp87–104.

126 Loro Horta, 'From Red to Blue: China and Peacekeeping', *Australian Army Journal*, v (5), Autumn 2008, p107.

127 Richard Robison, Ian Wilson and Adrianus Meliala, '"Governing the Ungovernable": Dealing with the Rise of Informal Security in Indonesia', *Asia Pacific Research Centre Policy Brief*, No. 1, June 2008, Asia Pacific Research Centre, Murdoch University.

128 '10 PNTL officers to join the UN mission in Kosovo', *UNMIT press release*, as found at http://www.unmit.org/UNMISETWebSite.nsf/60325cf12626b2a349256f0a003ef7d8/9dbdd35f81817778492570d1001fd98e?OpenDocument, accessed 7/4/2008.

Chapter 3 Kosovo and East Timor

1 William Shawcross, *Deliver Us from Evil: Warlords and Peacekeepers in a World of Endless Conflict* (London: Bloomsbury, 2000), p323.

2 Paul Heinbecker and Rob McRae, 'The Kosovo Air Campaign', *Human Security and the New Diplomacy: Protecting People, Promoting Peace*, eds. Rob McRae and Don Hubert (Montreal: McGill-Queen's University Press, 2001), p124.

3 Senior UN Official cited in William Shawcross, *Deliver Us from Evil: Warlords and Peacekeepers in a World of Endless Conflict* (London: Bloomsbury, 2000), p349.

4 NATO, 'Kosovo Force (KFOR); How did it evolve?', as found at http://www.nato.int/issues/kfor/evolution.html, accessed on 1/10/2007, this document also mentions that in August 2005 KFOR was restructured. The four

existing multinational brigades were replaced by five task forces which placed more emphasis on intelligence-led operations, with forces working more closely with local police and populations.

5 Roland Paris, *At War's End: Building Peace after Civil Conflict* (Cambridge: Cambridge University Press, 2004), p213.

6 Renata Dwan, 'Civilian tasks and capabilities in EU operations', *A Human Security Doctrine for Europe: Project, Principles, Practicalities*, eds. Marlies Glasius and Mary Kaldor (London and New York: Routledge, 2006), p268.

7 UNMIK Police: Kosovo Police Service diagram, as found at http://www.civpol.org/unmik/KPS.htm, accessed on 21/12/2005.

8 OSCE, 'Police Education: Establishing Kosovo Police Service', as found at http://www.osce.org/kosovo/13216.html, accessed on 20/12/2005.

9 OSCE-UNMIK police cooperation, as found at http://www.civpol.org/unmik/KPS.htm, accessed on 21/12/2005.

10 'UNMIK Police Mandate', as found at http://www.civpol.org/unmik/mandate.htm, accessed on 21/12/2005.

11 UN, 'Report of the Secretary General on the United Nations Interim Administration in Kosovo', 12 July 1999, S/1999/799, as found at http://daccess-dds.un.org/doc/UNDOC/GEN/N99/204/10/PDF/N9920410.pdf?OpenElement, accessed 21/12/2005.

12 *Guidelines for Governments Contributing Special Police Units to UNMIK* (New York: CPD/DPKO, 1999), p9.

13 UNMIK, 'Frequently Asked Questions; General information about the International Police in Kosovo', as found at http://www.unmikonline.org/civpol/newfaq.htm#11, accessed 8/1/2006.

14 UN, 'Report of the Secretary General on the United Nations Interim Administration in Kosovo', 12 July 1999, S/1999/799, as found at http://daccessdds.un.org/doc/UNDOC/GEN/N99/204/10/PDF/N9920410.pdf?OpenElement, accessed 21/12/2005.

15 'UNMIK Tasks', as found at http://www.civpol.org/unmik/mandate.htm, accessed on 21/12/2005.

16 'Kosovo Police Service School', as found at http://www.civpol.org/unmik/KPS.htm, accessed on 21/12/2005.

17 Robert Perito, 'US Police in Peace and Stability Operations', *USIP Special Report*, #191, August 2007, p9.

18 OSCE, 'Police Education Factsheet', March 2005, as found at http://www.osce.org/documents/mik/2004/09/3822_en.pdf, accessed on 21/12/2005.

19 Espen Barth Eide and Tor Tanke Holm, 'Postscript: Towards Executive Authority Policing? The Lessons of Kosovo', *Peacebuilding and Police Reform*, eds. Tor Tanke Holm and Espen Barth Eide (London and Portland OR: Frank Cass, 2000), p212.

20 William Shawcross, *Deliver Us from Evil: Warlords and Peacekeepers in a World of Endless Conflict* (London: Bloomsbury, 2000), p351.

21 Robert Perito, 'US Police in Peace and Stability Operations', *USIP Special Report*, #191, August 2007, p9.

22 As argued by Andreas Heinemann-Gruder and Igor Grebenschikov, 'Security Governance by Internationals: The Case of Kosovo', *International Peacekeeping*, 13 (1), March 2006, p56 amongst others.

23 Nicholas Wood, 'Division and Disorder Still Tearing at Kosovo', *The Washington Post*, 22 June 2002, p89.
24 Renata Dwan, 'Civilian tasks and capabilities in EU operations', *A Human Security Doctrine for Europe: Project, Principles, Practicalities*, eds. Marlies Glasius and Mary Kaldor (London and New York: Routledge, 2006), p272.
25 Annika S. Hansen, *From Congo to Kosovo: Civilian Police in Peace Operations*, Adelphi Paper 343 (Oxford: IISS, 2002), p25.
26 See: http://www.un.org/Depts/dpko/dpko/civpol/3.htm, accessed on 23/03/2005.
27 Espen Barth Eide and Tor Tanke Holm, 'Postscript: Towards Executive Authority Policing? The Lessons of Kosovo', *Peacebuilding and Police Reform*, eds. Tor Tanke Holm and Espen Barth Eide (London and Portland OR: Frank Cass, 2000), p217.
28 William G. O'Neill, *Kosovo: 'An Unfinished Peace'* (Boulder CO: Lynne Reinner, 2002), pp99–101.
29 Ray Murphy, *UN Peacekeeping in Lebanon, Somalia and Kosovo: Operational and Legal Issues in Practice* (Cambridge: Cambridge University Press, 2007), p92.
30 For a review of some of these tensions and contrasting agendas see International Crisis Group, *Kosovo Countdown: A Blueprint for Transition*, Europe Report #188, 6 December 2007, as found at http://www.crisisgroup.org/home/index.cfm?id=5201, accessed 20/1/2008.
31 See: the Human Rights Watch report *Failure to Protect: Anti-Minority Violence in Kosovo, March 2004*, as found at http://www.hrw.org/english/docs/2004/07/27/ serbia9136.htm, accessed on 28/07/2004. OSCE, 'Police Education Factsheet', March 2005, as found at http://www.osce.org/documents/mik/2004/09/3822_en.pdf, accessed on 21/12/2005 states that in response the OSCE's Department of Police and Education increased the focus on the relationship between the police and youth within the KPS School.
32 Ray Murphy, *UN Peacekeeping in Lebanon, Somalia and Kosovo: Operational and Legal Issues in Practice* (Cambridge: Cambridge University Press, 2007), p197.
33 'Police step up security in Kosovo', News From *Russia Online*, December 29 2005, http://newsfromrussia.com/world/2005/12/29/70702.htm, accessed on 8/1/2006.
34 International Crisis Group, 'Kosovo's First Month', *International Crisis Group Briefing*, Pristina/Belgrade/Brussels, 18 March 2008.
35 Andreas Heinemann-Gruder and Igor Grebenschikov, 'Security Governance by Internationals: The Case of Kosovo', *International Peacekeeping*, 13 (1), March 2006, p48.
36 Thanks to discussions with NATO officials and personnel.
37 Andreas Heinemann-Gruder and Igor Grebenschikov, 'Security Governance by Internationals: The Case of Kosovo', *International Peacekeeping*, 13 (1), March 2006, p51.
38 Amnesty International figures cited in Ekrem Krasniqi, 'UN Kosovo police arrested for sex trafficking', *International Relations and Security Network*, 01/09/2005, as found at http://www.isn.ethz.ch/news/sw/details.cfm?ID=12681, accessed on 10/1/2006.

39 Ekrem Krasniqi, 'UN Kosovo police arrested for sex trafficking', *International Relations and Security Network*, 01/09/2005, as found at http://www.isn.ethz.ch/news/sw/details.cfm?ID=12681, accessed on 10/1/2006.
40 NATO, 'Statement on the situation in the Balkans', issued at the Meeting of the North Atlantic Council in Defence Ministers Session held in Brussels, Press Release M-DNAC-D-1 (2001) 88, 7 June 2001, as found at http://www.nato.int/docu/pr/2001/p01-088e.htm, accessed on 6/6/2007.
41 Andreas Heinemann-Gruder and Igor Grebenschikov, 'Security Governance by Internationals: The Case of Kosovo', *International Peacekeeping*, 13 (1), March 2006, p44.
42 See: Aidan Hehir, 'Autonomous Province Building: Identification Theory and the Failure of UNMIK', *International Peacekeeping*, 13 (2), June 2006, pp200–13.
43 Renata Dwan, 'Civilian tasks and capabilities in EU operations', *A Human Security Doctrine for Europe: Project, Principles, Practicalities*, eds. Marlies Glasius and Mary Kaldor (London and New York: Routledge, 2006), p269.
44 Thomas R. Mockaitis, *Civil Military Cooperation in Peace Operations: The Case of Kosovo* (Carlisle Barracks: SSI, October 2004), p10.
45 UNDP poll cited in Kosovo Early Warning Reports, as found at http://www.kosovo.undp.org/repository/docs/Facts_EWS_14.doc, accessed 13/3/2008.
46 Footnote 51, International Crisis Group, *Kosovo Countdown: A Blueprint for Transition*, Europe Report No. 188, 6 December 2007, p7.
47 OSCE, 'Police Education Factsheet', March 2005, as found at http://www.osce.org/documents/mik/2004/09/3822_en.pdf, accessed on 21/12/2005.
48 Andreas Heinemann-Gruder and Igor Grebenschikov, 'Security Governance by Internationals: The Case of Kosovo', *International Peacekeeping*, 13 (1), March 2006, p51.
49 United Nations Development Programme, *Human Development Report – Kosovo 2004*, as found at http://hdr.undp.org/docs/reports/national/KOS_Kosovo/Kosovo_2004_en.pdf, accessed on 21/03/2006.
50 Some such as Roland Paris, *At War's End: Building Peace after Civil Conflict* (Cambridge: Cambridge University Press, 2004), p216 have claimed that 'it is difficult to understand how the empowerment of Kosovo separatists through democratic elections serves the interests of achieving long-term peaceful solution to the Kosovo problem' and suggests that this form of rapid democratisation may simply have been a means for UNMIK to extract itself from Kosovo prematurely.
51 Ian Martin and Alexander Mayer-Rieckh, 'The United Nations and East Timor: From Self-Determination to State-Building', *International Peacekeeping*, 12 (1), Spring 2005, p109.
52 William Shawcross, *Deliver Us from Evil: Warlords and Peacekeepers in a World of Endless Conflict* (London: Bloomsbury, 2000), p356.
53 Michael Elmquist, *CIMIC in East Timor: An Account of Civil-Military Cooperation, Coordination and Collaboration in the Early Phases of the East Timor Relief Operation* (Geneva: OCHA 1999).
54 S. Ayling and S. Guise, 'UNTAC and INTERFET – A Comparative Analysis', *Australian Defence Force Journal*, No. 150 Sept/Oct 2001, p51.
55 See for example, New Zealand Defence Force Media Release, 'New Zealand Military Police investigate East Timor Graves', *Scoop*, 26 October 1999, as

found at http://www.scoop.co.nz/stories/HL9910/S00152.htm, accessed on 21/03/2006.

56 UNSC, *UNSC Resolution 1272*, S/RES/1272 (1999), adopted on 25 October 1999, as found at http://www.un.org/peace/etimor/docs/9931277E. htm, accessed 11/7/2007.

57 'East Timor: UNTAET, Background', *UN Website*, http://www.un.org/peace/etimor/UntaetB.htm, accessed on 5/12/2005.

58 UN Secretary General Kofi Annan, *Report of the Secretary General on the United Nations Transitional Administration in East Timor*, S/2001/983, 18 October 2001, paragraph 83, p11.

59 'East Timor: UNTAET, Background', *UN Website*, http://www.un.org/peace/etimor/UntaetB.htm, accessed on 5/12/2005.

60 Human Rights Watch, 'East Timor: Human Rights Developments', *World Report 2000*, as found at http://www.hrw.org/wr2k1/asia/etimor.html, accessed on 7/12/2005.

61 UN News Service, 'Security Council extends Timor-Leste mission for 1 year, boosts police', *UN Police Magazine*, 2nd edn, June 2007, p9.

62 Thanks to discussions held at the Round Table on 'The Pacific Island States: Peace, Security and Development in a Difficult Environment – A Comparison of Australian and European Neighbourhood Policies', hosted by the National Europe Centre and the Asia-Pacific College of Diplomacy, 2–3 October 2007, ANU, Canberra.

63 Australian Embassy Dili, *Status of Forces Agreement May 26 2006*, Note No. 159/2006, as found at http://www/laohamatuk.org/reports/UN/06SOFAs.html, accessed 12/12/2007.

64 UN News Service, 'Timor-Leste: UN envoy pays special tribute to police for peaceful presidential elections', *UN Police Magazine*, 2nd edn, June 2007, p8.

65 'Police and Justice: Australia-East Timor Police Development Program', as found at http://www.ausaid.gov.au/country/country.cfm?CountryID=911&Region=EastAsia, accessed on 1/12/2005.

66 Police and Justice: Law and Justice Development Program', as found at http://www.ausaid.gov.au/country/country.cfm?CountryID=911&Region=EastAsia, accessed on 1/12/2005.

67 International Policy Institute, 'Rule of Law and Administration of Justice', East Timor Report, Kings College London, as found at http://ipi.sspp.kcl.ac.uk/rep006/s05.html, accessed 21/03/2006.

68 Annika S. Hansen, *From Congo to Kosovo: Civilian Police in Peace Operations*, Adelphi Paper 343 (Oxford: IISS, 2002), pp72–3.

69 For further comment on Report of the Secretary-General on the Situation in East Timor, S/1999/1024, 4 October 1999 see UN Press Release SC/6745, 'Security Council Establishes UN Transitional Administration in East Timor for Initial Period Until 31 January', as found at http://www.un.org/news/Press/docs/1999/19991025.sc6745.doc.html, accessed 13/3/2007.

70 UNMISET, 'Timeline of UN Presence in East Timor', http://www.unmiset.org/UNMISETWebSite.nsf/TimeLineofUNMISET.htm?OpenPage, accessed 12/1/2006.

71 Amnesty International, 'Timor-Leste: Briefing to Security Council Members on Policing and Security in Timor-Leste', 6 March 2006, http://web.amnesty.org/library/Index/ENGASA570012003?open&of=ENG-TMP, accessed 12/1/2006.

72 UNSC, UNSC Resolution 1410, S/RES/1410 (2002) (adopted 17 May 2002, as found at http://www.unmit.org/UNMISETwebsite.nsf/p9999/$FILE/S-RES-1410%20(2002).pdf, accessed 13/3/2007.
73 Ian Martin and Alexander Mayer-Rieckh, 'The United Nations and East Timor: From Self-Determination to State-Building', *International Peacekeeping*, 12 (1), Spring 2005, p140.
74 Source: La'o Hamutuk Group, 'UN Missions and Security', *The La'o Hamutuk Bulletin*, 4 (2), 2003, as found at http://www.laohamutuk.org/Bulletin/2003/May/bulletinv4n2.html, accessed 12/1/2006.
75 UN News Service, 'Timor-Leste: UN envoy pays special tribute to police for peaceful presidential elections', *UN Police Magazine*, 2nd edn, June 2007, p7.
76 Bu V.E. Wilson, 'Smoke and Mirrors: Institutionalising fragility in the Policia Nacional Timor Leste', paper delivered to the Democratic Governance in Timor-Leste: Reconciling the National and Local Conference, Charles Darwin University, Darwin, 7–8 February 2008, p2.
77 United Nations Secretary General Ban Ki-Moon, *Report of the Secretary General on the United Nations Mission in Timor Leste*, 2007 S/2007/513, as found at http://www.un.org/Docs/journal/asp/ws.asp?m=S/PV.5740, accessed 12/10/2007.
78 David M. Law, 'Conclusion: Security Sector (Re)Construction in Post-Conflict Settings', *International Peacekeeping*, 13 (1), March 2006, p115 and also Ludovic Hood, 'Missed Opportunities: The United Nations, Police Service and Defence Force Development in Timor-Leste, 1999–2004', *Civil Wars*, 8 (2), June 2006, pp143–62.
79 Ian Martin and Alexander Mayer-Rieckh, 'The United Nations and East Timor: From Self-Determination to State-Building', *International Peacekeeping*, 12 (1), Spring 2005, p141 and Ludovic Hood, 'Security Sector Reform in East Timor', *International Peacekeeping*, 13 (1), March 2006, p61.
80 As noted in reports such as *A Review of Peace Operations: A Case for Change – East Timor, Conflict, Security and Development Group*, King's College London, 10 March 2003, as found at http://www.jsmp.minihub.org/Reports/other-resources/Peace4Timor_10_3_03.pdf, accessed 7/4/2008.
81 Ludovic Hood, 'Missed Opportunities: The United Nations, Police Service and Defence Force Development in Timor-Leste, 1999–2004', *Civil Wars*, 8 (2), June 2006, p154.
82 Human Rights Watch, 'East Timor: Human Rights Developments', *World Report 2000*, as found at http://www.hrw.org/wr2k1/asia/etimor.html, accessed on 7/12/2005. Similar critiques can be found in Ian Martin and Alexander Mayer-Rieckh, 'The United Nations and East Timor: From Self-Determination to State-Building', *International Peacekeeping*, 12 (1), Spring 2005, p134.
83 Bu V.E. Wilson, 'Smoke and Mirrors: institutionalising fragility in the Policia Nacional Timor Leste', paper delivered to the Democratic Governance in Timor-Leste: Reconciling the National and Local Conference, Charles Darwin University, Darwin, 7–8 February 2008, p9.
84 Ian Martin and Alexander Mayer-Rieckh, 'The United Nations and East Timor: From Self-Determination to State-Building', *International Peacekeeping*, 12 (1), Spring 2005, p142.

85 Ludovic Hood, 'Missed Opportunities: The United Nations, Police Service and Defence Force Development in Timor-Leste, 1999–2004', *Civil Wars*, 8 (2), June 2006, p146 and 149.

86 Ludovic Hood, 'Security Sector Reform in East Timor', *International Peacekeeping*, 13 (1), March 2006, p61.

87 *A Review of Peace Operations: A Case for Change – East Timor, Conflict, Security and Development Group*, King's College London, 10 March 2003, as found at http://www.jsmp.minihub.org/Reports/otherresources/Peace4Timor_10_3_03.pdf, accessed 7/4/2008.

88 International Crisis Group, *Timor Leste: Security Sector Reform*, Asia Report #143, as found at http://www.crisisgroup.org/home/index.cfm?id=5264, accessed 7/4/2008.

89 La'o Hamutuk Group, 'An Assessment of the UN's Police Mission in East Timor', *The La'o Hamutuk Bulletin*, 3 (1), 2002, as found at http://www.laohamutuk.org/Bulletin/2002/Feb/bulletinv3n1.html#Japanese%20Self-Defense%20Force, accessed 12/1/2006.

90 La'o Hamutuk Group, 'An Assessment of the UN's Police Mission in East Timor', *The La'o Hamutuk Bulletin*, 3 (1), 2002, as found at http://www.laohamutuk.org/Bulletin/2002/Feb/bulletinv3n1.html#Japanese%20Self-Defense % 20Force, accessed 12/1/2006.

91 Lt Col Antony Hayward, *East Timor: A Case Study in Humanitarian Intervention*, New Zealand Army Military Studies Institute Occasional Paper Series (Wellington: Military Studies Institute, 2003), p15.

92 Bu V.E. Wilson, 'Smoke and Mirrors: institutionalising fragility in the Policia Nacional Timor Leste', paper delivered to the Democratic Governance in Timor-Leste: Reconciling the National and Local Conference, Charles Darwin University, Darwin, 7–8 February 2008, p5.

93 La'o Hamutuk Group, 'The World Bank in East Timor', *The La'o Hamutuk Bulletin*, 1 (4), 31 December 2000, as found at http://www.etan.org/li/bulletin04.html, accessed 12/10/2007.

94 Jarat Chopra and Tanja Hohe, 'Participatory Peacebuilding', *Building Sustainable Peace*, eds. Tom Keating and W. Andy Knight (Saskatchewan: UN University Press and The University of Alberta Press, 2004), pp249–52. Chopra is, in fact, the former UNTAET head of the Office of District Administration.

95 La'o Hamutuk Group, 'Japanese Peacekeepers in East Timor', *The La'o Hamutuk Bulletin*, 3 (6), 2002, as found at http://www.laohamutuk.org/Bulletin/2002/Aug/bulletinv3n6.html#Japanese%20Peacekeepers%20in%20East%20Timor, accessed 12/1/2006.

96 Human Rights Watch, 'East Timor: Human Rights Developments', *World Report 2000*, as found at http://www.hrw.org/wr2k1/asia/etimor.html, accessed on 7/12/2005.

97 Jill Jolliffe, 'Justice at crossroads in East Timor', *Asia Times Online*, 24 February 2005, as found at http://www.atimes.com/atimes/Southeast_Asia/GB24Ae03.html, accessed on 8/1/2006.

98 Amnesty International, *Timor-Leste: Briefing to Security Council Members on Policing and Security in Timor-Leste*, 6 March 2006, http://web.amnesty.org/library/Index/ENGASA570012003?open&of=ENG-TMP, accessed 12/1/2006.

99 US State Department, 'East Timor' *Country Reports on Human Rights Practices: 2004*, as found at http://www.state.gov/g/drl/rls/hrrpt/2004/41641.htm, accessed 8/1/2006.

100 Ben Moxham, 'Market-imposed hunger adds to Timor misery', *Asia Times Online*, 16 February 2005, as found at http://www.atimes.com/atimes/Southeast_Asia/GB16Ae02.html, accessed on 12/1/2006.
101 La'o Hamutuk Group, 'UN Missions and Security', *The La'o Hamutuk Bulletin*, 4 (2), 2003, as found at http://www.laohamutuk.org/Bulletin/2003/May/bulletinv4n2.html, accessed 12/1/2006.
102 Lt Col Antony Hayward, *East Timor: A Case Study in Humanitarian Intervention*, New Zealand Army Military Studies Institute Occasional Paper Series (Wellington: Military Studies Institute, 2003), p10.
103 Ludovic Hood, 'Security Sector Reform in East Timor', *International Peacekeeping*, 13 (1), March 2006, p64.
104 Ludovic Hood, 'Security Sector Reform in East Timor', *International Peacekeeping*, 13 (1), March 2006, p73.
105 *UNOHCR Report of the United Nations Independent Special Commission of Inquiry for Timor-Leste* (Geneva: UN, 2006).
106 Bob Lowry, 'After the 2006 crisis: Australia's interests in Timor-Leste', *ASPI Strategic Insights*, #38 (Canberra: Australian Strategic Policy Institute, 2007), p14.
107 Bernard Kouchner cited in R. Jeffrey Smith, 'Kosovo still seethes as UN Official nears exit', *The Washington Post*, 19 December 2000, pA20.

Chapter 4 RAMSI

1 Paul D. McLean (ed.) *Solomon Islands: Report of a Study Group* (Wellington: NZIIA, 2001), pp20–1.
2 See: Sandra Tarte and Tarcisius Tara Kabutaulaka, 'Rethinking Security in the South Pacific: Fiji and the Solomon Islands', *The Unraveling of Island Asia? Governmental, Communal and Regional Instability*, ed. Bruce Vaughn (Westport CO and London: Praeger, 2002), for an overview of the time leading up to RAMSI.
3 The Guale population hails from Guadalcanal.
4 Item Nine in the New Zealand Ministry of Foreign Affairs and Trade, 'Solomon Islands: Strengthened Assistance', Defence Cabinet Document Covering Submission and Cabinet Paper, 23 June 2003, SLB/4, p2.
5 RAMSI, 'RAMSI's work', as found at http://www.ramsi.org/node/2, accessed 10/3/2008.
6 RAMSI, 'RAMSI Organisation Chart', created 16/02/2008, found at http://www.ramsi.org/node/269/print, accessed on 10/03/2008.
7 Articles Six and Seven, New Zealand Ministry of Foreign Affairs and Trade, 'Solomon Islands: Possible Intervention', Defence Cabinet Document – Submission and Annex, 23 May 2003, SLB/4, p4.
8 Indeed, as James Watson, *A Model Pacific Solution? A Study of the Deployment of the Regional Assistance Mission to Solomon Islands*, Land Warfare Studies Centre Working Paper No. 126, Canberra, October 2005, p25 points out an alleged incident did occur and the contributing country, in this case Australia, dealt with the matter themselves.
9 *Facilitation of International Assistance Act 2003* as cited in Footnote 1, James Watson, *A Model Pacific Solution? A Study of the Deployment of the Regional*

Assistance Mission to Solomon Islands, Land Warfare Studies Centre Working Paper No. 126, Canberra, October 2005, p1.

10 See Elsina Wainwright, 'How is RAMSI faring? Progress, Challenges and Lessons Learned', *ASPI Strategic Insights* (Canberra: Australian Strategic Police Institute, 2005) for commentary on these phases.

11 Item Six, New Zealand Ministry of Foreign Affairs and Trade, 'Solomon Islands: Strengthened Assistance', Defence Cabinet Document, Cabinet Paper plus attachment, 9 June 2003, p2.

12 Item Seventeen, New Zealand Ministry of Foreign Affairs and Trade, 'Solomon Islands: Strengthened Assistance', Defence Cabinet Document Covering Submission and Cabinet Paper, 23 June 2003, SLB/4, p4.

13 Item Ten, New Zealand Ministry of Foreign Affairs and Trade, 'Solomon Islands: Possible New Zealand Involvement in Strengthened Assistance', Defence Cabinet Document, Cabinet Paper, 24 June 2003, p2.

14 Item Thirteen, New Zealand Cabinet, 'Report of the Cabinet External Relations and Defence Committee', Period Ended 4 July 2003, Defence Cabinet Document, Cabinet Minute of Decision, 7 July 2003, CAB Min (03) 6/6.

15 Items Thirteen to Eighteen, New Zealand Ministry of Foreign Affairs and Trade, 'Solomon Islands: Strengthened Assistance: NZ Concept Paper', Defence Cabinet Document, Submission, 26 June 2003, pp4–5.

16 Item Seventeen, New Zealand Ministry of Foreign Affairs and Trade, 'Solomon Islands: Strengthened Assistance', Defence Cabinet Document Covering Submission and Cabinet Paper, 23 June 2003, SLB/4, p4.

17 Dr John Roughan, '100 Days of RAMSI', State, Society and Governance in Melanesia Working Paper 03/3, as found at http://eprints.anu.edu.au/archive/00002780/20/9/2004 describes how effective RAMSI has been and pointed out that the establishment of over 16 police posts in the provinces had been an important part of that success.

18 Sinclair Dinnen, Abby McLeod and Gordon Peake, 'Police-building in Weak States: Australian Approaches in Papua New Guinea and Solomon Islands', *Civil Wars*, 8 (2), June 2006, p99.

19 Item 26, New Zealand Cabinet, 'Report of the Cabinet External Relations and Defence Committee', Period Ended 4 July 2003, Defence Cabinet Document, Cabinet Minute of Decision, 7 July 2003, CAB Min (03) 6/6.

20 Item 27, New Zealand Cabinet, 'Report of the Cabinet External Relations and Defence Committee', Period Ended 4 July 2003, Defence Cabinet Document, Cabinet Minute of Decision, 7 July 2003, CAB Min (03) 6/6.

21 Item 22, New Zealand Cabinet, 'Report of the Cabinet External Relations and Defence Committee', Period Ended 4 July 2003, Defence Cabinet Document, Cabinet Minute of Decision, 7 July 2003, CAB Min (03) 6/6.

22 Garth van den Heyer, 'Stabilising the Solomons: A regional response', *New Zealand International Review*, 32 (4), July/August 2007, p19.

23 James Watson, *A Model Pacific Solution? A Study of the Deployment of the Regional Assistance Mission to Solomon Islands*, Land Warfare Studies Centre Working Paper No. 126, Canberra, October 2005, p21.

24 James Watson interviewed in Russell Glenn, *Counter-Insurgency in a Test Tube: Analyzing the Success of the Regional Assistance Mission to Solomon Islands (RAMSI)* (Santa Monica CA: RAND, 2007), p98.

25 Russell Glenn, *Counter-Insurgency in a Test Tube: Analyzing the Success of the Regional Assistance Mission to Solomon Islands (RAMSI)* (Santa Monica CA: RAND, 2007), p61.
26 In an interview with Superintendent Tony McLeod, National Manager of Operations, New Zealand Police, 16/08/2004, this difference became quite apparent in the retelling of one incident regarding the need for a search and rescue effort. Lead police requested help from the ADF to launch a search and rescue effort to rescue some local people that were stuck out at sea, but the ADF were unwilling to comply, asserting that this particular incident did not correspond directly with their given mandate. The working relationship between the AFP and the ADF has improved markedly as a result of working more closely together in RAMSI.
27 James Watson, *A Model Pacific Solution? A Study of the Deployment of the Regional Assistance Mission to Solomon Islands*, Land Warfare Studies Centre Working Paper No. 126, Canberra, October 2005, p20.
28 James Watson, *A Model Pacific Solution? A Study of the Deployment of the Regional Assistance Mission to Solomon Islands*, Land Warfare Studies Centre Working Paper No. 126, Canberra, October 2005.
29 For more detail on the last of these see: Russell Glenn, *Counter-Insurgency in a Test Tube: Analyzing the Success of the Regional Assistance Mission to Solomon Islands (RAMSI)* (Santa Monica CA: RAND, 2007), p63.
30 James Watson, *A Model Pacific Solution? A Study of the Deployment of the Regional Assistance Mission to Solomon Islands*, Land Warfare Studies Centre Working Paper No. 126, Canberra, October 2005, p28 and p16. See: Rosaleen Smyth, Nii-K Plange and Neil Burdess, 'Big Brother? Australia's Image in the South Pacific', *Australian Journal of International Affairs*, 51 (1), April 1997 for further discussion of how Australia is perceived in the region.
31 That RAMSI was still 'perceived predominantly as an Australian exercise' has been mentioned in a number of sources including the rather conservative Report of the Pacific Islands Forum Eminent Persons Group, *A Review of the Regional Assistance Mission to Solomon Islands*, May 2005 (Suva: PIF, 2005) in Point Ten of its Summary of Key Findings and Recommendations.
32 Paul Roughan, B.K. Greener-Barcham, and Manuhuia Barcham, *Where to now for RAMSI?*, CIGAD Briefing Notes, 1/2006, April 2006, p2.
33 See Matthew Allen, 'Dissenting Voices: Local Perspectives on the Regional Assistance Mission to Solomon Islands', *Pacific Economic Bulletin*, 21 (2), 2005, pp56–71 and Michael Morgan and Abby McLeod, 'Have we failed our neighbour? *Australian Journal of International Affairs*, 60 (3), 2006 pp412–28.
34 Sinclair Dinnen, Abby McLeod and Gordon Peake, 'Police-building in Weak States: Australian Approaches in Papua New Guinea and Solomon Islands', *Civil Wars*, 8 (2), June 2006, p99.
35 ANU Enterprise Pty Limited and ANU, *RAMSI Peoples Survey Pilot 2006: Final Report* (Honiara 2006), p31.
36 RAMSI, 'Special Features', as found at http://www.ramsi.org/node/17, accessed on 12/3/2008.
37 AUSAID, *Solomon Islands: Transitional Country Strategy 2006–7* (Canberra: AUSAID, 2006), p24.
38 See: Mary Louise O'Callaghan, RAMSI: The Challenges Ahead, paper presented at Solomon Islands: Where to now? Workshop, State, Society and

Governance in Melanesia Project and the Pacific Centre, College of Asia and the Pacific, Australian National University, Canberra, Friday, 5 May 2006, for further discussion of this particular issue.

39 Such stories have been relayed to the author in a number of informal settings.

40 See: Anita Butler, 'An Australian Government Perspective', paper presented at *Solomon Islands: Where to now? Workshop*, State, Society and Governance in Melanesia Project and the Pacific Centre, College of Asia and the Pacific, Australian National University, Canberra, Friday 5 May 2006 for a discussion of some of these and for a general overview of the official Australian view on then recent events in Solomons.

41 Peter Larmour and Manuhuia Barcham, *National Integrity Systems Pacific Overview Report 2004* (Blackburn SA: Transparency International, 2004), as found at http://www.transparency.org.au/documents/NISPACoverview04.pdf, accessed 10/5/2005.

42 As Russell Glenn, *Counter-Insurgency in a Test Tube: Analyzing the Success of the Regional Assistance Mission to Solomon Islands (RAMSI)* (Santa Monica CA: RAND, 2007), pxii points out the original pledge was for assistance up until 2008 at the least. This has since been talked of as at least a ten year commitment in Australian and New Zealand circles.

43 Dr John Roughan, '100 Days of RAMSI', State, Society and Governance in Melanesia Working Paper 03/3, as found at http://eprints.anu.edu.au/archive/00002780/, accessed on 20/9/2004 described how effective RAMSI was in a relatively short time, pointing out that the establishment of over 16 police posts in the provinces had been an important part of that success. Elsina Wainwright, 'How is RAMSI faring? Progress, Challenges and Lessons Learned', *ASPI Strategic Insights* (Canberra: Australian Strategic Police Institute, 2005), p3 also claims that RAMSI was an 'effective circuit breaker'. This has also been recognised by Report of the Pacific Islands Forum Eminent Persons Group, *A Review of the Regional Assistance Mission to Solomon Islands*, May 2005 (Suva: PIF, 2005), p8.

44 RAMSI, 'Law and Justice', as found at http://www.ramsi.org/node/268, accessed on 12/3/2008.

45 ANU Enterprise Pty Limited and ANU, *RAMSI Peoples Pilot Survey: Final Report* (Honiara, 2006).

46 See: ANU Enterprise Pty Limited and ANU, *RAMSI Peoples Pilot Survey: Final Report* (Honiara, 2006). Garth van den Heyer, 'Stabilising the Solomons: A regional response', *New Zealand International Review*, 32 (4), July/August 2007, p19.

47 AUSAID, *Solomon Islands: Transitional Country Strategy 2006–7* (Canberra: AUSAID, 2006), p7.

48 United Nations Development Programme, *Solomon Islands Peace and Conflict Development Analysis: Emerging Priorities in Preventing Future Conflict* (Honiara: UNDP, 2004) and Pacific Islands Forum, *Mission Helpem Fren: A Review of the Regional Assistance Mission to Solomon Islands Report of the Pacific Islands Forum Eminent Persons Group* (Suva: Pacific Islands Forum, 2005).

49 Mary Louise O'Callaghan, RAMSI: The Challenges Ahead, paper presented at Solomon Islands: Where to now? Workshop, State, Society and Governance in Melanesia Project and the Pacific Centre, College of Asia and the Pacific,

Australian National University, Canberra, Friday 5 May 2006, p1. The AUSAID report *Solomon Islands: Transitional Country Strategy 2006–7* (Canberra: AUSAID, 2006) points to the strengths of the economy as being gold and nickel deposits, palm oil plantations, logging and tuna fishing, but as most of these are unsustainable it also points to the need to attract private investment, to work on tourism and other more sustainable development projects. The ANU Enterprise Pty Limited and ANU, *RAMSI Peoples Survey Pilot 2006: Final Report* (Honiara, 2006), p6 on the other hand, highlights local concerns about the economic situation too with 63 per cent believing the economic situation would be worse or at best the same in two to three years.

50 ANU Enterprise Pty Limited and ANU, *RAMSI Peoples Survey Pilot 2006: Final Report* (Honiara, 2006), p7.

Chapter 5 Afghanistan and Iraq

1 The official name of the Bonn Agreement is the Agreement on Provisional Arrangements in Afghanistan Pending Re-establishment of Permanent Institutions. The agreement brought into being the AIA and invited an international security force to maintain security. UNSCR 1386 mandated ISAF to operate for an initial six-month period. International Resources Group et al., *Filling the Vacuum: Prerequisites to Security in Afghanistan* (Washington DC: International Resources Group, 2002), p12.

2 Steven Metz and Raymond Millen, 'Intervention, Stabilization and Transformation Operations: The Role of Landpower in the New Strategic Environment', *Parameters*, Spring 2005, pp41–51. Here in SSR, as pointed out in NATO, 'NATO support to Afghan National Army', as found at http://www.nato.int/issues/afghanistan/factsheets/ana-support.html, accessed 2/10/2007, the US has played the lead role in developing the Afghan National Army (ANA), with NATO providing Operational Mentor and Liaison Teams (OMLT) to help coordinate and 'de-conflict' relations between the ANA and ISAF, and to support training and deploy in an advisory role.

3 International Resources Group et al., *Filling the Vacuum: Prerequisites to Security in Afghanistan* (Washington DC: International Resources Group, 2002), p12.

4 Robert Perito, *Where is the Lone Ranger When We Need Him? America's Search for a Post-Conflict Stability Force* (Washington DC: USIP, 2004), p289.

5 William Maley, 'International force and political reconstruction: Cambodia, East Timor and Afghanistan', *Security Sector Reform and Post-Conflict Peacebuilding*, eds. Albrecht Schnabel and Hans-Georg Ehrhart (Tokyo: UN University Press, 2005), p297.

6 NATO, 'NATO in Afghanistan', as found at http://www.nato.int/issues/afghanistan/index.html, accessed on 1/10/2007.

7 Robert Perito, *Where is the Lone Ranger When We Need Him? America's Search for a Post-Conflict Stability Force* (Washington DC: USIP, 2004), p292.

8 Tonita Murray, 'Police-Building in Afghanistan: A Case Study of Civil Security Reform', *International Peacekeeping*, 14 (1), January 2007, p109.

9 NATO, 'Revised Operational Plan for NATO's expanding mission in Afghanistan', *NATO official website*, as found at http://www.nato.int/issues/afghanistan_ stage3/index.html, accessed 20 March 2006.

10 Michael Dziedzic and Colonel Michael Seidl, 'Provincial Reconstruction Teams and Military Relations with International and Non-Governmental Organisations in Afghanistan', *USIP Special Report*, n147, September 2005, p2.
11 Michael Dziedzic and Colonel Michael Seidl, 'Provincial Reconstruction Teams and Military Relations with International and Non-Governmental Organisations in Afghanistan', *USIP Special Report*, n147, September 2005, p4.
12 Robert Perito, *Where is the Lone Ranger When We Need Him? America's Search for a Post-Conflict Stability Force* (Washington: USIP, 2004), p290.
13 Tonita Murray, 'Police-Building in Afghanistan: A Case Study of Civil Security Reform', *International Peacekeeping*, 14 (1), January 2007, p111.
14 International Crisis Group, *Reforming Afghanistan's Police*, Asia Report #138, 30 August 2007, as found at http://www.crisisgroup.org/home/index.cfm?id=5052&l=1, accessed 10/10/2007, p6.
15 The London Conference on Afghanistan, *The Afghanistan Compact*, 31 January–1 February 2006, as found at http://www.unama-afg.org/news/_londonConf/_docs/06jan30-AfghanistanCompact-Final.pdf, accessed 12/10/2007, p2.
16 The London Conference on Afghanistan, *The Afghanistan Compact*, 31 January–1 February 2006, as found at http://www.unama-afg.org/news/_londonConf/_docs/06jan30-AfghanistanCompact-Final.pdf, accessed 12/10/2007, Annex I (Security) Afghan National and Border Police, p6.
17 Excerpts, Police Law, Article 5, Official Gazette no. 862, 22 September 2005. Translation provided by German Technical Cooperation (GTZ) as cited in International Crisis Group, *Reforming Afghanistan's Police*, Asia Report #138, 30 August 2007, as found at http://www.crisisgroup.org/home/index.cfm?id=5052&l=1, accessed 10/10/2007, p4.
18 NATO, 'NATO in Afghanistan: Reconstruction and Development (June 2007)', as found at http://www.nato.int/issues/afghanistan/factsheetsreconst_develop.html, accessed on 1/10/2007.
19 Tonita Murray, 'Police-Building in Afghanistan: A Case Study of Civil Security Reform', *International Peacekeeping*, 14 (1), January 2007, p108.
20 Human Rights Watch, *Afghanistan: Police Reconstruction Essential for the Protection of Human Rights*, ASA 11/003/2003, as found at http://web.amnesty.org/library/Index/ENGASA110032003, accessed 13/03/2006, p5.
21 Tonita Murray, 'Police-Building in Afghanistan: A Case Study of Civil Security Reform', *International Peacekeeping*, 14 (1), January 2007, p110.
22 Pam O'Toole, 'Afghan Police "Under-Equipped"', *BBC News Online*, 13 July 2007, as found at http://news.bbc.co.uk/1/hi/world/south_asia/6897051.stm, accessed 10/10/2007.
23 International Crisis Group, *Reforming Afghanistan's Police*, Asia Report #138, 30 August 2007, as found at http://www.crisisgroup.org/home/index.cfm?id=5052&l=1, accessed 10/10/2007, p10.
24 Mark Sedra, 'Security Sector Reform in Afghanistan: The Slide Towards Expediency', *International Peacekeeping*, 13 (1), March 2006, p95.
25 Thanks to discussions at the European Commission.
26 Leigh Toomey and J. Alexander Thier, 'Bridging Modernity and Tradition: Rule of Law and Search for Justice in Afghanistan', *USIPeace Briefing* October 2007, as found at http://www.usip.org/pubs/usipeace_briefings/2007/1031_afghanistan. html, accessed on 12/12/2007.

27 William Maley, 'International force and political reconstruction: Cambodia, East Timor and Afghanistan', *Security Sector Reform and Post-Conflict Peace-building*, eds. Albrecht Schnabel and Hans-Georg Ehrhart (Tokyo: UN University Press, 2005), p307.
28 'Securing Afghanistan's Future, Technical Annex: National Police and Law Enforcement', January 2004 as cited in International Crisis Group, *Reforming Afghanistan's Police*, Asia Report #138, 30 August 2007, as found at http://www.crisisgroup.org/home/index.cfm?id=5052&l=1, accessed 10/10/2007, p3
29 Thanks to discussions with NATO officials and personnel.
30 Tonita Murray, 'Police-Building in Afghanistan: A Case Study of Civil Security Reform', *International Peacekeeping*, 14 (1), January 2007, p123.
31 Human Rights Watch, *Afghanistan: Police Reconstruction Essential for the Protection of Human Rights*, ASA 11/003/2003, as found at http://web.amnesty.org/library/Index/ENGASA110032003, accessed 13/03/2006, pp21–2.
32 Tonita Murray, 'Police-Building in Afghanistan: A Case Study of Civil Security Reform', *International Peacekeeping*, 14 (1), January 2007, p113.
33 Tonita Murray, 'Police-Building in Afghanistan: A Case Study of Civil Security Reform', *International Peacekeeping*, 14 (1), January 2007, p111.
34 Thanks to discussions at NATO HQ, see also Judy Dempsey, 'Letter from Germany: Bickering between NATO and EU hampers training of Afghan police', *International Herald Tribune*, 23 August 2007, as found at http://www.iht.com/articles/2007/08/23/europe/letter.php, accessed 10/10/2007.
35 Touku Piiparinen, 'A Clash of Mindsets? An Insider's Account of Provincial Reconstruction Teams', *International Peacekeeping*, 14 (1), 2005, pp143–57.
36 Tonita Murray, 'Police-Building in Afghanistan: A Case Study of Civil Security Reform', *International Peacekeeping*, 14 (1), January 2007, p109.
37 Touku Piiparinen, 'A Clash of Mindsets? An Insider's Account of Provincial Reconstruction Teams', *International Peacekeeping*, 14 (1), 2005, pp143–57.
38 Thanks to discussions at the Liu Institute, University of British Columbia, October 2007.
39 International Crisis Group, *Reforming Afghanistan's Police*, Asia Report #138, 30 August 2007, as found at http://www.crisisgroup.org/home/index.cfm?id=5052&l=1, accessed 10/10/2007, Abstract and p15.
40 Mark Sedra, 'Security Sector Reform in Afghanistan: The Slide Towards Expediency', *International Peacekeeping*, 13 (1), March 2006, p97.
41 Mark Sedra, 'Security Sector Reform in Afghanistan: The Slide Towards Expediency', *International Peacekeeping*, 13 (1), March 2006, p98.
42 International Crisis Group, *Reforming Afghanistan's Police*, Asia Report #138, 30 August 2007, as found at http://www.crisisgroup.org/home/index.cfm?id=5052&l=1, accessed 10/10/2007, pp13–14.
43 Tonita Murray, 'Police-Building in Afghanistan: A Case Study of Civil Security Reform', *International Peacekeeping*, 14 (1), January 2007, pp108–24.
44 International Crisis Group, *Reforming Afghanistan's Police*, Asia Report #138, 30 August 2007, as found at http://www.crisisgroup.org/home/index.cfm?id=5052&l=1, accessed 10/10/2007, pp1–2.
45 Tonita Murray, 'Police-Building in Afghanistan: A Case Study of Civil Security Reform', *International Peacekeeping*, 14 (1), January 2007, p115 says there are 160–180 women in the police, about one-third of 1 per cent. She further asserts that most of them were recruited before the civil war and that recruitment has not been effectively handled.

46 Tonita Murray, 'Police-Building in Afghanistan: A Case Study of Civil Security Reform', *International Peacekeeping*, 14 (1), January 2007, pp116–17.
47 Jon Boone, 'Blackwater scandal revives reform efforts', *Financial Times*, Friday 2 November 2007, p6.
48 Graham Day and Christopher Freeman, 'Policekeeping is the Key: Rebuilding the Internal Security Architecture of Postwar Iraq', *International Affairs*, 2 (79), March 2003, pp299–313.
49 Rice cited in Steven Metz, *Learning from Iraq: Counterinsurgency in American Strategy* (Carlise PA: SSI US Army War College, January 2007), p21.
50 Robert Perito, 'US Police in Peace and Stability Operations', *USIP Special Report*, #191, August 2007, p9.
51 Thomas R. Mockaitis, *The Iraq War: Learning from the Past, Adapting to the Present and Planning for the Future* (Carlisle Barracks: SSI, February 2007), p34.
52 For further comment on a lack of strategic planning for SSR in Iraq in general see: Christoph Wilcke, 'A Hard Place: The United States and the Creation of a New Security Apparatus in Iraq', *Civil Wars*, 8 (2), June 2006, pp124–42.
53 Brooks cited in Robert Perito, *Where is the Lone Ranger When We Need Him? America's Search for a Post-Conflict Stability Force* (Washington DC: USIP, 2004), p314.
54 Steven Metz, *Learning from Iraq: Counterinsurgency in American Strategy* (Carlise PA: SSI US Army War College, January 2007), p26.
55 Robert Perito, 'US Police in Peace and Stability Operations', *USIP Special Report*, #191, August 2007, pp9–10. Perito also cites (p2) an American general who, in the face of looting, said 'I do not shoot people for stealing television sets and mattresses.'
56 International Crisis Group, *In their Own Words: Reading the Iraq Insurgency*, Middle East Report #50, June 2006, as found at http://www.crisisgroup.org/home/index.cfm?id=3953&l=1, accessed 10/2/2008.
57 BBC News, 'Iraqi Police Deaths Hit 12,000', 24 December 2006, *BBC News Online*, as found at http://news.bbc.co.uk/2/hi/middle_east/6208331.stm, accessed 14/4/2007. Discussion about the accuracy of such numbers can be found in Mathieu Deflem and Suzanne Sutphin, 'Policing Post-War Iraq: Insurgency , Civilian Police and the Reconstruction of Society', *Sociological Focus*, 39 (4), November 2006, pp273–6.
58 Steve Fainaru, 'For Police Recruits, Risk is Constant Companion', *The Washington Post*, September 2005, pA1.
59 Robert Perito, 'US Police in Peace and Stability Operations', *USIP Special Report*, #191, August 2007, p9.
60 Robert Perito, 'Reforming the Iraqi Interior Ministry, Police and Facilities Protection Service', *USIPeace Briefing*, February 2007, as found at http://www.usip.org/pubs/usipeace_briefings/2007/0207_iraqi_interior_ministry.html, accessed on 8/10/2007.
61 James A. Baker III and Lee Hamilton, co-chairs, *The Iraq Study Group Report: The Way Forward – A New Approach* (New York: Vintage Books, 2006), pp78–83.
62 As told by a departing Coalition division commander to Tony Pfaff, *Development and Reform of the Iraqi Police Forces* (Carlisle SA: Strategic Studies Institute US Army War College, 2007), as noted on p1.

63 Robert Perito, 'US Police in Peace and Stability Operations', *USIP Special Report*, #191, August 2007, pp10–11.
64 Robert Perito, 'Reforming the Iraqi Interior Ministry, Police and Facilities Protection Service', *USIPeace Briefing*, February 2007, as found at http://www.usip.org/pubs/usipeace_briefings/2007/0207_iraqi_interior_ministry.html, accessed on 8/10/2007.
65 Robert Perito, 'Provincial Reconstruction Teams in Iraq', *USIP Special Report*, #185, March 2007, p4.
66 Robert Perito, 'Provincial Reconstruction Teams in Iraq', *USIP Special Report*, #185, March 2007, p2.
67 Robert Perito, 'Embedded Provincial Reconstruction Teams', *USIPeace Briefing*, March 2008, as found at http://www.usip.org/pubs/usipeace_briefings/2008/0305_prt.html, accessed on 10/3/2008.
68 Thomas R. Pickering, 'Does the UN have a role in Iraq?', *Survival*, 50 (1), February–March 2008, p133.
69 Michael Moss and David Rhode, 'Law and Disorder: Training Gap', multimedia presentation from *The New York Times Online* link found at http://www.nytimes.com/2006/05/22/world/middleeast/22security.html?_r=1&oref=slogin, accessed 15/4/2008.
70 Robert Perito, 'US Police in Peace and Stability Operations', *USIP Special Report*, #191, August 2007, pp10–11.
71 Robert Perito, 'US Police in Peace and Stability Operations', *USIP Special Report*, #191, August 2007, pp10–11.
72 Michael O'Hanlon and Jason Campbell, *Tracking Variables of Reconstruction and Security in Post Saddam Iraq* (Washington DC: Brookings Institute, 2007), p11.
73 Robert Perito, 'Reforming the Iraqi Interior Ministry, Police and Facilities Protection Service', *USIPeace Briefing*, February 2007, as found at http://www.usip.org/pubs/usipeace_briefings/2007/0207_iraqi_interior_ministry.html, accessed on 8/10/2007.
74 Robert Perito, 'US Police in Peace and Stability Operations', *USIP Special Report*, #191, August 2007, pp10–11.
75 Michael Moss, 'How Iraq Police Reform Became a Casualty of War', *The New York Times Online*, 22 May 2006, as found at http://www.nytimes.com/2006/05/22/world/middleeast/22security.html?_r=1&oref=slogin, accessed 15/04/2008.
76 Recommendation 50 and 51 of the James A. Baker III and Lee H. Hamilton, co-chairs, *The Iraq Study Group Report: The Way Forward – A New Approach* (New York: Vintage Books, 2006), pp78–9.
77 Recommendations 55 and 56 of the James A. Baker III and Lee H. Hamilton, co-chairs, *The Iraq Study Group Report: The Way Forward – A New Approach* (New York: Vintage Books, 2006), p81.
78 Tony Pfaff, *Development and Reform of the Iraqi Police Forces* (Carlisle SA: Strategic Studies Institute US Army War College, 2007), p6.
79 Christoph Wilcke, 'A Hard Place: The United States and the Creation of a New Security Apparatus in Iraq', *Civil Wars*, 8 (2), June 2006, p127.
80 Robert Perito, 'Provincial Reconstruction Teams in Iraq', *USIP Special Report*, #185, March 2007, p5.
81 Robert Perito, 'Embedded Provincial Reconstruction Teams', *USIPeace Briefing*, March 2008, as found at http://www.usip.org/pubs/usipeace_briefings/2008/0305_prt.html, accessed on 10/3/2008.

82 Robert Perito, 'Provincial Reconstruction Teams in Iraq', *USIP Special Report*, #185, March 2007, p5.

83 Tony Pfaff, *Development and Reform of the Iraqi Police Forces* (Carlisle SA: Strategic Studies Institute US Army War College, 2007), p10. Similarly as Robert Perito, 'Provincial Reconstruction Teams in Iraq', *USIP Special Report*, #185, March 2007, p5 notes, although there is a position entitled 'Rule of Law Coordinator' or ROLC who is a Department of Justice official who leads the rule of law team and is essentially there to monitor the Iraqi judicial system and to promote access to justice, there remain problems with coordination within the system. The ROLC provides advice and some training, and undertakes visits to police and corrections, reporting on these visits to the US Embassy.

84 Christoph Wilcke, 'A Hard Place: The United States and the Creation of a New Security Apparatus in Iraq', *Civil Wars*, 8 (2), June 2006, p129.

85 Steve Negus, 'Iraq focuses on prosecution of security groups', *Financial Times*, Wednesday 31 October, p6.

86 See, for example, BBC News, 'US-Iraq contract in "disarray", 23 October 2007, *BBC News Online*, as found at http://news.bbc.co.uk/2/hi/americas/7057629.stm, accessed 7/4/2008.

87 Mathieu Deflem and Suzanne Sutphin, 'Policing Post-War Iraq: Insurgency, Civilian Police and the Reconstruction of Society', *Sociological Focus*, 39 (4), November 2006, p278.

88 Christoph Wilcke, 'A Hard Place: The United States and the Creation of a New Security Apparatus in Iraq', *Civil Wars*, 8 (2), June 2006, p133.

89 Human Rights Watch, *The New Iraq? Torture and Ill Treatment of Detainees in Iraqi Custody*, 17 (1), January 2005, as found at http://www.hrw.org/reports/2005/iraq0105/, accessed 10/3/2007.

90 James A. Baker III and Lee H. Hamilton, co-chairs, *The Iraq Study Group Report: The Way Forward – A New Approach* (New York: Vintage Books, 2006), p80.

91 James A. Baker III and Lee H. Hamilton, co-chairs, *The Iraq Study Group Report: The Way Forward – A New Approach* (New York: Vintage Books, 2006), p80.

92 Tony Pfaff, *Development and Reform of the Iraqi Police Forces* (Carlisle SA: Strategic Studies Institute US Army War College, 2007).

93 Tony Pfaff, *Development and Reform of the Iraqi Police Forces* (Carlisle SA: Strategic Studies Institute US Army War College, 2007), p27.

94 Michael Moss, 'How Iraq Police Reform Became a Casualty of War', *The New York Times Online*, 22 May 2006, as found at http://www.nytimes.com/2006/05/22/world/middleeast/22security.html?_ r=1&oref=slogin, accessed 15/04/2008.

95 Steven Farrell and Qais Mizher, 'Iraq Dismisses 1,300 After Basra Offensive', *The New York Times Online*, 14 April 2008, as found at http://www.nytimes.com/2008/04/14/world/middleeast/14iraq.html?ref=middleeast, accessed 15/4/2008.

96 Jim Randle, 'Study Finds Iraqi Police Ineffective in Combating Terrorism', 14 October 2007, *Voice of America Online*, as found at http://www.voanews.com/english/archive/2007-10/2007-10-14-voa18.cfm?CFID=201034466&CFTOKEN=52128407, accessed 15/2/2008. Support for the rebuilding of Iraq's security sector was expressed at the NATO Heads of State and Government meeting Istanbul, 28 June 2004.

97 See Alice Hills, 'Fear and Loathing in Falluja', *Armed Forces & Society*, 32 (4), July 2006, pp623–39 for a lucid discussion of how the US focus on military objectives has obscured the need to determine where power relations lie in the political and social realm, thereby acting to prevent the achievement of a sustainable peace.
98 Thomas R. Pickering, 'Does the UN have a role in Iraq?', *Survival*, 50 (1), February–March 2008, pp133–42.

Chapter 6 The New International Policing in Theory

1 Anthony Giddens, *The Nation State and Violence* (Cambridge: Polity, 1987), p121.
2 See: Samuel Huntington, *The Soldier and the State: The Theory and Politics of Civil-Military Relations* (Cambridge MA: Belknap Press, 1957) for an exposition on how soldiers are intended to be the state's agents of external force.
3 Michael Walzer, *Just and Unjust Wars: A Moral Argument with Historical Illustrations* (Harmondsworth: Penguin, 1977), Chapter Three 'The Rules of War' outlines some of these extraordinary principles.
4 See: Morris Janowitz, *The Professional Soldier: A Social and Political Portrait* (London: The Free Press of Glencoe Collier-Macmillan Ltd., 1960).
5 For example, the Chapter on 'Managing Risks' – particularly the section on 'Operational Risks' – in the US Department of Defence, *Quadrennial Defense Review Report*, 30 September 2001, as found at http://www.defenselink.mil/pubs/qdr2001.pdf, accessed on 13/10/2004, promotes an aggressive power projection model as the preferred method for lessening operational risks to US military personnel. This is further discussed in Mockaitis, Thomas R., *Civil Military Cooperation in Peace Operations: The Case of Kosovo* (Carlisle Barracks: SSI, October 2004), pp15–16.
6 Naomi J. Weinberger, 'Peacekeeping Operations in Lebanon', *Middle East Journal*, 37 (3), Summer 1983, p347.
7 For an analysis of the variety of force protection postures utilised by NATO member states in their deployments to Bosnia (which highlights the differences between and even within national units), see: Walter E. Kretchik, 'Armed for Peace: National Attitudes and Force Protection Posture in Bosnia 1995–2001', *Small Wars and Insurgencies*, 15 (2), Autumn 2004, pp20–37. Kretchik in particular picks up on a European-American divide, and notes how the British, in particular, believed in a minimal force protection posture (to the extent that they were labelled 'cavalier' (p25) by some Canadian interviewees!).
8 Clive Emsley, 'The Origins of the Modern Police', *History Today*, 49 (4), April 1999, pp1–8.
9 Emilio Santoro, 'Crime and punishment', *Political Concepts*, eds. Richard Bellamy and Richard Mason (Manchester: Manchester University Press, 2003), p70.
10 See: Chapter Two, John Kleinig, *The Ethics of Policing* (Cambridge: Cambridge University Press, 1996), for an outline of these kinds of models.
11 David Bayley, *Police for the Future* (Oxford: Oxford University Press, 1994), p30.

12 Seumas Miller, John Blackler and Andrew Alexander, *Police Ethics* (St Leonards NSW: Allen and Unwin, 1997), pp38–9.

13 David H. Bayley, 'The Contemporary Practices of Policing: A Comparative View', *Civilian Police and Multinational Peacekeeping – A Workshop Series: A Role for Democratic Policing*, National Institute of Justice (Washington DC: US Department of Justice, 1999), p3.

14 Mark Malan, 'Peacebuilding in Southern Africa: Police Reform in Mozambique and South Africa', *Peacebuilding and Police Reform*, eds. Tor Tanke Holm and Espen Barth Eide (London and Portland OR: Frank Cass, 2000), p181.

15 Stephen P. Lab, 'Introduction: Community Policing and Crime Prevention', *International Perspectives on Community Policing and Crime Prevention*, eds. Stephen P. Lab and Dilip K. Das (New Jersey: Prentice Hall, 2003), pxvi – he also says that 'trying to define community policing is like trying to hold mercury in your hand'.

16 Steven P. Lab, 'Community Policing as Crime Prevention in the US', *International Perspectives on Community Policing and Crime Prevention*, eds. Stephen P. Lab and Dilip K. Das (New Jersey: Prentice Hall, 2003), pp5–6.

17 This term 'constabulary' is, I believe, quite confusing and the use of the term 'formed police unit' or 'stability police unit' is less so. This is because the term 'constabulary' has been used in a number of different contexts over time and place, so it is avoided here and preference is given to the term FPU.

18 Robert Reiner, *The Politics of the Police* 2nd edn (New York and London: Harvester Wheatsheaf, 1992), p256.

19 Michael Dziedzic and Colonel Christine Stark, 'Bridging the Security Gap: The Role of the Center of Excellence for Stability Police Units (CoESPU) in Contemporary Peace Operations', *USIPeace Briefing*, June 2006, as found at http://www.usip.org/pubs/usipeace_briefings/2006/0616_coespu.html, accessed on 8/10/2007.

20 Michael Dziedzic and Colonel Christine Stark, 'Bridging the Security Gap: The Role of the Center of Excellence for Stability Police Units (CoESPU) in Contemporary Peace Operations', *USIPeace Briefing*, June 2006, as found at http://www.usip.org/pubs/usipeace_briefings/2006/0616_coespu.html, accessed on 8/10/2007.

21 Joshua G. Smith, Victoria K. Holt and William J. Durch, 'From Timor-Leste to Darfur: New Initiatives for Enhancing UN Civilian Policing Capacity', *The Henry L. Stimson Center Issue Brief*, August 2007, p3.

22 Michael Dziedzic and Colonel Christine Stark, 'Bridging the Security Gap: The Role of the Center of Excellence for Stability Police Units (CoESPU) in Contemporary Peace Operations', *USIPeace Briefing*, June 2006, as found at http://www.usip.org/pubs/usipeace_briefings/2006/0616_coespu.html, accessed on 8/10/2007.

23 Additional forces similar in nature to the French and Italian units outlined here include the Spanish Guardia Civil, the Netherlands' Royal Constabulary (Marechausee), the Argentinian National Gendarmerie, and even, according to Robert Perito, *Where is the Lone Ranger When We Need Him? America's Search for a Post-Conflict Stability Force* (Washington: USIP, 2004), p51 the Texas rangers.

24 The term 'para-military' can be associated with the illegitimate use of force by non-state actors. Indeed some scholars, such as Alice Hills, 'International Peace Support Operations and CIVPOL: Should There Be a Permanent Global Gendarmerie?', *International Peacekeeping*, 5 (3), Autumn 1998, pp35–7, argues that this term should not be used to refer to such constabulary forces. However, I find the term constabulary too broad and also open to misuse – para-military to me brings across the fact that these police forces are much more aligned to military models and therefore is more descriptive (as long as this term is recognised as being one that is associated with other possible connotations).
25 P.A.J. Waddington, 'Armed and Unarmed Policing', *Policing Across the World: Issues for the Twenty-First Century*, ed. R.I. Mawby (London: University College London Press, 1999), p154.
26 Thanks to discussions at King's College London, October 2007 for this point.
27 Thanks to discussions with officials at NATO and elsewhere for further information on this.
28 Robert Perito, *Where is the Lone Ranger When We Need Him? America's Search for a Post-Conflict Stability Force* (Washington: USIP, 2004), p39.
29 Robert Perito, *Where is the Lone Ranger When We Need Him? America's Search for a Post-Conflict Stability Force* (Washington: USIP, 2004), p5.
30 Janet B.L. Chan with Chris Devery and Sally Doran, *Fair Cop: Learning the Art of Policing* (Toronto: University of Toronto Press, 2003), p36.
31 Robert Reiner, *The Politics of the Police*, 2nd edn (Hertfordshire: Harvester Wheatsheaf, 1992), p111.
32 David H. Bayley, *Democratizing the Police Abroad: What to Do and How to Do It* (Washington DC: US Department of Justice, 2001), p54.
33 See the work of Bruce Russett, John Mueller, Robert Kaplan Samuel Huntington, respectively.
34 Mary Kaldor, *New and Old Wars: Organized Violence in a Global Era* (Cambridge: Polity Press, 1999).
35 See: International Commission on Intervention and State Sovereignty, *The Responsibility to Protect* (Ottawa: International Development Research Centre, 2001).
36 Nicholas Wheeler, *Saving Strangers: Humanitarian Intervention in International Society* (Oxford: Oxford University Press, 2000).
37 Francis Fukuyama, *The End of History and the Last Man* (New York: Free Press, 1992).
38 Recent decades have seen a number of works dedicated to the topic of 'changing conceptions of security as noted in Daniel Baldwin, 'The Concept of Security', *Review of International Studies*, 23 (1), 1997, pp5–26, and Steve Smith, 'The Increasing Insecurity of Security Studies: Conceptualising Security in the Last Twenty Years', *Contemporary Security Policy*, 20 (3), December 1999. Throughout the 1990s in particular a number of scholars sought to challenge traditional security paradigms that focused on state-centred and politico-military notions of security. Scholars therefore suggested that it was time to include 'freedom from want' alongside more traditional foci on 'freedom from fear' as legitimate security concerns. Here, for example, security studies by author Ken Booth, 'Security as Emancipation', *Review of International Studies*,

17, 1991, pp313–26, suggested that security should be reconceptualised as an issue of 'emancipation' – the freedom of individuals (who were to be the 'referent' for security rather than the state) to be able to function in all aspects of human life was thus in itself the crux of security and insecurity. Other scholars such as Ronnie D. Lipschutz, ed. *On Security* (New York: Columbia University Press, 1995) sought to ask deeper questions both about this nature of 'security' and 'insecurity', and about the effects of labelling such issues as 'security'.

39 Morris Janowitz, *The Professional Soldier: A Social and Political Portrait* (London: The Free Press of Glencoe Collier-Macmillan Ltd. 1960), pp418–19. Gustav Daniker, *The Guardian Soldier: On the Nature and Use of Future Armed Forces*, Research Paper #36, UNIDIR (New York and Geneva: United Nations, 1995).

40 Morris Janowitz, *The Professional Soldier: A Social and Political Portrait* (London: The Free Press of Glencoe Collier-Macmillan Ltd. 1960), p418.

41 See: Michael C. Williams, *Civil-Military Relations and Peacekeeping*, Adelphi Paper No. 321 (London: International Institute for Strategic Studies, 1998).

42 Alan Vick et al., *Preparing the US Air Force for Military Operations other than War* (Santa Monica CA: RAND, 1997), p2. Indeed, in one scenario that the NZDF was heavily involved in, that is enforcing the peace process on Bougainville, the NZDF contingent was *unarmed* – confusing the military-maximum (armed) force and police-minimum (preferably unarmed) force rules of thumb.

43 John Allen Williams, 'The Postmodern Military Reconsidered', *The Postmodern Military: Armed Forces after the Cold War*, eds. Charles C. Moskos et al. (Oxford: Oxford University Press, 2000), p275.

44 For work on the increasing civilianisation of armed forces see the work of scholars such as Christopher Dandeker, such as his Keynote Paper, 'The military and social change in the post-Cold War era: the need for a strategic approach to personnel issues in the armed forces', *Proceedings of the 42nd Annual Conference of the International Military Testing Association*, Edinburgh 2002, as found at http://www.internationalmta.org/2000/00IMTAproceedings.pdf, accessed on 13/10/2004.

45 Adam Roberts, 'Law and the Use of Force After Iraq', *Survival*, 45 (2), Summer 2003, p34, states that 'the numerous crises of the post-Cold War world have exposed a curious and little-noted problem: that the very success of international law may itself have contributed, at least occasionally, to the perceived necessity to use force'.

46 Michael Ignatieff, *Virtual War: Kosovo and Beyond* (New York: Metropolitan Books, 2000), pp100–1 highlights the intense involvement of military lawyers in all phases of the Kosovo campaign.

47 Peter Andreas and Richard Price, 'From War-fighting to Crime Fighting: Transforming the American National Security State', *International Studies Review*, 3 (3), Fall 2001, p51.

48 Sir Michael Howard cited in Tania Branigan, 'Al-Qaeda is winning war Allies warned', 31 October 2001, *The Guardian*, as found at http://www.guardian.co.uk/waronterror/story/0,1361,583789,00.html, accessed on 11/10/2004, believed that a 'terrible and irreversible' mistake had been made by declaring a war on terror as it granted the terrorists a status they did not deserve. Howard thought that a police operation under UN auspices with international court involvement would have been the best strategy.

49 See: Adam Roberts, 'Law and the Use of Force After Iraq', *Survival*, 45 (2), Summer 2003, pp31–56.

50 Ray Takeyh and Nikolas Gvosdev, 'Do Terrorist Networks Need a Home?', *The Washington Quarterly*, 25 (3), Summer 2002, and Ken Menkhaus, *Somalia: State Collapse and the Threat of Terrorism*, Adelphi Paper 364 (Oxford: IISS, 2004), Beth K. Greener-Barcham and Manuhuia Barcham, 'Terrorism in the South Pacific? Thinking Critically About Approaches to Security in the Region', *Australian Journal of International Affairs*, 60 (1), March 2006, pp67–82.

51 Thomas R. Mockaitis, *The Iraq War: Learning from the Past, Adapting to the Present and Planning for the Future* (Carlisle Barracks: SSI, February 2007), p12.

52 General David Petraeus as cited in 'Brains not Bullets', *The Economist*, 29 October 2007, p16.

53 This notion of security-development nexus is referred to in literature on human security and human development and indeed there is much concern about the securitisation of development goals. There has also been mention of this nexus in policing literature too. Here Otwin Marenin's, *Restoring Policing Systems in Conflict Torn Nations: Process, Problems, Prospects* (Geneva: Geneva Centre for the Democratic Control of Armed Forces, 2005), p2, suggests that 'police reform projects have been influenced by two parallel but diverse discourses, policy streams and contexts at the international, transnational, and regional levels: one might be called the discovery of the development-security nexus, leading, in turn, to policy discussions on the need by the global community and transnational actors to be involved in peace-building, the promotion of human security broadly defined, and security sector reform (SSR); the second policy stream has centred on and responded to developments in the field of police and policing, including the emergence of international democratic policing regimes, and general approaches to reform and innovation of policing organizations and policing and public security systems'.

54 Oliver P. Richmond, 'UN Peace Operations and the Dilemmas of the Peacebuilding Consensus', *International Peacekeeping*, 11 (1), Spring 2004, pp83–101.

55 Roland Paris, *At War's End: Building Peace After Civil Conflict* (Cambridge: Cambridge University Press, 2004), p11.

56 Peter Andreas and Richard Price, 'From War-fighting to Crime Fighting: Transforming the American National Security State', *International Studies Review*, 3 (3), Fall 2001, p32.

57 Michael Hardt and Antonio Negri, *Empire* (London, Cambridge: Harvard University Press, 2000), p189.

58 Mitchell Dean, 'Military Intervention as "Police Action"', *The New Police Science: The Police Power in Domestic and International Governance*, eds. Markus D. Dubber and Mariana Valverde (Stanford CA: Stanford University Press, 2006), p201.

59 Otwin Marenin, *Restoring Policing Systems in Conflict Torn Nations: Process, Problems, Prospects* (Geneva: Geneva Centre for the Democratic Control of Armed Forces, 2005), p39.

60 Thanks to discussions at the Liu Institute, University of British Columbia, October 2007 for teasing out this point.

61 Skolnick (1972) p4 cited in Robert Reiner, *The Politics of the Police*, 2nd edn (New York and London: Harvester Wheatsheaf, 1992), p2.
62 Jacques Rancière, *Disagreement: Politics and Philosophy* [Translated by Julie Rose] (Minneapolis: University of Minnesota Press, 1999), p28.
63 Kimberley C. Field and Robert M. Perito, 'Creating a Force for Peace Operations: Ensuring Stability with Justice', *Parameters*, Winter 2002–3, p79.
64 Jeff Penrose, 'Peace Support Operations and Policing: An Explosive Human Skills Mix', *The Human in Command: Peace Support Operations*, eds. Peter Essens et al. (Breda: KMA Royal Netherlands Academy, 2001), p120.
65 See: John McFarlane and William Maley, 'Civilian police in UN peace operations: Some lessons from recent Australian experience', *United Nations Peacekeeping Operations: Ad Hoc Missions, Permanent Engagement*, eds. Ramesh Thakur and Albrecht Schnabel (Tokyo: United Nations University Press, 2001). John McFarlane further expanded upon these points in a discussion with the author.
66 This point was made by a number of NATO personnel and officials.
67 Renata Dwan, 'Civilian tasks and capabilities in EU operations', *A Human Security Doctrine for Europe: Project, Principles, Practicalities*, eds. Marlies Glasius and Mary Kaldor (London and New York: Routledge, 2006), p266.
68 Eirinn Mobekk, *Identifying Lessons in United Nations International Policing Missions* (Geneva: Geneva Centre for the Democratic Control of the Armed Forces, 2005), p3.
69 Wesley Clark, *Waging Modern War: Bosnia, Kosovo and the Future of Combat* (New York: Public Affairs, 2001), p458.
70 Don Kraus, 'The Need for UN Police', *Foreign Policy in Focus*, 5 June 2003, as found at http://www.globalpolicy.org/security/peacekpg/reform/2003/0605 police.htm, accessed on 01/02/2005.
71 Further, traditional demarcations for policing versus military roles are clearly laid out within older official documents that outline procedures for international deployments. The 1979 UN *Code of Conduct for Law Enforcement Officials*, Commentary A Article 3, p2, for example, emphasises that 'the use of force by law enforcement officials should be exceptional; while it implies that law enforcement officials may be authorized to use force as is reasonably necessary under the circumstances for the prevention of crime or in effecting or assisting in the lawful arrest of offenders or suspected offenders, no force going beyond that may be used'. The *Code*, Commentary C Article 3, p2, also argues that 'the use of firearms is to be considered an extreme measure. Every effort should be made to exclude the use of firearms'.
72 David Bayley, *Police for the Future* (Oxford: Oxford University Press, 1994), p9.
73 Chuck Call and Michael Barnett, 'Looking for a Few Good Cops: Peacekeeping, Peacebuilding and CIVPOL', *Peacebuilding and Police Reform*, eds. Tor Tanke Holm and Espen Barth Eide (London and Portland OR: Frank Cass, 2000), p43.
74 International Crisis Group, *Reforming Afghanistan's Police*, Asia Report #138, 30 August 2007, as found at http://www.crisisgroup.org/home/index.cfm?id=5052&l=1, accessed 10/10/2007.
75 For a critical view on this, and one that will be referred to in the conclusion of this book, see Oliver P. Richmond, 'UN Peace Operations and the Dilemmas

of the Peacebuilding Consensus', *International Peacekeeping*, 11 (1), Spring 2004, pp83–101.

76 Elsina Wainwright (with contributions from John McFarlane), 'Police Join the Front Line: Building Australia's International Policing Capability', *ASPI Strategic Insights* (Canberra: Australian Strategic Policy Institute, 2004), p3.

Chapter 7 The New International Policing

1 Peter Andreas and Ethan Nadelmann, *Policing the Globe: Criminalization and Crime Control in International Relations* (Oxford: Oxford University Press, 2006), p13.

2 Kimberley C. Field and Robert M. Perito, 'Creating a Force for Peace Operations: Ensuring Stability with Justice', *Parameters*, Winter 2002–3, p79.

3 'UN Police Presentation', Third Meeting of the International Policing Advisory Council, 30–31 August 2007, National Museum of Australia, Canberra.

4 S. Jones, et al., *Establishing Law and Order After Conflict* (Washington DC: The RAND Corporation, 2005), pxv.

5 Morris Janowitz, *The Professional Soldier: A Social and Political Portrait* (London: The Free Press of Glencoe Collier-Macmillan Ltd. 1960), p418.

6 Michael Berkow, 'Practical Issues in Providing Policing Assistance Abroad', *Civilian Police and Multinational Peacekeeping – A Workshop Series: A Role for Democratic Policing*, National Institute of Justice (Washington DC: US Department of Justice, 1999), p15.

7 Annika S. Hansen, *From Congo to Kosovo: Civilian Police in Peace Operations*, Adelphi Paper 343 (Oxford: IISS, 2002), pp70–2. Alice Hills, 'The Inherent Limits of Military Forces in Policing Peace Operations', *International Peacekeeping*, 8 (3), Autumn 2001, p92f.

8 S. Jones, et al., *Establishing Law and Order After Conflict* (Washington DC: The RAND Corporation, 2005), pxii.

9 Eirinn Mobekk, *Identifying Lessons in United Nations International Policing Missions* (Geneva: Geneva Centre for the Democratic Control of the Armed Forces, 2005), pp19–27.

10 Chuck Call and Michael Barnett, 'Looking for a Few Good Cops: Peacekeeping, Peacebuilding and CIVPOL', *Peacebuilding and Police Reform*, eds. Tor Tanke Holm and Espen Barth Eide (London and Portland OR: Frank Cass, 2000), p51.

11 Annika S. Hansen, *From Congo to Kosovo: Civilian Police in Peace Operations*, Adelphi Paper 343 (Oxford: IISS, 2002), p58.

12 Even here with the case of DynCorp, though, which theoretically has stronger accountability mechanisms at work, Antony Barnett and Solomon Hughes, 'British Firm Accused in UN "Sex Scandal": International Police in Bosnia Face Prostitution Claims', as found at http://www.globalpolicy.org/socecon/inequal/0729un.htm, accessed on 01/02/2005, indicate how Kathryn Bolkovac, an American policewoman, was hired by DynCorp for a UN post aimed at investigating sexual abuse and forced prostitution in Bosnia. She claims to have been fired after having amassed evidence that UN police were taking part in the trafficking of young women from Eastern Europe as sex slaves. Bolkovac claims she tried to report this to her supervisors who 'didn't want to know'.

Bolkovac sued DynCorp for unfair dismissal – following a previous suit by air mechanic Ben Johnston who says he was sacked for uncovering evidence that DynCorp employees were involved in sex slavery and selling arms.

13 James Dobbin, 'New directions for transatlantic security cooperation', *Survival*, 47 (4), Winter 2005–6, p47.

14 Annika S. Hansen, *From Congo to Kosovo: Civilian Police in Peace Operations*, Adelphi Paper 343 (Oxford: IISS, 2002), p19.

15 A. Kaplan, 'Capacity Building: shifting the paradigms of practice', *Development in Practice*, 10 (3–4), 2000, pp517–26.

16 Lynn M. Thomas, 'Peace Operations and the Need to Prioritize the Rule of Law through Legal System Reform: Lessons from Somalia and Bosnia', *Small Wars and Insurgencies*, 15 (2), Autumn 2004, pp70–6. Andreas Heinemann-Gruder and Igor Grebenschikov, 'Security Governance by Internationals: The Case of Kosovo', *International Peacekeeping*, 13 (1), March 2006, p56.

17 Eirinn Mobekk, *Identifying Lessons in United Nations International Policing Missions* (Geneva: Geneva Centre for the Democratic Control of the Armed Forces, 2005), p9.

18 Renata Dwan, 'Civilian tasks and capabilities in EU operations', *A Human Security Doctrine for Europe: Project, Principles, Practicalities*, eds. Marlies Glasius and Mary Kaldor (London and New York: Routledge, 2006), p272.

19 Renata Dwan, 'Civilian tasks and capabilities in EU operations', *A Human Security Doctrine for Europe: Project, Principles, Practicalities*, eds. Marlies Glasius and Mary Kaldor (London and New York: Routledge, 2006), p272.

20 Annika S. Hansen, *From Congo to Kosovo: Civilian Police in Peace Operations*, Adelphi Paper 343 (Oxford: IISS, 2002), p30.

21 Eirinn Mobekk, *Identifying Lessons in United Nations International Policing Missions* (Geneva: Geneva Centre for the Democratic Control of the Armed Forces, 2005), p10.

22 Tarcisius Kabutaulaka, 'Crowded Stage: Actors, Actions and Issues', *Securing a Peaceful Pacific*, eds. John Henderson and Greg Watson (Christchurch: University of Canterbury Press, 2005), p409.

23 Andrew Goldsmith and Colleen Lewis, 'Introduction', *Civilian Oversight of Policing: Governance, Democracy and Human Rights*, eds. Andrew J. Goldsmith and Colleen Lewis (Oxford and Portland OR: Hart Publishing, 2000), p9.

24 Mathieu Deflem and Suzanne Sutphin, 'Policing Post-War Iraq: Insurgency, Civilian Police and the Reconstruction of Society', *Sociological Focus*, 39 (4), November 2006, p279.

25 Peter Andreas and Ethan Nadelmann, *Policing the Globe: Criminalization and Crime Control in International Relations* (Oxford: Oxford University Press, 2006), pp252–3.

26 Ron Levi and John Hagan, 'International Police', *The New Police Science: The Police Power in Domestic and International Governance*, eds. Markus D. Dubber and Mariana Valverde (Stanford CA: Stanford University Press, 2006), p233.

27 Oliver P. Richmond, 'UN Peace Operations and the Dilemmas of the Peacebuilding Consensus', *International Peacekeeping*, 11 (1), Spring 2004, p90 and p95.

28 The Enhanced Cooperation Program (ECP) was mooted in 2003 and was originally intended to place up to 260 Australian police officers to executive

policing positions within the Royal Papua New Guinea Constabulary (RPNGC) to have direct involvement in day-to-day policing with shared command responsibilities, and to have certain immunities. This final point proved the undoing of the ECP as the PNG court found such powers unconstitutional and the project was quickly reversed, leaving a handful of police advisors only in place. This situation underlined a perceived unfairness in the negotiations between the two countries, with numerous rumours of neo-colonialism on behalf of the Australians as well as consternation over where money was being spent, as well as the fact that centralised police efforts will find it difficult to make headway in such a diverse, rurally-based country where authority is often much more local. Papua New Guinea has been beset by major law and order problems in recent years; both in terms of criminal elements and in terms of corruption and disciplinary problems within the RPNGC. Indeed Human Rights Watch, *Making their Own Rules: Police Beatings, Rape and Torture of Children in Papua New Guinea* (New York: Human Rights Watch, 2005), documents numerous problems within the RPNGC. Here even the PNG police minister, Bire Kimisopa (cited in the *Papua New Guinea Post Courier*, 26 July 2004 as cited in Alpers, Philip, *Gun Violence, Crime and Politics in the Southern Highlands, Community Interviews and a Guide to Military-Style Small Arms in Papua New Guinea*, Background Paper Small Arms Survey (Geneva: Small Arms Survey, 2004), p6, had described the RPNGC as:

> incapacitated left, right and centre....plagued by inadequate funding with very little attention paid to any structural reform in order to meet the needs of all stakeholders of our community. Our police force is infested with corruption, collusion and incompetence....its inability to maintain an honourable record on prosecutions has rendered the operations of the PNG police totally inoperable and dysfunctional.

Moreover the ECP was to include the placement of a large number of economic, finance, planning, justice and security officials to help shore up other arms of government. The budget as a whole – encompassing law and order reform, judicial and prison system reform, financial governance and border and airport security efforts – came to almost $1 billion. The duration of the package was to be for at least a five-year term. Critics were rife, with Charles Hawksley, 'The Enhanced Cooperation Programme between Australia and PNG: the intervention you have when you're not having an intervention'?, paper presented to the First Oceanic International Studies Conference, 14–16 July 2004, Australian National University, Canberra, p3, calling the ECP an ongoing part of Australia's 'colossal self-interest...[which] arguably undermine[s] PNG's capacity to be an effective sovereign state'. Problems also stemmed from the disparity between the amount of monies set aside for the wages, accommodation, logistics and operational costs of the AFP ($745 million) versus the arguably paltry amount of money set aside for the Royal Papua New Guinean Constabulary (RPNGC) – a mere $55 million in comparison.

29 Thanks to discussions at UN Police Division, November 2007.

30 International Policing Advisory Council, *Summary Meeting Report of the Third Meeting of the International Policing Advisory Council (IPAC)*, Canberra, Australia, 30–31 August 2007, p12.

31 John Kleinig, *The Ethics of Policing* (Cambridge: Cambridge University Press, 1996), p237.
32 Peter Andreas and Ethan Nadelmann, *Policing the Globe: Criminalization and Crime Control in International Relations* (Oxford: Oxford University Press, 2006), p8.
33 David H. Bayley, *Democratizing the Police Abroad: What to Do and How to Do It* (Washington DC: US Department of Justice, 2001), pp13–15.
34 Otwin Marenin, *Restoring Policing Systems in Conflict Torn Nations: Process, Problems, Prospects* (Geneva: Geneva Centre for the Democratic Control of Armed Forces, 2005), pp37–8 and p60.
35 Roland Paris, 'International Peacebuilding and the "Mission Civilisatrice"', *Review of International Studies*, 28 (4), 2002, pp642–5. Andreas Andersson, 'Democracies and UN Peacekeeping Operations, 1990–1996', *International Peacekeeping*, 7 (2), Summer 2000, p17, and others also argue that peacekeeping is driven by the desire to spread liberal democracy.
36 Chuck Call and Michael Barnett, 'Looking for a Few Good Cops: Peacekeeping, Peacebuilding and CIVPOL', *Peacebuilding and Police Reform*, eds. Tor Tanke Holm and Espen Barth Eide (London and Portland OR: Frank Cass, 2000), p58.
37 See: Martha Finnemore, *The Purpose of Intervention; Changing Beliefs about the Use of Force* (Ithaca and London: Cornell University Press, 2003). Nicholas Wheeler, *Saving Strangers; Humanitarian Intervention in International Society* (Oxford: Oxford University Press, 2000). International Commission on Intervention and State Sovereignty, *The Responsibility to Protect* (Ottawa: International Development Research Centre, 2001).
38 The Convention on the Privileges and Immunities of the United Nations, 1 U.N.T.S. 15, February 1946, section 23 relates to the issue of immunity in UN missions is currently one whereby UNPOL personnel are generally not subject to local laws although these immunities can be withdrawn by the UN Secretary General, and officers are also subject to the laws of their own country.
39 Stephen D. Krasner, *Sovereignty: Organized Hypocrisy* (Princeton NJ: Princeton University Press, 1999).
40 Emilio Santoro, 'Crime and punishment', *Political Concepts*, eds. Richard Bellamy and Richard Mason (Manchester: Manchester University Press, 2003), p72. For the term 'risk creating agents', Santoro cites Hazel Kemshall, *Reviewing Risk: A Review of Research on the Assessment Management of Risk and Dangerousness: Implications for Policy and Practice in the Probation Service* (Croydon, Report for the Home Office, Research and Statistics Directorate, 1996), p35. Similarly Janet B.L. Chan with Chris Devery and Sally Doran, *Fair Cop: Learning the Art of Policing* (Toronto: University of Toronto Press, 2003), p269, also suggests that recent changes within policing institutions have seen the rise of risk management, particularly in an era of the increasing transnational nature of crime and poverty.
41 Otwin Marenin, *Restoring Policing Systems in Conflict Torn Nations: Process, Problems, Prospects* (Geneva: Geneva Centre for the Democratic Control of Armed Forces, 2005), p4.
42 Christopher Coker, *Globalisation and Insecurity in the Twenty-First Century: NATO and the Management of Risk*, Adelphi Paper 345 (Oxford: IISS, 2002), pp62–3.

43 Robert D. Kaplan, 'The Coming Anarchy', *Atlantic Monthly*, February 1994, as found at http://www.theatlantic.com/doc/199402/anarchy, accessed 8/4/2008, and Robert Cooper, *The Postmodern State and World Order* (London: Demos, 2000).
44 Eşref Aksu, *The United Nations, Intra-state Peacekeeping and Normative Change* (Manchester, New York: Manchester University Press, 2003), p92.
45 For interesting recent article on issue of the division over such norms of intervention seen through an exploration of the work of Kant and Pufendorf see: Richard Devetak, 'Between Kant and Pufendorf: humanitarian interventionism, statist anti-cosmopolitanism and critical international theory', *Review of International Studies*, 23, 2007, pp151–74.
46 Annika S. Hansen and Sharon Wihata, *The Transition to a Just Order-Establishing Local Ownership after Conflict: A Policy Report* (Stockholm: Folke Bernadotte Academy, 2007), pxvi.
47 Jarat Chopra and Tanja Hohe, 'Participatory Peacebuilding', *Building Sustainable Peace*, eds. Tom Keating and W. Andy Knight (Saskatchewan: UN University Press and The University of Alberta Press, 2004), p243.
48 Otwin Marenin, *Restoring Policing Systems in Conflict Torn Nations: Process, Problems, Prospects* (Geneva: Geneva Centre for the Democratic Control of Armed Forces, 2005), p58.
49 Oliver P. Richmond, 'UN Peace Operations and the Dilemmas of the Peacebuilding Consensus', *International Peacekeeping*, 11 (1), Spring 2004, p92.
50 Charles Call, *Challenges in Police Reform: Promoting Effectiveness and Accountability*, IPA Policy Report, 2003, as found at http://www.justiceinitiative.org/db/resource2?res_id=101709, accessed 8/4/2008, p4.
51 Neclâ Tschirgi, *Post-Conflict Peacebuilding Revisited: Achievements, Limitations, Challenges* (New York: International Peace Academy, 2004), pii.
52 Oliver P. Richmond, 'UN Peace Operations and the Dilemmas of the Peacebuilding Consensus', *International Peacekeeping*, 11 (1), Spring 2004, p90 and p92.
53 Danilo Zolo, *Cosmopolis: Prospects for World Government* (Cambridge: Polity Press, 1997), pp14–15.
54 Christopher Murphy, 'The Cart Before the Horse: Community Oriented Versus Professional Models of International Police Reform', *Crafting Transnational Policing: Police Capacity-Building and Global Policing Reform*, eds. Andrew Goldsmith and James Sheptycki (Oxford and Portland OR: Hart Publishing, 2007), p258. Murphy also shows how similar arguments are to be found in Neild (2001) and Mendes (1999).
55 William Lewis and Edward Marks, 'Overview', *Civilian Police and Multinational Peacekeeping – A Workshop Series: A Role for Democratic Policing*, National Institute of Justice (Washington DC: US Department of Justice, 1999), pp1–2.

Bibliography

Adebajo, Adekeye, 'West Africa's Tragic Twins; Building Peace in Liberia and Sierra Leone', *Building Sustainable Peace*, eds. Tom Keating and W. Andy Knight (Saskatchewan: UN University Press and The University of Alberta Press, 2004).

Ahlquist, Leif et al., 'The Command and Control of UN Peace Support Operations', *The Human in Command: Peace Support Operations*, eds. Peter Essens et al. (Breda: KMA Royal Netherlands Academy, 2001).

Ahmed, Salman, Paul Keating and Ugo Solinas, 'Shaping the future of UN peace operations: is there a doctrine in the house?' *Cambridge Review of International Affairs*, 20 (1), 2007, pp11–28.

Ajello, Aldo and Patrick Wittman, 'Mozambique', *The UN Security Council: From the Cold War to the 21st Century*, ed. David Malone (Boulder CO and London: Lynne Reinner, 2004).

Aksu, Eşref, *The United Nations, Intra-state Peacekeeping and Normative Change* (Manchester and New York: Manchester University Press, 2003).

Ali Mahmoud, 'UN Operation in Mozambique (ONUMOZ)', *The Role and Functions of Civilian Police in United Nation's Peace-keeping Operations: Debriefing and Lessons*, Report and Recommendations of the International Conference Singapore December 1995 (London: Kluwer Law International, 1995).

Allen, Matthew, 'Dissenting Voices: Local Perspectives on the Regional Assistance Mission to Solomon Islands', *Pacific Economic Bulletin*, 21 (2), 2005, pp56–71.

Alpers, Philip, *Gun Violence, Crime and Politics in the Southern Highlands, Community Interviews and a Guide to Military-Style Small Arms in Papua New Guinea, Background Paper Small Arms Survey* (Geneva: Small Arms Survey, 2004).

Anderson, Malcolm, *Policing the World: Interpol and the Politics of International Police Cooperation* (Oxford: Clarendon Press, 1989).

Anderson, Mary B. and Lara Olsen with assistance from Kristin Doughty, *Confronting War: Critical Lessons for Peace Practitioners* (Cambridge MA: Collaborative for Development Action, 2003).

Andersson, Andreas, 'Democracies and UN Peacekeeping Operations, 1990–1996', *International Peacekeeping*, 7 (2), (Summer, 2000).

Andreas, Peter and Ethan Nadelmann, *Policing the Globe: Criminalization and Crime Control in International Relations* (Oxford: Oxford University Press, 2006).

Andreas, Peter and Richard Price, 'From War-fighting to Crime Fighting: Transforming the American National Security State', *International Studies Review*, 3 (3), Fall 2001, pp31–52.

Ayling, S. and S. Guise, 'UNTAC and INTERFET – A Comparative Analysis', *Australian Defence Force Journal*, No. 150, Sept/Oct 2001, pp47–56.

Bailey, Michael, Robert Maguire and J. O'Neil and G. Pouliot, 'Haiti: Military-Police Partnership for Public Security', *Policing the New World Disorder: Peace Operations and Public Security* eds. Robert B. Oakley et al. (Washington DC: National Defense University Press, 1998).

Baker, James A. III and Lee H. Hamilton, co-chairs, *The Iraq Study Group Report: The Way Forward – A New Approach* (New York: Vintage Books, 2006).

Baldwin, Daniel, 'The Concept of Security', *Review of International Studies*, 23 (1), 1997, pp5–26.
Barry, Robert, *The OSCE: A Forgotten Transatlantic Security Organisation*, BASIC Research Report July 2002 (London: British American Security Information Council, 2002).
Bayley, David H., 'The Police and Political Development in Europe', *The Formation of National States in Europe*, ed. C. Tilly (Princeton NJ: Princeton University Press, 1975).
——, *Police for the Future* (Oxford: Oxford University Press, 1994).
——, 'A Foreign Policy for Democratic Policing', *Policing and Society*, 5 (2), 1995, pp79–94.
——, 'The Contemporary Practices of Policing: A Comparative View', *Civilian Police and Multinational Peacekeeping – A Workshop Series: A Role for Democratic Policing*, National Institute of Justice (Washington DC: US Department of Justice, 1997).
——, 'Policing: The World Stage', *Policing Across the World: Issues for the Twenty-First Century*, ed. R.I. Mawby (London: University College London Press, 1999).
——, *Democratizing the Police Abroad: What to Do and How to Do It* (Washington DC: US Department of Justice, 2001).
Beck, Ulrich, *World Risk Society* (Cambridge: Polity Press, 1999).
——, 'The Terrorist Threat: World Risk Society Revisited', *Theory, Culture and Society*, 19 (4), 2002, pp39–55.
Benyon, J., 'Policing the European Union: the changing basis of cooperation on law enforcement', *International Affairs*, 70 (3), 1994, pp417–517.
Berdal, Mats, *European Security After the Cold War*, Adelphi Paper 284 (London: IISS, 1994).
——, 'United Nations Peacekeeping in the Former Yugoslavia', *Beyond Traditional Peacekeeping*, eds. Donald C.F. Daniel and Bradd C. Hayes (London: Macmillan, 1995).
Berkow, Michael, 'Practical Issues in Providing Policing Assistance Abroad', *Civilian Police and Multinational Peacekeeping – A Workshop Series: A Role for Democratic Policing*, National Institute of Justice (Washington DC: US Department of Justice, 1997).
Booth, Ken, 'Security as Emancipation', *Review of International Studies*, 17, 1991, pp313–26.
——, 'Ten Flaws of Just Wars', *The Kosovo Tragedy: The Human Rights Dimension*, ed. Ken Booth (London: Frank Cass, 2001).
Bronson, Rachel, 'When Soldiers Become Cops', *Foreign Affairs*, 81 (6), November–December 2002, pp122–32.
Brown, Gavin, Barry Barker and Terry Burke, *Police as Peacekeepers; The History of the Australian and New Zealand Police serving with the United Nations Force in Cyprus 1964–1984* (Victoria Australia: UNCIVPOL, 1984).
Butler, Anita, 'An Australian Government Perspective', paper presented at Solomon Islands: Where to now? Workshop, Australian National University, Canberra, Friday, 5 May 2006.
Buzan, Barry, 'Environment as a Security Issue', *Geopolitical Perspectives on Environmental Security*, ed. Paul Painchaud (Quebec: Cahier du GERPE Universite Laval, 2005).
Call, Chuck and Michael Barnett, 'Looking for a Few Good Cops: Peacekeeping, Peacebuilding and CIVPOL', *Peacebuilding and Police Reform*, eds. Tor Tanke

Holm and Espen Barth Eide (London and Portland OR: Frank Cass, 2000).

Carothers, Thomas, *Aiding Democracy Abroad: The Learning Curve* (Washington DC: Carnegie Endowment, 1999).

Caygill, Howard, 'Perpetual Peace? Kosovo and the Elision of Police and Military Violence', *European Journal of Social Theory*, 4 (1), 2001, pp73–80.

Chan, Janet B.L. with Chris Devery and Sally Doran, *Fair Cop: Learning the Art of Policing* (Toronto: University of Toronto Press, 2003).

Chatterton, M.R., 'Reflections on International Police Cooperation: Putting Police Cooperation in Its Place – An Organisational Perspective', *International Police Cooperation: A World Perspective*, eds. Daniel J. Koenig and Dilip K. Das (Lanham MD: Lexington Books, 2001).

Cheik, Oumar Diarra, 'United Nations Assistance Mission for Rwanda (UNAMIR)', *The Role and Functions of Civilian Police in United Nations Peace-keeping Operations: Debriefing and Lessons*, Report and Recommendations of the International Conference Singapore December 1995 (London: Kluwer Law International, 1995).

Chopra, Jarat and Tanja Hohe, 'Participatory Peacebuilding', *Building Sustainable Peace*, eds. Tom Keating and W. Andy Knight (Saskatchewan: UN University Press and The University of Alberta Press, 2004).

Clark, Wesley, *Waging Modern War: Bosnia, Kosovo and the Future of Combat* (New York: Public Affairs, 2001).

Coker, Christopher, *Globalisation and Insecurity in the Twenty-First Century: NATO and the Management of Risk*, Adelphi Paper 345 (Oxford: IISS, 2002).

Collantes Celador, Gemma, 'Police Reform: Peacebuilding Through 'Democratic Policing'?, *International Peacekeeping*, 12 (3), Autumn 2005, pp364–76.

Cooper, Robert, *The Postmodern State and World Order* (London: Demos, 2000).

Cousens, Elizabeth, 'Introduction', *Peacebuilding as Politics: Cultivating Peace in Fragile Societies*, eds. Elizabeth Cousens and Chetan Kumar with Karin Wermester (Boulder CO: Lynne Reinner, 2001).

Covey, J. et al. eds. *The Quest for Viable Peace: International Intervention and Strategies for Conflict Transformation* (Washington DC: USIP, 2005).

Dandeker, Christopher, Keynote Paper, 'The military and social change in the post-Cold War era: the need for a strategic approach to personnel issues in the armed forces', Proceedings of the 42nd Annual Conference of the International Military Testing Association, Edinburgh 2002, as found at http://www.internationalmta.org/2000/00IMTAproceedings.pdf, accessed on 13/10/2004.

Daniker, Gustav, *The Guardian Soldier: On the Nature and Use of Future Armed Forces*, Research Paper #36, UNIDIR (New York and Geneva: United Nations, 1995).

Das, Dilip K. and Peter C. Kratcoski, 'International Police Cooperation: A World Perspective', *International Police Cooperation: A World Perspective*, eds. Daniel J. Koenig and Dilip K. Das (Lanham MD: Lexington Books, 2001).

Day, Graham and Christopher Freeman, 'Policekeeping is the Key: Rebuilding the Internal Security Architecture of Postwar Iraq', *International Affairs*, 2 (79), March 2003, pp299–313.

Dean, Mitchell, 'Military Intervention as "Police Action"', *The New Police Science: The Police Power in Domestic and International Governance*, eds. Markus D. Dubber and Mariana Valverde (Stanford CA: Stanford University Press, 2006).

Deflem, Mathieu, *Policing World Society: Historical Foundations of International Police Cooperation* (Oxford: Oxford University Press, 2002).

Deflem, Mathieu and Suzanne Sutphin, 'Policing Post-War Iraq: Insurgency, Civilian Police and the Reconstruction of Society', *Sociological Focus*, 39 (4), November 2006, pp265–83.

Devetak, Richard, 'Between Kant and Pufendorf: humanitarian interventionism, statist anti-cosmopolitanism and critical international theory', *Review of International Studies*, 23, 2007, pp151–74.

Dinnen, Sinclair, Anita Jowitt and Tess Newton Cain (eds.) *A Kind of Mending – Restorative Justice in the Pacific Islands* (Canberra: Pandanus Books, 2003).

Dinnen, Sinclair, Abby McLeod and Gordon Peake, 'Police-building in Weak States: Australian Approaches in Papua New Guinea and Solomon Islands', *Civil Wars*, 8 (2), June 2006, pp87–108.

Dinnen, Sinclair and Edwina Thompson, 'Gender and Small Arms Violence in Papua New Guinea', *State, Society and Governance in Melanesia Discussion Paper*, 2004/8 (Canberra: SSGM ANU, 2004).

Dobbin, James, et al., *America's Role in Nation-building from Germany to Iraq* (Santa Monica CA: RAND, 2003).

Dobbin, James, 'New directions for transatlantic security cooperation', *Survival*, 47 (4), Winter 2005–6, pp39–54.

Doyle, Michael W. et al. (eds.) *Keeping the Peace: Multidimensional UN Operations in Cambodia and El Salvador* (Cambridge: Cambridge University Press, 1997).

Doyle, Michael W., 'Peacebuilding in Cambodia: Legitimacy and Power', *Peacebuilding as Politics: Cultivating Peace in Fragile Societies*, eds. Elizabeth Cousens et al. (Boulder CO and London: Lynne Reinner, 2001).

Dupont, Benoit and Samuel Tanner, 'Not always a happy ending: The organisational challenges of deploying and reintegrating civilian police peacekeepers: A Canadian perspective', paper presented to Community Policing in Three Dimensions Workshop, December 12–14 2007, Canberra, Australia, co-sponsored by the Regulatory Institutions Network, ANU and the Berkeley Centre for International Justice.

Dwan, Renata, *Executive Policing: Enforcing the Law in Peace Operations* (Stockholm: SIPRI, 2002).

——, 'Civilian tasks and capabilities in EU operations', *A Human Security Doctrine for Europe: Project, Principles, Practicalities*, eds. Marlies Glasius and Mary Kaldor (London and New York: Routledge, 2006).

Dziedzic, Michael J., 'Introduction', *Policing the New World Disorder: Peace Operations and Public Security* eds. Robert Oakley et al. (Washington DC: National Defense University Press, 1998).

Dziedzic, Michael, and Colonel Christine Stark, 'Bridging the Security Gap: The Role of the Center of Excellence for Stability Police Units (CoESPU) in Contemporary Peace Operations', *USIPeace Briefing*, June 2006, as found at http://www.usip.org/pubs/usipeace_briefings/2006/0616_coespu.html, accessed on 8/10/2007.

Dziedzic, Michael, and Colonel Michael Seidl, 'Provincial Reconstruction Teams and Military Relations with International and Non-Governmental Organisations in Afghanistan', *USIP Special Report*, n147, September 2005.

Ebbe, Obi N.I., 'International Police Cooperation in Africa', *International Police Cooperation: A World Perspective*, eds. Daniel J. Koenig and Dilip K. Das (Lanham MD: Lexington Books, 2001).

Eide, Espen Barth and Tor Tanke Holm, 'Postscript: Towards Executive Authority Policing? The Lessons of Kosovo', *Peacebuilding and Police Reform*, eds. Tor

Tanke Holm and Espen Barth Eide (London and Portland OR: Frank Cass, 2000).

Elmquist, Michael, *CIMIC in East Timor: An Account of Civil-military Cooperation, Coordination and Collaboration in the Early Phases of the East Timor Relief Operation* (Geneva: OCHA, 1999).

Emsley, Clive, 'The Origins of the Modern Police', *History Today*, 49 (4), April 1999, pp1–8.

Fannin, Stephen, 'UN Peace Settlement Plan for Namibia (UNTAG)', *The Role and Functions of Civilian Police in United Nations Peace-keeping Operations: Debriefing and Lessons*, Report and Recommendations of the International Conference Singapore December 1995 (London: Kluwer Law International, 1995).

Ferguson, Chris, 'Police Reform, Peacekeeping and SSR: The Need for Closer Synthesis', *Journal of Security Sector Management*, 2 (3), September 2004, pp1–13.

Field, Kimberly C. and Robert M. Perito, 'Creating a Force for Peace Operations: Ensuring Stability with Justice', *Parameters*, Winter 2002–3, pp77–87.

Finnemore, Martha, *The Purpose of Intervention: Changing Beliefs about the Use of Force* (Ithaca and London: Cornell University Press, 2003).

Fortier, Patricia, 'The Evolution of Peacekeeping', *Human Security and the New Diplomacy: Protecting People, Promoting Peace*, eds. Rob McRae and Don Hubert (Montreal: McGill-Queen's University Press, 2001).

Fukuyama, Francis, *The End of History and the Last Man* (New York: Free Press, 1992).

Giddens, Anthony, *The Nation State and Violence* (Cambridge: Polity, 1987).

Glenn, Russell, *Counter-Insurgency in a Test Tube: Analyzing the Success of the Regional Assistance Mission to Solomon Islands (RAMSI)* (Santa Monica CA: RAND, 2007).

Goldsmith, Andrew, 'Police Accountability Reform in Colombia: The Civilian Oversight Experiment', *Civilian Oversight of Policing: Governance, Democracy and Human Rights*, eds Andrew J. Goldsmith and Colleen Lewis (Oxford and Portland OR: Hart Publishing, 2000).

——, 'Policing Weak States: Citizen Safety and State Responsibility', *Policing and Society*, 13 (1), 2003, pp3–21.

Goldsmith, Andrew and Colleen Lewis, 'Introduction', *Civilian Oversight of Policing: Governance, Democracy and Human Rights*, eds. Andrew J. Goldsmith and Colleen Lewis (Oxford and Portland OR: Hart Publishing, 2000).

Goulding, Marrack, 'The Evolution of United Nations Peacekeeping', *International Affairs*, 69 (3), June 1993, pp451–64.

Gray, Anthony and Maxwell Manwaring, 'Panama: Operation *Just Cause', Policing the New World Disorder: Peace Operations and Public Security* eds. Robert Oakley et al. (Washington DC: National Defense University Press, 1998).

Greener-Barcham, Beth and Manuhuia Barcham, 'Terrorism in the South Pacific? Thinking Critically about Approaches to Security in the Region', *Australian Journal of International Affairs*, 60 (1), March 2006, pp67–82.

Greener-Barcham, B.K., 'Crossing the Green or Blue Line? Exploring the Military-Police Divide', *Small Wars and Insurgencies*, 18 (1), March 2007, pp90–112.

——, 'Liberalism, Liberal States and Military Force', *Global Change, Peace and Security*, 19 (2), June 2007, pp67–81.

Hansen, Annika S., *From Congo to Kosovo: Civilian Police in Peace Operations*, Adelphi Paper 343 (Oxford: IISS, 2002).

Hansen, Annika S. and Sharon Wihata, *The Transition to a Just Order-Establishing Local Ownership after Conflict: A Policy Report* (Stockholm: Folke Bernadotte Academy, 2007).
Harris, Geoff, 'The military as a resource for peace-building: time for a reconsideration?', *Conflict, Security and Development*, 6 (2), June 2006, pp241–52.
Hardt, Michael and Antonio Negri, *Empire* (London and Cambridge MA: Harvard University Press, 2000).
Hartz, Halvor, 'CIVPOL: The UN Instrument for Police Reform', *Peacebuilding and Police Reform*, eds. Tor Tanke Holm and Espen Barth Eide (London and Portland OR: Frank Cass, 2000).
Hawke, Allan, 'Regional Co-operation in the Pacific: An Australian('s) Perspective', paper presented to Redefining the Pacific? Regionalism, Past, Present and Future, Dunedin, 26 June 2004.
Hawksley, Charles, 'The MV Tampa, the "Pacific Solution" and the 2001 Federal Election', *APMRN Update*, No. 10, December 2001, pp3–4.
——, 'The Enhanced Cooperation Programme between Australia and PNG: the intervention you have when you're not having an intervention?', paper presented to the First Oceanic International Studies Conference, 14–16 July 2004, Australian National University, Canberra.
Hayward, Lt Col Antony, 'East Timor: A Case Study in Humanitarian Intervention', New Zealand Army Military Studies Institute Occasional Paper Series (Wellington: Military Studies Institute, 2003).
Hayward, Keith and Wayne Morrison, 'Locating "Ground Zero": Caught between the narratives of crime and war', *Law After Ground Zero*, ed. John Strawson (Sydney: Glasshouse Press, 2002).
Hearn, Roger, *UN Peacekeeping in Action: The Namibian Experience* (New York: Nova Science Publishers Inc., 1999).
Hehir, Aidan, 'Autonomous Province Building: Identification Theory and the Failure of UNMIK', *International Peacekeeping*, 13 (2), June 2006, pp200–13.
Heinbecker, Paul and Rob McRae, 'The Kosovo Air Campaign', *Human Security and the New Diplomacy: Protecting People, Promoting Peace*, eds. Rob McRae and Don Hubert (Montreal: McGill-Queen's University Press, 2001).
Heinemann-Gruder, Andreas and Igor Grebenschikov, 'Security Governance by Internationals: The Case of Kosovo', *International Peacekeeping*, 13 (1), March 2006, pp43–59.
Higden, Paul, 'Interpol's Role in International Police Cooperation', *International Police Cooperation: A World Perspective*, eds. Daniel J. Koenig and Dilip K. Das (Lanham MD: Lexington Books, 2001).
Hills, Alice, 'International Peace Support Operations and CIVPOL: Should There Be a Permanent Global Gendarmerie?', *International Peacekeeping*, 5 (3), Autumn 1998, pp26–41.
——, 'The Inherent Limits of Military Forces in Policing Peace Operations', *International Peacekeeping*, 8 (3), Autumn 2001, pp79–98.
——, 'Fear and Loathing in Falluja', *Armed Forces & Society*, 32 (4), July 2006, pp623–39.
Hood, Ludovic, 'Security Sector Reform in East Timor', *International Peacekeeping*, 13 (1), March 2006, pp60–77.
——, 'Missed Opportunities: The United Nations, Police Service and Defence Force Development in Timor-Leste, 1999–2004', *Civil Wars*, 8 (2), June 2006, pp143–62.

Horta, Loro, 'From Red to Blue: China and Peacekeeping', *Australian Army Journal*, v (5), Autumn 2008, pp105–14.

Huntington, Samuel P., *The Soldier and the State: The Theory and Politics of Civil-Military Relations* (Cambridge MA: Belknap Press, 1957).

Ignatieff, Michael, *Virtual War: Kosovo and Beyond* (New York: Metropolitan Books, 2000).

Jan, Ameen, 'Somalia: Building Sovereignty or Restoring Peace?', *Peacebuilding as Politics: Cultivating Peace in Fragile Societies*, eds. Elizabeth Cousens et al. (Boulder CO and London: Lynne Reinner, 2001).

Janowitz, Morris, *The Professional Soldier: A Social and Political Portrait* (London: The Free Press of Glencoe Collier-Macmillan Ltd., 1960).

Jones, S. et al., *Establishing Law and Order After Conflict* (Washington DC: The RAND Corporation, 2005).

Kabutaulaka, Tarcisius, 'Crowded Stage: Actors, Actions and Issues', *Securing a Peaceful Pacific*, eds. John Henderson and Greg Watson (Christchurch: University of Canterbury Press, 2005).

Kaldor, Mary, *New and Old Wars: Organized Violence in a Global Era* (Cambridge: Polity Press, 1999).

Kaplan, A., 'Capacity Building: shifting the paradigms of practice', *Development in Practice*, 10 (3–4), 2000, pp517–26.

Kaplan, Robert D., 'The Coming Anarchy', *Atlantic Monthly*, February 1994, as found at http://www.theatlantic.com/doc/199402/anarchy, accessed 8/4/2008.

Kemshall, Hazel, *Reviewing Risk: A Review of Research on the Assessment Management of Risk and Dangerousness: Implications for Policy and Practice in the Probation Service* (Croydon, Report for the Home Office, Research and Statistics Directorate, 1996).

Kleinig, John, *The Ethics of Policing* (Cambridge: Cambridge University Press, 1996).

Klobodu, Abraham K., 'A Perspective from Ghana', *International Police Cooperation: A World Perspective*, eds. Daniel J. Koenig and Dilip K. Das (Lanham MD: Lexington Books, 2001).

Krasner, Stephen D., *Sovereignty: Organized Hypocrisy* (Princeton NJ: Princeton University Press, 1999).

Kraus, Don, 'The Need for UN Police', *Foreign Policy in Focus*, June 5 2003, as found at http://www.globalpolicy.org/security/peacekpg/reform/2003/0605-police. htm, accessed on 01/02/2005.

Kretchik, Walter E., 'Armed for Peace: National Attitudes and Force Protection Posture in Bosnia 1995–2001', *Small Wars and Insurgencies*, 15 (2), Autumn 2004, pp20–37.

Kumar, Chetan, 'Peacebuilding in Haiti', *Peacebuilding as Politics: Cultivating Peace in Fragile Societies*, eds. Elizabeth Cousens et al. (Boulder CO and London: Lynne Reinner, 2001).

Lab, Stephen P., 'Community Policing as Crime Prevention in the US', *International Perspectives on Community Policing and Crime Prevention*, eds. Stephen P. Lab and Dilip K. Das (Englewood Cliffs NJ: Prentice Hall, 2003).

—— 'Introduction: Community Policing and Crime Prevention', *International Perspectives on Community Policing and Crime Prevention*, eds. Stephen P. Lab and Dilip K. Das (Englewood Cliffs NJ: Prentice Hall, 2003).

Law, David M., 'Conclusion: Security Sector (Re)Construction in Post-Conflict Settings', *International Peacekeeping*, 13 (1), March 2006, pp111–23.

Lee Kim, Cheryl M. and Mark Metrikas, 'Holding a Fragile Peace: The Military and Civilian Components of UNTAC', *Keeping the Peace: Multidimensional UN Operations in Cambodia and El Salvador*, eds. Michael W. Doyle et al. (Cambridge: Cambridge University Press, 1997).

Levi, Ron and John Hagan, 'International Police', *The New Police Science: The Police Power in Domestic and International Governance*, eds. Markus D. Dubber and Mariana Valverde (Stanford CA: Stanford University Press, 2006).

Lewis, William and Edward Marks, 'Overview', *Civilian Police and Multinational Peacekeeping – A Workshop Series: A Role for Democratic Policing*, National Institute of Justice (Washington DC: US Department of Justice, 1997).

Lewis, William, Edward Marks and Robert Perito, 'Enhancing International Civilian Police in Peace Operations', *USIP Special Report*, 22 April 2002.

Lipschutz, Ronnie D. (ed.) *On Security* (New York: Columbia University Press, 1995).

Lipson, Michael, 'Peacekeeping: Organized Hypocrisy', *European Journal of International Relations*, 13 (1), 2007, pp5–34.

Lipton, Deborah, *Risk* (London: Routledge, 1992).

Livingstone, Ken and Jerry Hart, 'The Wrong Arm of the Law? Public Images of Private Security', *Policing and Society*, 13 (2), 2003, pp159–70.

Lowry, Bob, 'After the 2006 Crisis: Australia's interests in Timor-Leste', *ASPI Strategic Insights*, #38 (Canberra: Australian Strategic Policy Institute, 2007).

Malan, Mark, 'Peacebuilding in Southern Africa: Police Reform in Mozambique and South Africa', *Peacebuilding and Police Reform*, eds. Tor Tanke Holm and Espen Barth Eide (London and Portland OR: Frank Cass, 2000).

Maley, William, 'International force and political reconstruction: Cambodia, East Timor and Afghanistan', *Security Sector Reform and Post-Conflict Peacebuilding*, eds. Albrecht Schnabel and Hans-Georg Ehrhart (Tokyo: UN University Press, 2005).

Mani, Rama, 'Contextualizing Police Reform: Security, the Rule of Law and Post-Conflict Peacebuilding', *Peacebuilding and Police Reform*, eds. Tor Tanke Holm and Espen Barth Eide (London and Portland OR: Frank Cass, 2000).

Marenin, Otwin, 'United States International Policing Activities: An Overview', *International Police Cooperation: A World Perspective*, eds. Daniel J. Koenig and Dilip K. Das (Lanham MD: Lexington Books, 2001).

——, *Restoring Policing Systems in Conflict Torn Nations: Process, Problems, Prospects* (Geneva: Geneva Centre for the Democratic Control of Armed Forces, 2005).

Mares, D.R., 'Securing Peace in the Americas in the Next Decade', *The Future of Inter-American Relations*, ed. J.I. Dominguez (New York: Routledge, 2000).

Martin, Ian and Alexander Mayer-Rieckh, 'The United Nations and East Timor: From Self-Determination to State-Building', *International Peacekeeping*, 12 (1), Spring 2005, pp125–45.

McDonald, William F. (ed.) *Crime and Law Enforcement in the Global Village* (Cincinnati OH: Anderson Publishing, 1997).

McFarlane, John, *Civilian Police in Peace Operations*, Working Paper No.64 (Canberra: SDSC ANU, 2001).

——, 'Regional and International Cooperation in Tackling Transnational Crime, Terrorism and the Problems of Disrupted States', paper presented to the CSCAP Study Group on Oceania: Law and Order, Wellington, 17 August 2004.

McFarlane, John and William Maley, 'Civilian police in UN peace operations: Some lessons from recent Australian experience', *United Nations Peacekeeping*

Operations; Ad Hoc Missions, Permanent Engagement, eds. Ramesh Thakur and Albrecht Schnabel (Tokyo: United Nations University Press, 2001).

McLean, Paul D. (ed.) *Solomon Islands: Report of a Study Group* (Wellington: NZIIA, 2001).

Menkhaus, Ken, *Somalia: State Collapse and the Threat of Terrorism*, Adelphi Paper 364 (Oxford: IISS, 2004).

Metz, Steven, *Learning from Iraq: Counterinsurgency in American Strategy* (Carlise PA: SSI US Army War College, January 2007).

Metz, Steven and Raymond Millen, 'Intervention, Stabilization and Transformation Operations: The Role of Landpower in the New Strategic Environment', *Parameters*, Spring 2005, pp41–51.

Miller, Seumas, John Blackler and Andrew Alexander, *Police Ethics* (St. Leonards NSW: Allen and Unwin, 1997).

Mobekk, Eirinn, *Policing Peace Operations: United Nations Civilian Police in East Timor*, A Monograph for the John D. and Catherine T. MacArthur Foundation Programme on Peace and International Co-operation (London: King's College London, 2001).

——, *Identifying Lessons in United Nations International Policing Missions* (Geneva: Geneva Centre for the Democratic Control of the Armed Forces, 2005).

Mockaitis, Thomas R., *Civil Military Cooperation in Peace Operations: The Case of Kosovo* (Carlisle Barracks: SSI, October 2004).

——, *The Iraq War: Learning from the Past, Adapting to the Present and Planning for the Future* (Carlisle Barracks: SSI, February 2007).

Morgan, Michael and Abby McLeod, 'Have we failed our neighbour?' *Australian Journal of International Affairs*, 60 (3), 2006, pp412–28.

Morrison, Alex, 'Methodology, Contents and Structure of UN Civilian Police Training Programmes', *The Role and Functions of Civilian Police in United Nations Peacekeeping Operations: Debriefing and Lessons*, ed. Nassrine Azimi (London: Kluwer Law International, 1996).

Muhammad, Anwarul Iqbal, 'An Overview of the CIVPOL Operations in Angola (UNAVEM)', *The Role and Functions of Civilian Police in United Nations Peacekeeping Operations: Debriefing and Lessons*, Report and Recommendations of the International Conference Singapore December 1995 (London: Kluwer Law International, 1995).

Murphy, Christopher, 'The Cart Before the Horse: Community Oriented Versus Professional Models of International Police Reform', *Crafting Transnational Policing: Police Capacity-Building and Global Policing Reform*, eds. Andrew Goldsmith and James Sheptycki (Oxford and Portland OR: Hart Publishing, 2007).

Murphy, Ray, *UN Peacekeeping in Lebanon, Somalia and Kosovo: Operational and Legal Issues in Practice* (Cambridge: Cambridge University Press, 2007).

Murray, Tonita, 'Police-Building in Afghanistan: A Case Study of Civil Security Reform', *International Peacekeeping*, 14 (1), January 2007, pp108–26.

Nadelmann, Ethan, *Cops Across Borders: The Internationalization of US Criminal Law Enforcement* (Philadelphia: Pennsylvania State Press, 1993).

Oakley, Robert B. et al. (eds.) *Policing the New World Disorder: Peace Operations and Public Security* (Washington DC: National Defense University Press, 1998).

O'Callaghan, Mary Louise, RAMSI: The Challenges Ahead, paper presented at Solomon Islands: Where to now? Workshop, Australian National University, Canberra, Friday 5 May 2006.

O'Hanlon, Michael and Jason Campbell, *Tracking Variables of Reconstruction and Security in Post Saddam Iraq* (Washington DC: Brookings Institute, 2007).
O'Neill, William G., *Kosovo: 'An Unfinished Peace'* (Boulder CO: Lynne Reinner, 2002).
Paris, Roland, 'International Peacebuilding and the "Mission Civilisatrice"', *Review of International Studies*, 28 (4), 2002, pp637–56.
——, *At War's End: Building Peace After Civil Conflict* (Cambridge: Cambridge University Press, 2004).
Peake, Gordon and Kaysie Studdard Brown, 'Policebuilding: the International Deployment Group in the Solomon Islands', *International Peacekeeping*, 12 (4), Winter 2005, pp520–32.
Penrose, Jeff, 'Peace Support Operations and Policing: An Explosive Human Skills Mix', *The Human in Command: Peace Support Operations*, eds. Peter Essens et al. (Breda: KMA Royal Netherlands Academy, 2001).
Perito, Robert, *Where is the Lone Ranger When We Need Him? America's Search for a Post-Conflict Stability Force* (Washington DC: USIP, 2004).
——, 'Provincial Reconstruction Teams in Iraq', *USIP Special Report*, #185, March 2007.
——, 'US Police in Peace and Stability Operations', *USIP Special Report*, #191, August 2007.
——, 'Reforming the Iraqi Interior Ministry, Police and Facilities Protection Service', *USIPeace Briefing*, February 2007, as found at http://www.usip.org/pubs/usipeace_briefings/2007/0207_iraqi_interior_ministry.html, accessed on 8/10/2007.
——, 'Embedded Provincial Reconstruction Teams', *USIPeace Briefing*, March 2008, as found at http://www.usip.org/pubs/usipeace_briefings/2008/0305_prt.html, accessed on 10/3/2008.
Pfaff, Tony, *Development and Reform of the Iraqi Police Forces* (Carlisle Barracks SA: Strategic Studies Institute US Army War College, 2007).
Pickering, Thomas R., 'Does the UN have a role in Iraq?', *Survival*, 50 (1), February–March 2008, pp133–42.
Piiparinen, Touku, 'A Clash of Mindsets? An Insider's Account of Provincial Reconstruction Teams', *International Peacekeeping*, 14 (1), 2005, pp143–57.
Pugh, Michael, 'Peacekeeping and Critical Theory', *International Peacekeeping*, 11 (1), March 2004, pp39–58.
Pumphrey, Carolyn, 'Introduction', Transnational Threats: Blending Law Enforcement and Military Strategies, ed. Carolyn W. Pumphrey (Carlisle Barracks USA: Strategic Studies Institute, 2000).
Rancière, Jacques, *Disagreement: Politics and Philosophy*, trans. Julie Rose (Minneapolis MN and London: University of Minnesota Press, 1999).
Rauchs, Georges and Daniel J. Koenig, 'Europol', *International Police Cooperation: A World Perspective*, eds. Daniel J. Koenig and Dilip K. Das (Lanham MD: Lexington Books, 2001).
Reagan, A.J. and R.J. May, 'Reassessing Australia's Role in Papua New Guinea and the Island Pacific', *The National Interest in a Global Era: Australia in World Affairs 1996–2000* (Oxford: Oxford University Press, 2000).
Reimann, Jurgen, 'Debriefing on CIVPOL Experiences: United Nations Mission for the Referendum in Western Sahara (MINURSO)', *The Role and Functions of Civilian Police in United Nations Peace-keeping Operations: Debriefing and Lessons,*

Report and Recommendations of the International Conference Singapore December 1995 (London: Kluwer Law International, 1995).

Reiner, Robert, *The Politics of the Police*, 2nd edn. (New York and London: Harvester Wheatsheaf, 1992).

Richmond, Oliver P., 'UN Peace Operations and the Dilemmas of the Peacebuilding Consensus', *International Peacekeeping*, 11 (1), Spring 2004, pp83–101.

Roberts, Adam, 'Law and the Use of Force After Iraq', *Survival*, 45 (2), Summer 2003, pp31–56.

Robison, Richard, Ian Wilson and Adrianus Meliala, '"Governing the Ungovernable": Dealing with the Rise of Informal Security in Indonesia', *Asia Pacific Research Centre Policy Brief*, No. 1 June 2008, Asia Pacific Research Centre, Murdoch University.

Rosenau, James, *Along the Foreign Domestic Frontier: Exploring Governance in a Turbulent World* (Cambridge: Cambridge University Press, 1997).

Roughan, John, *100 Days of RAMSI*, State, Society and Governance in Melanesia Working Paper 03/3, as found at http://eprints.anu.edu.au/archive/00002780/ 20/9/2004.

Roughan, Paul, B.K. Greener-Barcham and Manuhuia Barcham, *Where to now for RAMSI?*, CIGAD Briefing Notes, 1/2006, April 2006.

Rupp, Richard, 'High Hopes and Limited Prospects: Washington's Security and Nation-Building Aims in Afghanistan', *Cambridge Review of International Affairs*, 19 (2), June 2006, pp285–98.

Santoro, Emilio, 'Crime and punishment', *Political Concepts*, eds. Richard Bellamy and Richard Mason (Manchester: Manchester University Press, 2003).

Sargent, Wendy, *Civilizing Peace Building: Twenty-first Century Global Politics* (Aldershot: Ashgate, 2007).

Schear, James and Karl Farris, 'Policing Cambodia: The Public Security Dimensions of UN Peace Operations', *Policing the New World Disorder: Peace Operations and Public Security*, eds. Robert Oakley et al. (Washington DC: National Defense University Press, 1998).

Schmidl, Erwin A., 'Police Functions in Peace Operations: An Historical Overview', *Policing the New World Disorder: Peace Operations and Public Security* eds. Robert Oakley et al. (Washington DC: National Defense University Press, 1998).

Schnabel, Albrecht and Hans-Georg Ehrhart (eds.) *Security Sector Reform and Post Conflict Peacebuilding* (New York: United Nations University Press, 2005).

Sedra, Mark, 'Security Sector Reform in Afghanistan: The Slide Towards Expediency', *International Peacekeeping*, 13 (1), March 2006, pp94–110.

Selwyn, Mettle, 'Operation in Somalia (UNOSOM)', *The Role and Functions of Civilian Police in United Nations Peace-keeping Operations: Debriefing and Lessons*, Report and Recommendations of the International Conference Singapore December 1995 (London: Kluwer Law International, 1995).

Shawcross, William, *Deliver Us from Evil: Warlords and Peacekeepers in a World of Endless Conflict* (London: Bloomsbury, 2000).

Sheptycki, J.W E., 'Transnational policing and the makings of the postmodern state', *British Journal of Criminology*, 35 (4), Autumn 1995, pp613–35.

——, 'The Constabulary Ethic and the Transnational Condition', *Crafting Transnational Policing: Police Capacity-Building and Global Policing Reform*, eds. Andrew Goldsmith and James Sheptycki (Oxford and Portland OR: Hart Publishing, 2007).

Sismanidis, Roxanne, *Police Functions in Police Operations: Report from a Workshop Organized by the United States Institute of Peace*, Peaceworks 14 (Washington: USIP, 1997).

Smith, Hugh (ed.) *International Peacekeeping: Building on the Cambodian Experience* (Canberra: ADFA, 1994).

Smith, Joshua G., Victoria K. Holt and William J. Durch, 'From Timor-Leste to Darfur: New Initiatives for Enhancing UN Civilian Policing Capacity', *The Henry L. Stimson Center Issue Brief*, August 2007.

Smith, Steve, 'The increasing insecurity of security studies: conceptualising security in the last twenty years', *Critical Reflections on Security and Change*, eds. Stuart Croft and Terry Terriff (Portland OR: Frank Cass, 2000).

Smyth, Rosaleen, Nii-K Plange and Neil Burdess, 'Big Brother? Australia's Image in the South Pacific', *Australian Journal of International Affairs*, 51 (1), April 1997, pp37–52.

Stedman, S., 'International implementation of peace agreements in civil wars', *Turbulent Peace: The Challenge of Managing International Conflict*, eds. C. Croker et al. (Washington DC: USIP, 2001).

Takeyh, Ray and Nikolas Gvosdev, 'Do Terrorist Networks Need a Home?', *The Washington Quarterly*, 25 (3), Summer 2002, pp97–108.

Tarte, Sandra and Tarcisius Tara Kabutaulaka, 'Rethinking Security in the South Pacific: Fiji and the Solomon Islands', *The Unraveling of Island Asia? Governmental, Communal and Regional Instability*, ed. Bruce Vaughn (Westport CO and London: Praeger, 2002).

Teck, Teo Kian, 'Singapore's Experience with International Police Cooperation', *International Police Cooperation: A World Perspective*, eds. Daniel J. Koenig and Dilip K. Das (Lanham MD: Lexington Books, 2001).

Thomas, Lynn M., 'Peace Operations and the Need to Prioritize the Rule of Law through Legal System Reform: Lessons from Somalia and Bosnia', *Small Wars and Insurgencies*, 15 (2), Autumn 2004, pp70–6.

Thornberry, Cedric, 'Namibia', *The UN Security Council: From the Cold War to the 21st Century*, ed. David Malone (Boulder CO and London: Lynne Reinner, 2004).

Toomey, Leigh and J. Alexander Thier, 'Bridging Modernity and Tradition: Rule of Law and Search for Justice in Afghanistan', *USIPeace Briefing* October 2007, as found at http://www.usip.org/pubs/usipeace_briefings/2007/1031_afghanistan.html, accessed on 12/12/2007.

Tschirgi, Neclâ, *Post-Conflict Peacebuilding Revisited: Achievements, Limitations, Challenges* (New York: International Peace Academy, 2004).

Van den Heyer, Garth, 'Stabilising the Solomons: A regional response', *New Zealand International Review*, 32 (4), July/August 2007, pp17–21.

Vick, Alan et al., *Preparing the US Air Force for Military Operations Other than War* (Santa Monica CA: RAND, 1997).

Von Einsiedel, Sebastian and David M. Malone, 'Haiti', *The UN Security Council: From the Cold War to the 21st Century*, ed. David Malone (Boulder CO and London: Lynne Reinner, 2004).

Waddington, P.A.J., 'Armed and Unarmed Policing', *Policing Across the World: Issues for the Twenty-First Century*, ed. R.I. Mawby (London: University College London Press, 1999).

Waever, Ole, 'Securitization and Desecuritization', *On Security*, ed. Ronnie D. Lipschutz (New York: Columbia University Press, 1995).

Wainwright, Elsina, 'How is RAMSI faring? Progress, Challenges and Lessons Learned', *ASPI Strategic Insights* (Canberra: Australian Strategic Police Institute, 2005).
Wainwright, Elsina (with contributions from John McFarlane), 'Police Join the Front Line: Building Australia's International Policing Capability', *ASPI Strategic Insights* (Canberra: Australian Strategic Policy Institute, 2004).
Walzer, Michael, *Just and Unjust Wars: A Moral Argument with Historical Illustrations* (Harmondsworth: Penguin, 1977).
Watson, Greg, 'Conflict Overview', *Securing a Peaceful Pacific*, eds. John Henderson and Greg Watson (Christchurch: University of Canterbury Press, 2005).
Watson, James, *A Model Pacific Solution? A Study of the Deployment of the Regional Assistance Mission to Solomon Islands*, Land Warfare Studies Centre Working Paper No. 126, Canberra, October 2005.
Weinberger, Naomi J., 'Peacekeeping Operations in Lebanon', *Middle East Journal*, 37 (3), Summer 1983, pp342–60.
Wheeler, Nicholas, *Saving Strangers: Humanitarian Intervention in International Society* (Oxford: Oxford University Press, 2000).
Whitworth, Sandra, 'Where is the politics in peacekeeping?', *International Journal*, 50, Spring 1995, pp427–35.
Wilcke, Christoph, 'A Hard Place: The United States and the Creation of a New Security Apparatus in Iraq', *Civil Wars*, 8 (2), June 2006, pp124–42.
Williams, Alex J. and Paul Williams, 'Conclusion: What Future for Peace Operations? Brahimi and Beyond', *International Peacekeeping*, 11 (1), Spring 2004, pp183–212.
Williams, John Allen, 'The Postmodern Military Reconsidered', *The Postmodern Military: Armed Forces After the Cold War*, eds. Charles C. Moskos et al. (Oxford: Oxford University Press, 2000).
Williams, Michael C., *Civil-Military Relations and Peacekeeping*, Adelphi Paper No. 321 (London: International Institute for Strategic Studies, 1998).
Wilson, Bu V.E., 'Smoke and Mirrors: Institutionalising fragility in the Policia Nacional Timor Leste', paper delivered to the Democratic Governance in Timor-Leste: Reconciling the National and Local Conference, Charles Darwin University, Darwin, 7–8 February 2008.
Zhongying, Pang, 'China's Changing Attitude to UN Peacekeeping', *International Peacekeeping*, 12 (1), Spring 2005, pp87–104.
Zolo, Danilo, *Cosmopolis: Prospects for World Government* (Cambridge: Polity Press, 1997).

Documents and Reports

Amnesty International, *Timor-Leste: Briefing to Security Council Members on policing and security in Timor-Leste*, 6 March 2006, http://web.amnesty.org/library/Index/ENGASA5700120 03?open&of=ENG-TMP, accessed 12/1/2006.
ANU Enterprise Pty Limited and ANU, *RAMSI Peoples Survey Pilot 2006: Final Report* (Honiara 2006).
APEC, 'Bangkok Declaration on Partnership for the Future', 21 October 2003, as found at http://www.apec.org/apec/leaders_declarations/2003.html, accessed on 21/03/2006.
A Review of Peace Operations: A Case for Change – East Timor, Conflict, Security and Development Group, King's College London, 10 March 2003, as found at http://

www.jsmp.minihub.org/Reports/otherresources/Peace4Timor_10_3_03.pdf, accessed 7/4/2008.

Asia-Pacific Regional Initiative, International Peacekeeping Operations Seminar; Reference Documents, 22–26 September 2003, Manila, the Philippines, Hosted by the Department of National Defense Republic of the Philippines, the United Nations, and the United States Pacific Command, Executed by the Center of Excellence in Disaster Management and Humanitarian Assistance.

AUSAID, *Solomon Islands: Transitional Country Strategy 2006–7* (Canberra: AUSAID, 2006).

Australian Department of Foreign Affairs and Trade, 'First Australians deployed in enhanced PNG-Australia cooperation', Statement by Alexander Downer Minister of Foreign Affairs 12 February 2004, as found at http://www.foreign-minister.gov.au/releases/2004/fa022_04.html, accessed on 14/12/2005.

Australian Embassy Dili, *Status of Forces Agreement*, 26 May 2006, Note No.159/2006, as found at http://www/laohamatuk.org/reports/UN/06SOFAs.html., accessed 12/12/2007.

Call, Charles, *Challenges in Police Reform: Promoting Effectiveness and Accountability*, IPA Policy Report, 2003, as found at http://www.justiceinitiative.org/db/resource2?res_id=101709, accessed 8/4/2008.

CDA Collaborative Learning Projects, *Has Peacebuilding Made a Difference in Kosovo: A Study of the Effectiveness of Peacebuilding in Preventing Violence: Lessons Learned from the March 2004 Riots in Kosovo*, Executive Summary, July 2006 as CDA Website, http://www.cdainc.com/cdawww/pdf/book/kosovo_peacebuilding_report_summary_of_findings_Pdf3.pdf, accessed 24/7/2007.

'East Timor: UNTAET, Background', UN Website, as found at http://www.un.org/peace/etimor/UntaetB.htm, accessed on 5/12/2005.

European Council, *EU Training Programme in ESDP 2007–9 Handout* (Brussels: European Council, 2007).

Guidelines for Governments Contributing Special Police Units to UNMIK (New York UN CPD/DPKO, 1999).

Human Rights Watch, *Failure to Protect: Anti-Minority Violence in Kosovo*, March 2004, as found at http://www.hrw.org/english/docs/2004/07/27/serbia9136.htm, accessed on 28/07/2004.

——, 'East Timor: Human Rights Developments', *World Report 2000*, as found at http://www.hrw.org/wr2k1/asia/etimor.html, accessed on 7/12/2005.

——, *Making their Own Rules: Police Beatings, Rape and Torture of Children in Papua New Guinea* (New York: Human Rights Watch, 2005).

——, *Afghanistan: Police Reconstruction Essential for the Protection of Human Rights*, ASA 11/003/2003, as found at http://web.amnesty.org/library/Index/ENGASA-110032003, accessed 13/03/2006.

——, *The New Iraq? Torture and Ill Treatment of Detainees in Iraqi Custody*, 17 (1), January 2005, as found at http://www.hrw.org/reports/2005/iraq0105/, accessed 10/3/2007.

International Commission on Intervention and State Sovereignty, *The Responsibility to Protect* (Ottawa: International Development Research Centre, 2001).

International Crisis Group, *Securing Afghanistan: The Need for More International Action*, Asia Briefing #13, 15 March 2002, as found at http://www.crisis-group.org/home/index.cfm?id=1819&l=1, accessed 25/6/2006.

——, *Peacebuilding in Afghanistan*, Asia Report #64, 29 September 2003, as found at http://www.crisisgroup.org/home/index.cfm?id=2293&l=1, accessed 13/5/2006.

——, *Disarmament and Reintegration in Afghanistan*, Asia Report #65, 30 September 2003, as found at http://www.crisisgroup. org/home/index.cfm?id=2292&l=1, accessed 13/5/2006.

——, *Central Asia: The Politics of Police Reform*, Asia Report #42, 10 December 2002, as found at http://www.crisisgroup.org/home/index.cfm?id=1444&l=1, accessed 25/6/2006.

——, *Reforming Afghanistan's Police*, Asia Report #138, 30 August 2007, as found at http://www.crisisgroup.org/home/index.cfm?id=5052&l=1, accessed 10/10/2007.

——, *Resolving Timor-Leste's Crisis*, Asia Report #120, 10 October 2006, as found at http://www.crisisgroup.org/home/index.cfm?id=4438&l=1, accessed 10/10/2007.

——, *Countering Afghanistan's Insurgency: No Quick Fixes*, Asia Report #123, 2 November 2006, as found at http://www.crisisgroup.org/home/index.cfm?id=4485&l=1, accessed 10/10/2007.

——, *Kosovo Countdown: A Blueprint for Transition*, Europe Report #188, 6 December 2007, as found at http://www.crisisgroup.org/home/index.cfm?id=5201, accessed 20/1/2008.

——, *In their Own Words: Reading the Iraq Insurgency*, Middle East Report #50 June 2006, as found at http://www. crisisgroup.org/home/index.cfm?id=3953&l=1, accessed 10/2/2008.

——, 'Kosovo's First Month', *International Crisis Group Briefing*, Pristina/Belgrade/Brussels, 18 March 2008.

——, *Timor Leste: Security Sector Reform*, Asia Report #143, as found at http://www.crisisgroup.org/home/index.cfm?id=5264, accessed 7/4/2008.

International Policing Advisory Council, *Summary Meeting Report of the First Meeting of the International Policing Advisory Council (IPAC)*, 16–17 August 2006, Wilton Park, United Kingdom.

——, *Summary Meeting Report of the Second Meeting of the International Policing Advisory Council (IPAC)*, Transcorp Hilton, Abuja, Nigeria, 22–23 January 2007.

——, *Summary Meeting Report of the Third Meeting of the International Policing Advisory Council (IPAC)*, Canberra, Australia, 30–31 August 2007.

International Policy Institute, *East Timor Report* (London: Kings College London, 2006), as found at http://ipi.sspp.kcl.ac.uk/rep006/toc.html, accessed 21/03/2006.

International Resources Group et al., *Filling the Vacuum: Prerequisites to Security in Afghanistan* (Washington DC: International Resources Group, 2002).

Larmour, Peter and Manuhuia Barcham, *National Integrity Systems Pacific Overview Report 2004* (Blackburn SA: Transparency International, 2004), as found at http://www.transparency.org.au/documents/NISPACoverview04.pdf, accessed 10/5/2005.

London Conference on Afghanistan, *The Afghanistan Compact*, 31 January–1 February 2006, as found at http://www.unama-afg.org/news/_londonConf/_docs/06jan30-AfghanistanCompact-Final.pdf, accessed 12/10/2007.

National Institute of Justice, *Civilian Police and Multinational Peacekeeping – A Workshop Series: A Role for Democratic Policing* (Washington DC: US Department of Justice, 1999).

NATO, 'Kosovo Force (KFOR); How did it evolve?', as found at http://www.nato.int/ issues/kfor/evolution.html, accessed on 1/10/2007.

NATO, 'NATO in Afghanistan', as found at http://www.nato.int/issues/afghanistan/index.html, accessed on 1/10/2007.

NATO, 'NATO in Afghanistan: Reconstruction and Development (June 2007)', as found at http://www.nato.int/issues/afghanistan/factsheets/reconst_develop.html, accessed on 1/10/2007.

NATO, 'NATO support to Afghan National Army', as found at http://www.nato.int/issues/afghanistan/ factsheets/ana-support.html, accessed 2/10/2007.

NATO, 'Revised Operational Plan for NATO's expanding mission in Afghanistan', as found at http://www.nato.int/issues/afghanistan_stage3/index.html, accessed 20/3/2006.

NATO, 'Revised Operational Plan for NATO's expanding mission in Afghanistan', as found at http://www.nato.int/issues/afghanistan_stage3/index.html, accessed 20/3/2006.

NATO, 'Statement on the situation in the Balkans', Issued at the Meeting of the North Atlantic Council in Defence Ministers Session held in Brussels, Press Release M-DNAC-D-1 (2001) 88, 7 June 2001, as found at http://www.nato.int/docu/pr/2001/p01-088e.htm, accessed on 6/6/2007.

NATO, The Alliance's New Strategic Concept, Agreed by the Heads of State and Government participating in the meeting of the North Atlantic Council on Rome on 7–8 November 1991, as found at http://www.nato.int/docu/comm/49-95/c911107a.htm, accessed on 10/2/03.

NATO, The Alliance's Strategic Concept Approved by the Heads of State and Government participating in the meeting of the North Atlantic Council, Washington D.C. 23–24 April 1999 (Brussels: NATO Office of Information and Press, 1999).

New Zealand Cabinet, 'Report of the Cabinet External Relations and Defence Committee', Period Ended 4 July 2003, Defence Cabinet Document, Cabinet Minute of Decision, 7 July 2003, CAB Min (03) 6/6.

New Zealand Cabinet External Relations and Defence Committee, 'Report of the Cabinet External Relations and Defence Committee: Period Ended 8 August 2003', Defence Cabinet Document Cabinet Minute of Decision, 11 August 2003, CAB Min (03) 27/2.

New Zealand Ministry of Foreign Affairs and Trade, 'Solomon Islands: Possible Intervention', Defence Cabinet Document, Submission and Annex, 23 May 2003, SLB/4.

——, 'Solomon Islands: Strengthened Assistance', Defence Cabinet Document, Cabinet Paper plus attachment, 9 June 2003.

——, 'Solomon Islands: Strengthened Assistance', Defence Cabinet Document Covering Submission and Cabinet Paper, 23 June 2003, SLB/4.

——, 'Solomon Islands: Possible New Zealand Involvement in 'Strengthened Assistance', Defence Cabinet Document, Cabinet Paper, 24 June 2003.

——, 'Solomon Islands: Strengthened Assistance: NZ Concept Paper', Defence Cabinet Document, Submission, 26 June 2003.

New Zealand Police, New Zealand Police Statement of Intent 2003/2004, Presented to the House of Representatives pursuant to Section 34A of the Public Finance Act 1989 (Wellington: Police, 2004).

NZAID, *Bougainville Community Policing Project Phase 3 2004–6* (Wellington: MFAT, 2005).

OECD DAC, *Security System Reform and Governance: Policy and Good Practice*, A DAC Reference Document (Paris: OECD, 2004).

Pacific Islands Chiefs of Police, *Future Directions in Pacific Policing: Beyond 2010, vols 1 and 2* (Wellington: PICP, 2007).
Pacific Islands Forum, *Mission Helpem Fren: A Review of the Regional Assistance Mission to Solomon Islands Report of the Pacific Islands Forum Eminent Persons Group* (Suva: Pacific Islands Forum, 2005).
Police and Justice Team, *Peace Support Operations: Information and Guidance for UK Personnel*, April 2007 (London: Foreign and Commonwealth Office, 2007).
RAMSI, 'Law and Justice', as found at http://www.ramsi.org/node/268, accessed on 12/3/2008.
RAMSI, 'Special Features', as found at http://www.ramsi.org/node/17, accessed on 12/3/2008.
RAMSI, 'RAMSI Organisation Chart', created 16/02/2008, found at http://www.ramsi.org/node/269/print, accessed on 10/03/2008.
RAMSI, 'RAMSI's work', as found at http://www.ramsi.org/node/2, accessed 10/3/2008.
Report of the Pacific Islands Forum Eminent Persons Group, *A Review of the Regional Assistance Mission to Solomon Islands*, May 2005 (Suva: PIF, 2005).
The Commonwealth of Australia, *Cambodia: An Australian Police Proposal*, Working papers prepared for the Informal Meeting on Cambodia, held at Jakarta, 26–28 February 1990 (Canberra: R.D. Rubie Commonwealth Government Printer, 1990).
United Nations Crime Prevention and Criminal Justice Branch, *United Nations Criminal Justice Standards for Peace-keeping Police* (Vienna: UN Office at Vienna, 1994).
United Nations Development Programme, *Human Development Report – Kosovo 2004*, as found at http://hdr.undp.org/docs/reports/national/KOS_Kosovo/kosovo_2004_en.pdf, accessed on 21/03/2006.
United Nations Development Programme, *Kosovo Early Warning Reports*, as found at http://www.kosovo.undp.org/repository/docs/Facts_EWS_14.doc, accessed 13/3/2008.
United Nations Development Programme, *Solomon Islands Peace and Conflict Development Analysis: Emerging Priorities in Preventing Future Conflict* (Honiara: UNDP, 2004).
UN Department of Peacekeeping Operations, Monthly Military and Civilian Police Contributions to UN PKO, as found at www.un.org/dpko/dpko/contributors.
UN Department of Peacekeeping Operations, *Selection Standards and Training Guidelines for United Nations Civilian Police* (New York: UN, 1997).
UN Department of Peacekeeping Operations, *United Nations Police Officers Course* (New York: UN, 2000).
UNMIK, 'Frequently Asked Questions: General information about the International Police in Kosovo', as found at http://www.unmikonline.org/civpol/newfaq.htm#11, accessed 8/1/2006.
UNMISET, 'Timeline of UN Presence in East Timor', http://www.unmiset.org/UNMISETWebSite.nsf/TimeLineofUNMISET.htm?OpenPage, accessed 12/1/2006.
UN Press Release SC/6745, Security Council Establishes UN Transitional Administration in East Timor for Initial Period Until 31 January, as found at http://www.un.org/news/Press/docs/1999/19991025.sc6745.doc.html, accessed 13/3/2007.
UNOHCR, *Report of the United Nations Independent Special Commission of Inquiry for Timor-Leste* (Geneva: UN, 2006).

UN Police Presentation, Third Meeting of the International Policing Advisory Council, 30–31 August 2007, National Museum of Australia, Canberra.
UN Secretary General's Special Representative in Bosnia and Herzegovina Jacques Paul Klein as cited in 'Police Reform in Bosnia and Herzegovina Signals a Mandate Completed', http://www.un.org/Depts/dpko/yir/english/page5.html, accessed on 01/02/2005.
United Nations Secretary General Kofi Annan, Report of the Secretary General on the United Nations Transitional Administration in East Timor, S/2001/983, 18 October 2001, as found at http://daccessdds.un.org/doc/UNDOC/GEN/N01/583/27/IMG/N0158327.pdf?OpenElement, accessed 12/10/2007.
United Nations Secretary General Ban Ki-Moon, Report of the Secretary General on the United Nations Mission in Timor Leste, 2007 S/2007/513, as found at http://www.un.org/Docs/journal/asp/ws.asp?m=S/PV.5740, accessed 12/10/2007.
United Nations Secretary General Boutros-Boutros Ghali, *An Agenda for Peace* (New York: UN, 1992).
United Nations Secretariat, Report of the Panel on United Nations Peace Operations, UN Doc. A/ff/305, S/2000/809 (21 August 2000), p7, as found at http://www. un.org/peace/report/peace_operations, accessed 8/10/2005.
UNSC, UNSC Resolution 1272, S/RES/1272 (1999) adopted on 25 October 1999, as found at http://www.un.org/peace/etimor/docs/9931277E.htm, accessed 11/7/2007.
UNSC, UNSC Resolution 1410, S/RES/1410 (2002) adopted 17 May 2002, as found at http://www.unmit.org/UNMISETwebsite.nsf/p9999/$FILE/SRES1410%20(2002). pdf, accessed 13/3/2007.
UN Website, 'UN Peacekeeping: Capstone Doctrine', as found at http://pbpu.unlb.org/pbps/Pages/Public/viewprimarydoc.aspx?docid=481, accessed on 6 December 2007.
US Department of Defence, Quadrennial Defense Review Report, 30 September 2001, as found at http://www.defenselink.mil/pubs/qdr2001.pdf, accessed on 13/10/2004.
US State Department, 'East Timor' Country Reports on Human Rights Practices 2004, as found at http://www.state.gov/g/drl/rls/hrrpt/2004/41641.htm, accessed 8/1/2006.
Washington Office on Latin America (WOLA), *Demilitarising Public Order: The International Community, Police Reform and Human Rights in Central America and Haiti* (Washington DC: WOLA, 1995).

Media Articles and Group Newsletters

AAP, 'Immunity for police must stay: Howard', *The Age*, 14 May 2005, as found at http://www.theage.com.au/news/National/Immunity-for-police-must-stay-Howard/2005/05/14/1116024403115.html, accessed on 30/6/2005.
'After smart weapons, smart soldiers', *The Economist*, 27 October 2007, pp33–5.
Barnett, Antony and Solomon Hughes, 'British Firm Accused in UN "Sex Scandal": International Police in Bosnia Face Prostitution Claims', as found at http://www.globalpolicy.org/socecon/inequal/0729un.htm, accessed on 01/02/2005.
BBC News, 'Iraqi Police Deaths Hit 12,000', 24 December 2006, *BBC News Online*, as found at http://news.bbc.co.uk/2/hi/middle_east/6208331.stm, accessed 14/4/2007.
BBC News, 'US-Iraq contract in 'disarray'', 23 October 2007, *BBC News Online*, as found at http://news.bbc.co.uk/2/hi/americas/7057629.stm, accessed 7/4/2008.
'Brains not Bullets', *The Economist*, 29 October 2007, p16.

'Bosnian Politics: Cracking Up', *The Economist*, 27 October 2007, p43.

Boone, Jon, 'Blackwater scandal revives reform efforts', *Financial Times*, Friday 2 November 2007, p6.

——, 'UN issues aid plea to Taliban', *Financial Times*, Tuesday 30 October 2007, p5.

Branigan, Tania, 'Al-Qaeda is winning war Allies warned', *The Guardian*, 31 October 2001, as found at http://www.guardian.co.uk/waronterror/story/0,1361,583789,00. html, accessed on 11/10/2004.

'China to Build Asia's Largest UN Police Training Center', *Peoples Daily Online*, as found at http://english1.people.com.cn/200208/20/print20020820_101732.html, accessed on 08/02/2005.

Crossette, Barbara, 'The UN's Unhappy Lot: Perilous Police Duties Multiplying', *New York Times*, 22 February 2000, pA3.

Dempsey, Judy, 'Letter from Germany: Bickering between NATO and EU hampers training of Afghan police', *International Herald Tribune*, 23 August 2007, as found at http://www.iht.com/articles/2007/08/23/europe/letter.php, accessed 10/10/2007.

Elshtain, Jean Bethke, 'A Just War?', *Boston Globe*, 10 June 2002.

Fainaru, Steve, 'For Police Recruits, Risk is Constant Companion', *The Washington Post*, September 2005, pA1.

Farrell, Steven and Qais Mizher, 'Iraq Dismisses 1,300 After Basra Offensive', *New York Times Online*, 14 April 2008, as found at http://www.nytimes.com/2008/04/14/world/middleeast/14iraq.html?ref=middleeast, accessed 15/4/2008.

Hughes, Helen and Susan Windybank, 'Nose cut off to spite the face', *The Courier Mail*, 31 May 2005, as found at http://www.cis.org.au/exechigh/Eh2005/EH27905.htm, accessed on 30/6/2005.

Jolliffe, Jill, 'Timorese police mimic violence of ex-masters', *Asia Times Online*, 28 January 2004, as found at http://www.atimes.com/atimes/Southeast_Asia/FA28Ae05.html, accessed on 8/1/2006.

Jones, Lloyd, 'Ruling Threat to Aussie police aid', *News.com.au*, as found at http://www.news.com.au/story/print/0,10119,15273255,00.html, as accessed on 30/6/2005.

Kerin, J., 'You police the Pacific: US', *The Australian*, 5 March 2004, p1.

Krasniqi, Ekrem, 'UN Kosovo police arrested for sex trafficking', *International Relations and Security Network*, 01/09/2005, as found at http://www.isn.ethz.ch/news sw/details.cfm? ID=12681, accessed on 10/1/2006.

La'o Hamutuk Group, 'An Assessment of the UN's Police Mission in East Timor', *The La'o Hamutuk Bulletin*, 3 (1), 2002, as found at http://www.laohamutuk.org/Bulletin/2002/Feb/bulletinv3n1.html#Japanese%20Self-Defense%20Force, accessed 12/1/2006.

La'o Hamutuk Group, 'Japanese Peacekeepers in East Timor', *The La'o Hamutuk Bulletin*, 3 (6), 2002, as found at http://www.laohamutuk.org/Bulletin/2002/Aug/bulletinv3n6.html#Japanese%20Peacekeepers%20in%20East%20Timor, accessed 12/1/2006.

La'o Hamutuk Group, 'The World Bank in East Timor', *The La'o Hamutuk Bulletin*, 1 (4), 31 December 2000, as found at http://www.etan.org/li/bulletin04.html, accessed 12/10/2007.

La'o Hamutuk Group, 'UN Missions and Security', *The La'o Hamutuk Bulletin*, 4 (2), 2003, as found at http://www.laohamutuk.org/Bulletin/2003/May/bulletinv4n2.html, accessed 12/1/2006.

Moss, Michael, 'How Iraq Police Reform Became a Casualty of War', *New York Times Online*, 22 May 2006, as found at http://www.nytimes.com/2006/05/22/world/middleeast/22security.html?_r=1&oref=slogin, accessed 15/04/2008.

Moss, Michael and David Rhode, 'Law and Disorder: Training Gap', multimedia presentation from *New York Times Online*, link found at http://www.nytimes.com/2006/05/22/world/middleeast/22security.html?_r=1&oref=slogin, accessed 15/4/2008.

Moxham, Ben, 'Market-imposed hunger adds to Timor misery', *Asia Times Online*, 16 February 2005, as found at http://www.atimes.com/atimes/Southeast_Asia/GB16Ae02.html, accessed on 12/1/2006.

Negus, Steve, 'Iraq focuses on prosecution of security groups', *Financial Times*, Wednesday 31 October, p6.

New Zealand Defence Force Media Release, 'New Zealand Military Police investigate East Timor Graves', *Scoop*, 26 October 1999, as found at http://www.scoop.co.nz/stories/HL9910/S00152.htm, accessed on 21/03/2006.

O'Toole, Pam, 'Afghan Police "Under-Equipped"', *BBC News Online*, 13 July 2007, as found at http://news.bbc.co.uk/1/hi/world/south_asia/6897051.stm, accessed 10/10/2007.

'Police probe WHP crime allegations', *Papua New Guinea Post-Courier Online*, Weekend Edition Friday–Sunday, 9–11 December 2005, as found at http://www.postcourier.com.pg/20051209/frhome.htm, accessed on 12/12/2005.

Randle, Jim, 'Study Finds Iraqi Police Ineffective in Combating Terrorism', 14 October 2007, *Voice of America Online*, as found at http://www.voanews.com/english/archive/2007-10/2007-10-14-voa18.cfm?CFID=201034466&CFTOKEN=52128407, accessed 15/2/2008.

Smith, R. Jeffrey, 'Kosovo still seethes as UN Official nears exit', *The Washington Post*, 19 December 2000, pA20.

Straw, Jack, 'Failed and Failing States', Speech to the European Research Institute, Birmingham, 6 September 2002, as found at http://www.fco.gov.uk/resources/en/speech/2003/10/fco_nsp_060902_strawfailedstates, accessed 12/3/2003.

UN News Service, 'Security Council extends Timor-Leste mission for 1 year, boosts police', *UN Police Magazine*, 2nd edn, June 2007, p9.

UN News Service, 'Timor-Leste: UN envoy pays special tribute to police for peaceful presidential elections', *UN Police Magazine*, 2nd edn, June 2007, p7–8.

UN News Service, 'Top Contributing Countries Graph May 2007', *UN Police Magazine*, 2nd edn., June 2007, p11.

Washington Business Journal, 'DynCorp International wins NATO job in Kosovo', http://www.bizjournals.com/washington/stories/2008/03/24/daily31.html? ana=from_rss, accessed 7/4/2008.

White, H., 'Thin Blue Line Amounts to PNG takeover', *The Age*, 24 September 2003, as found at http://www.theage.com.au/articles/2003/09/23/106408299-1886. html, accessed 13/12/2005.

Wood, Nicholas, 'Division and Disorder Still Tearing at Kosovo', *The Washington Post*, 22 June 2002, p8.

Index